David P. Handlin
was born in Boston and educated
at Harvard College and the Harvard Graduate
School of Design. He has a PhD from the University
of Cambridge, England, where from 1973 to 1978 he
lectured in the Department of Architecture. From 1979
to 1985 he was Associate Professor of Architecture at
the Harvard Graduate School of Design. He is now
president and founding partner of Handlin, Garrahan,
Zachos and Associates, Inc., an architecture firm in
Cambridge, Massachusetts. He is the author
of *The American Home, Architecture and
Society, 1815–1915* (1979).

Thames & Hudson world of art

This famous series
provides the widest available
range of illustrated books on art in all its aspects.
If you would like to receive a complete list
of titles in print please write to:
THAMES & HUDSON
181A High Holborn, London WC1V 7QX
In the United States please write to:
THAMES & HUDSON INC.
500 Fifth Avenue, New York, New York 10110

Printed in Singapore

David P. Handlin **American Architecture**

Second edition

265 illustrations

 Thames & Hudson world of art

For Holly

First published in paperback in the United States of America
in 1985 by Thames & Hudson Inc., 500 Fifth Avenue,
New York, New York 10110

thamesandhudsonusa.com

Second edition 2004

Library of Congress Catalog Card Number 2003102189
ISBN 0-500-20373-3

Printed and bound in Singapore by C.S. Graphics

Contents

Introduction

More than 280,000,000 people now live in the United States. Yet the most important fact about the history of American architecture continues to be that there was a time when the land was all but uninhabited. For the past two hundred years, the haunting image of a virgin continent has dramatized the recentness and fragility of settlement. At the same time it has also underscored not the possibility, but the necessity, of renewal.

The obligation to fulfill the promise of the empty land has been both a burden and an opportunity. American architects and builders have responded to it in three ways. Some have tried to define an American equivalent of sorely missed traditions; others have produced works of invention and originality; still others have questioned whether architecture as a self-conscious art is necessary or desirable at all. These reactions have most often been divergent, but the best buildings have usually tried to reconcile all three.

The continuing interplay of these responses gives American architecture its unity, its Americanness. Given the emphasis on renewal, there have of necessity been many turning points in the way in which this complex state of mind has been manifested in buildings, but two pivotal events stand out. With the founding of the Republic, many Americans first began to think about the significance of architecture. This subject became even more pointed half a century later when a rapid transition from a traditional to a modern society started to take place. Since that time the forms and details of buildings have frequently changed, but the issues then raised have remained the foundation of American architecture.

To locate the critical turning points of American architectural history before the Civil War does not of course suggest that Americans have nothing to learn from buildings constructed earlier or from the architecture of other countries and cultures. On the contrary, the best of American architecture is compelling evidence for the relevance of buildings that are remote, even obscure, in time and distance. Henry Hobson Richardson, for example, was fascinated by the twelfth-century churches of the Auvergne, but he pursued that interest in order to give expression to the structures that housed the institutions of his day. Just as Richardson did not delude himself about the times in which he lived, in our study of the history of architecture we should not forget that ours continues to be a modern age. Indeed, one important reason to examine the architecture of the past is to learn how to reconcile our vision of the vast, once uninhabited continent with the inescapable conditions of contemporary life.

Many people have offered encouragement and assistance in the course of writing this book, but I would like to single out for special thanks Robin Middleton who initiated the project and had the patience to see it through.

1 The American Indian village of Secoton, c. 1585.

2 Restoration of Pueblo Bonito.

CHAPTER ONE

The Unbuilt Spire

The Architecture of the American Colonies

When the first European settlers arrived in the New World, the territory that later became the continental United States was inhabited by about one million native Americans. These people belonged to approximately two hundred nations, many of which had a distinctive culture and architecture. *1, 2* Little is known of their history and even less of their buildings. The images associated with words such as pueblo, wigwam, tepee, hogan, long house, and mound temple probably convey more about what nineteenth- and twentieth-century observers have imputed to the architecture of native Americans than they do about the intentions of the builders and inhabitants. A diverse architecture, which had evolved over a long time, is therefore still largely unknown.

Only the Spaniards, of all the European settlers, thought the building techniques of the native Americans worth incorporating. Nowhere were the native and European traditions of building more intertwined than in the

9

3 The Governor's Palace, Santa Fe, New Mexico, 1610–14.

4, 5 San Estevan, Acoma, New Mexico, c. 1630.

early settlements of what is now New Mexico. The governors and priests who established these small outposts of Spanish civilization considered impressive buildings essential to their rule. Because they had no architects and skilled workmen to assist them, they had to use local methods and materials. Thus, the Governor's Palace, which was erected between 1610 and 1614, was made of adobe. But rather than piling the clay up in layers and then molding it into shape, as was the native custom, the Spaniards introduced a system of making precast, sun-dried adobe bricks by using wooden boxes. A similar combination of techniques took place in framing. The Governor's Palace had a flat roof which was spanned by the projecting beams used in the pueblos, but the doors and windows were framed with wood, a material not used in pueblo construction.

3

The Spaniards soon learned that New Mexico would not be a significant source of wealth and it became primarily a field for missionary work. As a result, the churches constructed by Franciscan padres were the most prominent manifestations of the Spanish presence. Like the Governor's Palace, these were European in plan. They had a nave, which culminated in a sanctuary and occasionally a transept. However, roofing techniques resembled those used locally. No vaults or domes were attempted. Instead, all the New Mexican churches had flat roofs supported by beams, often honed into a rectangular section. The walls that supported the roof were

4, 5

6 San José y San Miguel de Aguayo, San Antonio, Texas, 1720–31.

built of adobe. Their tapered form gave these churches their simple, but substantial, appearance.

No aspect of these buildings better expressed the amalgamation of the cultures than the decoration of the interiors. The corbels that supported the roof beams were European in conception and in their elaborate profiles. Nevertheless, their painted ornamentation incorporated pueblo iconography, as did vigorously colored scenes on the nave walls and the painted wood panels that were sometimes located in the sanctuary. Many of the themes of these paintings came from seventeenth-century Spanish art, yet they were intertwined with pueblo motifs such as sun, rain, and thunder symbols.

The churches and missions built by the Franciscans in Arizona, Texas, and California in the eighteenth century were more elaborate than their antecedents in New Mexico. They had many characteristics of the baroque architecture of the Spanish and Mexican churches of the period. Roof systems were a case in point. The nave of San José y San Miguel de Aguayo in San Antonio, Texas (1720–31) was covered by three groin vaults and a hemispherical dome. San Xavier del Bac (1784–97), near Tucson, Arizona, was a fully developed cruciform church with five low domes over the nave

6

7, 8

12

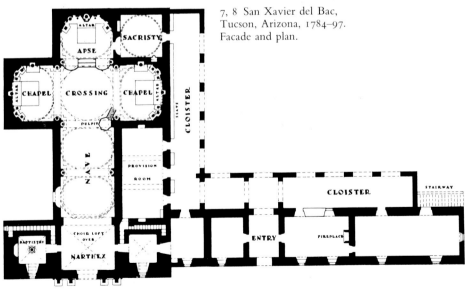

7, 8 San Xavier del Bac,
Tucson, Arizona, 1784–97.
Facade and plan.

transept, and apse and a high dome on an octagonal drum over the crossing. The churches of many of the twenty-one missions built in California were spanned with beams, but some of them also had domes and vaults.

Yet even the buildings with these sophisticated forms remained rooted in a local building tradition. The fusion of cultures was most forcefully represented in the facades of the great churches of Texas and Arizona. San José and San Xavier both had elaborately carved surroundings to their main entrance. But the exuberance of the gables, scrolls, pilasters, statues in niches, carved floral patterns, and articulated cornices was balanced by austere, solid walls. Built of adobe or a porous limestone covered with stucco, these clearly identified the churches with the local building culture.

At the end of the eighteenth century the Franciscan missions began to be secularized. By the 1820s most of them had fallen into disuse. Isolated from the main areas of settlement, they made no impact on the broader development of American architecture until the beginning of the twentieth century when interest in them was revived by those who were trying to establish a regional approach to architecture.

More consequential was the architecture erected by European settlers on the Atlantic seaboard. Like those of any period or place, the buildings of the American colonies can be studied to reflect something of the society for which they were made. Buildings can speak eloquently about politics, economics, the nature of agriculture and manufacturing, the role of women, the status of servants, the state of education, and dozens of other issues. They can also tell us much about how their clients, inhabitants, builders, and architects lived and what they thought.

Architecture should not and indeed never can be divorced from its cultural context, and in this book it certainly is not. Nevertheless, the architectural historian cannot write the history of the world, especially since other sources can usually disclose as much or more about the many issues which are intertwined with architecture. The focus of architectural history should, therefore, be buildings. But the historian's task is not simply to uncover a past that time has obscured. A principle of selection is also important. There is probably something of interest to say about every building, but some demonstrate the art of architecture more forcefully than others. Architectural historians should be allowed many diversions, but their first responsibility is to show how, through a compelling rendering of the elements of architecture and their assembly, vital ideas become transmuted into vivid and memorable form.

From this perspective, the most important question to ask about the architecture of the American colonies is why the early settlers did not attach more significance to it. Reasons sometimes cited for the meager architectural

14

achievement of the colonies have been the severe climate, the lack of skilled workers, and the disorienting nature of the first phases of settlement. The climate along the Atlantic seaboard certainly was more extreme than that in western Europe, and it is a fact that the colonists included only a few skilled artisans and no architects. In addition, the settlers quickly found that because they might move elsewhere, it did not make sense to put large amounts of capital and labor into a building.

While it is true that all these circumstances undoubtedly discouraged the construction of a substantial architecture, they alone do not account for the lack of significant buildings in the American colonies. Settlers in other areas of the world have often overcome equally difficult conditions to erect the buildings they considered important. They made special efforts to attract people with building skills to their settlements or, as in the case of the Spaniards in the Southwest, to obtain architectural plans and a labor force to execute them.

A more penetrating explanation has to do with the minor presence of government and, therefore, the lack of a concentration of authority to be manifested in buildings. The colonies were settled in different ways, but they were generally governed from a great distance with only a few minor officials making decisions on the spot. Whereas the court and all its governmental functions were increasingly celebrated in architecture in seventeenth- and eighteenth-century Europe, these institutions were all but absent from the colonies.

If there were few opportunities to give prominence to civil authority, then there was even less occasion to display private wealth or the presence of an established religion, because the pattern of land subdivision tended to disperse settlers; it did not draw people to a central point where they might come into daily contact with impressive houses and churches. This distinctive pattern of settlement occurred in several ways. For example, the Virginia Company established in 1610 a method of land apportionment that allowed individuals to accumulate large holdings. These plantations were situated along the many rivers of the area and were isolated from each other. Thus, there were only a few towns, and those were small and difficult to reach. Much of New England was originally settled in small compact towns by people who signed a covenant stipulating that all house lots were to front on a street that served as a boundary for an area of common land. Farm land was located beyond this cluster of houses. These conditions seemed to entail a centralized town, but this pattern of settlement was maintained for only one or two generations. By the end of the seventeenth century most New England towns were spread out over as much as a hundred square miles; the center usually contained only a meeting house and a few other straggling

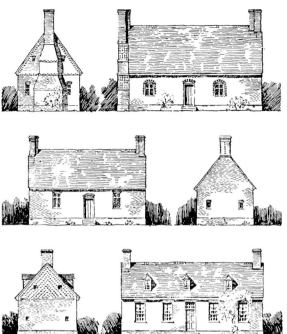

9 Medieval types of dwellings in Virginia.

buildings. Settlement in the other colonies took place in different ways, but in each case the result was the same; abundant land tended to disperse settlers.

Even though throughout the colonies a decentralized pattern of land settlement reinforced the effect created by an extreme climate and the low profile of government, none of these factors had as debilitating an influence on architecture as the uncertain attitude of the settlers toward the fine arts. Although they came to the New World from heterogeneous backgrounds, more arrived from England than from any other country. Thus, the English set the tone of the colonial cultural life.

During the seventeenth century, Puritans in England reacted against the extravagance of previous regimes, often citing lavish buildings as evidence of the excesses of the past. Colonists from England brought this attitude with them. If they were not overtly hostile to architecture as a fine art, then they were largely indifferent to it. As a result, most colonists did not wish to indulge the celebratory nature of architecture and were usually careful not to stray too far from immediate concerns of function and technique. Periods of economic uncertainty, of which there were many, always reinforced the fundamental lesson that a lavish expenditure on buildings was unwise.

By 1700 there were 275,000 settlers in the New World—106,000 in New England, 116,000 in the South Atlantic colonies, and 53,000 in the mid-

Atlantic areas. Given the conditions they encountered, this small and scattered population primarily erected modest variants of the buildings they knew in Europe.

Initially many settlers built shelters that were less sophisticated than those of the people they called Indians. These structures were made mainly of sticks and mud or were simple enclosures dug into a hillside. Such ephemeral houses were not endowed with the values associated with a permanent architecture and were rarely noticed, described, or preserved. So there are few remains of the shelters in which a large portion of the transient settlers of the seventeenth and eighteenth centuries housed themselves.

Evidence of even the more substantial farmhouses of Virginia, where by 1700 three-quarters of the people in the South Atlantic colonies lived, is also sketchy. Although bricks were made in Virginia as early as 1611, most houses were at least partially built of wood and have long since disappeared. Nevertheless, foundations and other fragmentary remains indicate that the Virginia farmhouse went through several phases of development. To begin *9* with, the vast majority were one-story buildings with two or three rooms, but by the middle of the seventeenth century a few prosperous planters were able to erect large houses. Bacon's Castle, for example, built in Surry *10* County in 1655, was an imposing building with five levels inside. The vertical tower that accommodated an entrance and stairway, the decorative chimneys, the side walls that culminated in what resembled a Flemish gable, and a simplified pediment all gave Bacon's Castle a presence which distinguished it from its predominantly unprepossessing neighbors. However, such large structures were not frequently built because by the end

10 Bacon's Castle, Surry County, Virginia, 1655. Reconstruction.

of the century it had become the custom for servants to live away from the main house in separate buildings.

Bacon's Castle may have been grand by the standards of the colonies, but it did not even begin to match the scale and sophistication of contemporary English manor houses. The same was certainly true of churches. Because the charter of the Virginia Company required that the Church of England be the official religion of the colony, churches had to be erected, and probably more than fifty were built in the seventeenth century. The English did not share the missionary zeal of other colonists, so these buildings were no more than simple parish churches which served the few settlers scattered throughout the immediate area. The majority were made of wood, and none of these remain. Of those in masonry, only St. Luke's in Isle of Wight County is still standing. Constructed in 1632, St. Luke's was probably typical of the other churches of the period. The configuration of the entrance tower at the west end leading to a nave is what one would have found in an English village, as were many details, such as the round-arched windows divided by brick tracery into two pointed arches. Like many English churches of the period, St. Luke's also had some rudimentary classical detailing, probably added in the 1650s or later.

The architecture of what is now New York and New Jersey had its own characteristics, but during the seventeenth century it followed the pattern of adaptation that existed elsewhere in the colonies. Thus, architectural traditions were imported from Holland to New Amsterdam and were disseminated as Dutch farmers settled along the Hudson River Valley. Once Dutch rule ended, the architecture of New Amsterdam and other towns came under English influence. But pockets of Dutch settlers remained for many years along the Hudson River and in their isolation were able to maintain a building tradition that showed signs of its descent from Holland. The same is true of the Flemish farmers who settled Long Island and parts of what is now New Jersey. They built a type of farmhouse which had a roof that flared or curved at broadly projecting eaves. Buildings with such roofs were constructed well into the eighteenth century, when the pitched profile was occasionally elaborated into several varieties of gambrel.

New England houses differed from those elsewhere in the colonies. Like those in Essex and East Anglia, from where most of the settlers of New England came, they were primarily made of wood. They were supported by a heavy timber frame, held together by mortise and tenon joints. Within this frame lighter studs and joists were used for partitions and floors. The spaces within the external frame were often filled with a mixture of clay and sticks or bricks. The walls were clad on the outside with clapboards; on the inside they were either plastered or, in the case of the most sumptuous houses,

18

11 St. Luke's, Isle of Wight County, Virginia, 1632.

12 Jan Ditmar's House, Flatlands, Brooklyn, New York, c. 1700.

covered with paneling. Because glass, which was not made in the colonies until late in the eighteenth century, had to be imported and was therefore scarce, windows were small. However, casement windows with small diamond-shaped panes set in lead bars were sometimes combined to give the appearance of a larger opening.

13

The plan of these houses also differed from that of other colonial houses. A one-room house had a chimney at one end. The front door opened toward it into an entrance hall. Directly across from this area, often intertwined with the chimney, was a steep stair that led to an attic or sleeping loft. In two-room houses the chimney was located in the center, but the building had the same entry sequence. Additional space could be created with a lean-to, often for a kitchen, at the back. Dormers or the transformation of the gable roof into a gambrel could expand the attic.

The New England colonies, unlike Virginia, were dominated by a powerful theocracy, which produced a system of independent churches that were conceived as an alternative to the pomp and ritual of the Church of England. The result in architecture was a unique building, a foursquare hall called a meeting house, which served both religious and secular functions. The meeting house was not organized with a long nave leading to an altar. Instead, the altar was replaced by a pulpit situated in the middle of the hall. This type of structure is the one original contribution of seventeenth-century American colonial architecture. The only remaining example is the Old Ship Meeting House in Hingham, Massachusetts. Built in 1681, it was altered in the eighteenth century, but its interior was restored in 1930. The Old

14, 15

14, 15 Old Ship Meeting House, Hingham, Massachusetts, 1681; additions 1731, 1755.

< 13 John Ward House, Salem, Massachusetts, 1684.

Ship Meeting House had a hipped roof with a belfry at the center. It was supported by three trusses made of forty-five-foot-long tie beams, king posts, and stiffening members. The stark grandeur of its interior must have made a striking contrast to the small rooms of nearby houses. This distinction between the sacred and worldly realms was further emphasized by the siting of the meeting house on a hill overlooking Hingham.

By the beginning of the Revolution the population of the colonies had increased markedly—to 2,507,000. Abundant land continued to be the lure of the New World. Therefore only a small percentage of this population resided in cities, of which Philadelphia was the largest with 20,000 inhabitants in 1765. Most colonists still lived off the land, but many of them were able to achieve a degree of comfort well beyond the grasp of their predecessors. This prosperity had mixed consequences for their architecture. On the one hand, it enabled colonists to follow more directly the architectural trends and tastes of Europe; on the other hand, because they could never take prosperity for granted, they could not dispel that deeply rooted sense that the art of architecture was essentially an indulgence.

By the time of the Revolution there was still no one in the colonies who was trained as an architect. The designing of buildings, therefore, was left to two groups. Carpenters and craftsmen, as earlier, were often called upon to supply designs, and they were joined by gentlemen amateurs who, following the example of their English counterparts, considered a knowledge of architecture a necessary attribute of refinement. Although craftsmen and gentlemen amateurs may have differed in other respects, both increasingly relied on the many architectural books then being published in England, where throughout the eighteenth century classical architecture imported from Italy was being absorbed into the local building culture.

These sources had direct consequences for colonial architecture, for though regional differences persisted, the same book was often used in both Massachusetts and Virginia and thus tended to produce a conformity of architecture throughout the colonies. Because the books arrived from England sporadically, often many years after they were published, colonists also tended to draw upon them indiscriminately. They were not attuned to the nuances of the discussion on architecture that was taking place in England. In fact, whereas in Europe this was a fertile period for architectural discourse and publication, in the New World there was virtually no written discussion on the subject. Thus, the distinctions that marked the sequence of interpretations of the classical language in the mother country were only dimly reflected in the buildings of the colonies.

Because so much colonial architecture was inspired by images in books, a degree of dilution was inevitable. Thus, the period's typical building—

16 City Tavern, New
Amsterdam (New York),
1641–42; used as Stadthuys
or Town House, 1654–99.

whether church, house, or for government—was a simple, cubic structure,
usually of wood. This basic volume was an efficient enclosure, typically
capped by a gable or hipped roof that could easily shed rain and snow. To
this format was added, as an emblem of refinement and achievement,
classical detailing at the doors, windows, and along the roofline, as well as at
critical places in the interior. Distance from sources should have given
colonists the freedom to interpret in a fresh way the fundamental question of
the relationship of the part to the whole and to make a statement, as French
designers were then doing, about the nature of the elements of architecture.
But none of the colonists had the background or inspiration to do this. Their
buildings were therefore not original in the sense of offering a vital
interpretation of the language of architecture, nor did they have the sense of
refinement that is sometimes characteristic of works which seek only to
make incremental extensions to a well established tradition. Instead, the
buildings of the American colonies were usually characterized either by a
sedulous concern for correctness or by a quality of abstraction which
achieved at best a naive elegance. These were the inevitable consequences of
an essentially provincial culture.

The difference between the architecture of the seventeenth and eighteenth
centuries was evident in all types of structures, but was most pronounced in
buildings erected for the conduct of public affairs. During the seventeenth
century there were few such buildings and all of them were modest. The
State House at St. Mary's, Maryland, for instance, consisted of one large
room with an entrance porch and stair tower at the back. The first State
House in Jamestown, Virginia, was actually composed of three connected
houses built in two stages in 1635 and 1655. Public buildings elsewhere were
equally unpretentious. In New Amsterdam the Stadthuys was a converted   16
tavern.

23

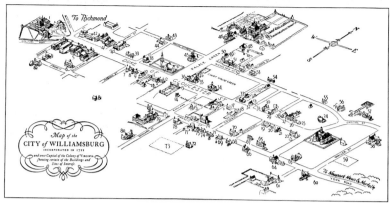

17 Plan of Williamsburg, Virginia.

A comparison of the first State House in Jamestown with the buildings that were erected with the removal of the Capitol to Williamsburg in 1699 illustrates the change that took place at the turn of the seventeenth century. A few seventeenth-century towns, most notably Philadelphia, had been laid out with deliberate plans, but these were usually only street grids with little
17   differentiation. Williamsburg was unusual because it was designed to give prominence to major buildings. The town was ordered around two streets. Duke of Gloucester Street—ninety-five feet wide, and seven-eighths of a mile long—culminated in the College of William and Mary at the west and the Capitol at the east. This thoroughfare was intersected by the Palace Green, which terminated at the Governor's Palace.

    The three major buildings of Williamsburg have many characteristics in
18   common. The design for the College of William and Mary was sent to the colonies from England and may have been conceived by Christopher Wren. It was a four-story brick block on axis with Duke of Gloucester Street. At the back there was a U-shaped court flanked by low wings containing the dining hall and chapel. The difference between front and back was one mark of subtlety that distinguished this building from its predecessors, but there were others. The accentuation of the center, the omission of windows at the end of the building to give a sense of solidity to the corners, and the strong vertical nature of the windows, dormers, and cupola were the gestures of a knowledgeable designer.
19   The Capitol had many of the same features and details as the college. It consisted of two wings connected by an open arcade with rooms above. The east wing contained a hall for the House of Burgesses; the west wing held the General Court and the Governor's Council. Of the three main buildings at

18 Christopher Wren (?): College of Williams and Mary, Williamsburg, Virginia, 1695–1700.

19 Henry Cary (overseer): Capitol, Williamsburg, Virginia, 1701–05; reconstructed 1928–34.

Williamsburg the Capitol was volumetrically the most sophisticated, because its two semicircular projections were capped by a hipped roof that covered the rest of the building. The decision to omit fireplaces left the roof free of punctuations and gave special prominence to the cupola.

20   The Palace of the Governors was the most sumptuous residence in the colonies. The Palace Green ended at the gate to a forecourt that was bounded by the palace and two service buildings. The steeply pitched roof, the vertical cupola, and the irregularly spaced windows all revealed a lack of ease with the principles of classical architecture. The building itself consisted of a hall that gave access on the right and left to a reception room and family dining room. Behind these spaces were a state dining room and stair hall. The second story included family bedrooms and a sitting room. Perhaps because this accommodation was not sufficient for official occasions, a ballroom, twenty-six by forty-seven feet, was added on at the back around 1750. Behind this was a smaller supper room.

These three buildings acted as the termini of the major streets of Williamsburg, but the rest of the town never developed in a manner that was commensurate with this generous plan. The town was crowded when government and court were in session, but when they were not, especially during the torrid summers, it was all but abandoned. The danger of overbuilding was heeded in other colonies. In 1742, the Maryland Assembly voted to grant money to build a governor's house that might have rivaled that in Virginia, but after two years of construction, the assembly had a change of heart, refused further funds, and for forty years the building stood unfinished.

21   The most prominent public building in Philadelphia was the Old State House or Independence Hall. It had a generous stairway, which led to a second-floor balcony, and two significant rooms—one originally for the Court of Common Pleas, the other for the Pennsylvania Assembly. The building's most prominent feature was its tower, which became progressively lighter the higher it ascended, thus making a transition from the solid base to the vertical cupola, steeple, and weather vane. This tower, possibly the most accomplished piece of American colonial architecture, took nearly a century to complete. Land for the State House was purchased in 1730, but because of numerous squabbles about the design, the site, and money, the building was not ready for use until 1745. Construction of the tower, which was part of the original design, only began in 1750. It took three years to finish but was then found to be so rickety that it had to be removed, finally to be restored in 1828.

The changes that occurred in public buildings were mirrored in ecclesiastical work. In New England the meeting-house type of church was

20 Henry Cary
(overseer): Palace of
the Governors,
Williamsburg,
Virginia, 1749–51;
reconstructed 1928–34.

21 Andrew Hamilton
and Edmund Woolley:
Independence Hall,
Philadelphia,
Pennsylvania, 1732–53
and later.

built throughout the eighteenth century. At their best these were straightforward rectangular boxes with gable roofs. Sometimes they had a two-story entrance element that also contained a staircase to a second-level gallery. The doors, windows, and cornice usually had some rudimentary ornament, but the power of these buildings came from the proportions of the basic volume and the relationship of window openings to stark clapboard walls.

The meeting house was gradually superseded by church buildings derived from works by Christopher Wren and James Gibbs. These had longitudinal plans and more elaborate detailing than the meeting house. The main entrance was often marked by a tower and spire and was located at one end of a long nave which was organized into box pews separated by side aisles. In Boston some of these characteristics first appeared in the Old Brick Meeting House, which was finished in 1713. A traditional meeting house in plan, its two-story entrance porch was located in the middle of the long side and was adorned with pilasters. Other bits of classical detailing set this building apart from its predecessors and made it the most elaborate structure of its kind in New England.

A more complete reevaluation of what a church should be soon followed this superimposition of classical elements onto a traditional building. By the early 1720s the makeshift church in which the increasingly prominent Anglican community in Boston worshiped was no longer adequate for the needs of its parishioners. A new building, Christ Church (Old North), was designed by William Price, a print seller who was probably familiar with drawings of Wren's London work. The building consisted of a rectangular block, preceded by a tower with a wooden spire that in its original state was 191 feet high. The interior had longitudinal aisles which led to box pews.

This format was also adopted by the Congregationalists of Boston. In the nearby Old South Meeting House (1729–30), the traditional meeting house entrance on the long side was retained, but the building had arched windows and, more important, a tower and spire, which set it apart from all previous Congregational churches. The successive octagonal stages of the spire were far more sophisticated than its neighbor's square elements. This fact was quickly acknowledged, and the Old South Meetinghouse's spire was copied in at least seven New England churches.

Elsewhere an increasingly affluent population also built churches that went well beyond what was possible earlier, though these buildings were still no more than imitations of what was being constructed in England. In Charleston, South Carolina, St. Michael's was far more elaborate than any of the small parish churches built during the first phases of settlement. Finished in 1753, the church was modeled after James Gibbs's St. Martin's-in-the-

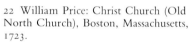

22 William Price: Christ Church (Old North Church), Boston, Massachusetts, 1723.

23 Robert Twelves: Old South Meeting House, Boston, Massachusetts, 1729–30.

24 St. Michael's, Charleston, South Carolina, completed 1753.

Fields. It had, compared to those in Boston, an unusually solid spire with a stout base surmounted by three diminishing octagons, none of which was elaborated by the pinnacles and balustrades characteristic of Wren's work.

St. Paul's Chapel, built in New York City in 1764–66, was also modeled after St. Martin's-in-the-Fields. A vaulted ceiling and engaged Corinthian columns gave its interior a rare spaciousness and opulence. Equally significant were its spire and portico. These were part of the original design, but, as so often happened in the colonies, were omitted in the initial construction and were only added after the Revolution, in 1794 and 1796.

The same tendencies that characterized civic and ecclesiastical architecture were evident in domestic work. The more substantial the house, the more likely there was to be continuity in form from colony to colony, as classical principles then being used in England were adopted. The fine houses of this period were uniformly larger than those built earlier. They either had H-shaped plans or, much more commonly, were variants of a rectangular block, usually with a transverse hall. In these houses the staircase was no longer intertwined with a fireplace. It was given a prominence of its own and was often freestanding. This generosity of space was matched in the heights of the rooms. Before 1700 it was not uncommon for the bottom of the summer beams in the lower story of a house to be less than six feet above the floor, but in many houses of the eighteenth century the parlor ceiling was

25, 26

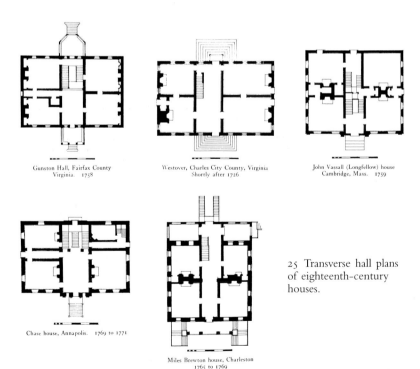

Gunston Hall, Fairfax County
Virginia. 1758

Westover, Charles City County, Virginia
Shortly after 1726

John Vassall (Longfellow) house
Cambridge, Mass. 1759

Chase house, Annapolis. 1769 to 1771

Miles Brewton house, Charleston
1765 to 1769

25 Transverse hall plans of eighteenth-century houses.

26 Westover, Charles City County, Virginia, 1726–30.

from ten to twelve feet high. Similarly, whereas two-and-a-half stories had previously been the highest house, in the eighteenth century many full three-story buildings were constructed.

Although these changes were significant, ·their implications for other aspects of the building were often not decisively acted upon. Houses in the colonies, even those on the largest Tidewater plantations, rarely exceeded four rooms to a floor, and though the staircase was sometimes given great prominence, more often than not it was handled with little finesse. Sometimes it was ungainly in scale, dominating the entrance hall; usually its designer did not know how to extend its language of details to other parts of the space in which it was situated. Similarly, it was usually considered enough to erect a large house; the coordination of outbuildings to make an architectural entity was not generally undertaken. In a few Virginia plantations the main structure was flanked by secondary elements, but these efforts were informed by nothing more than a routine knowledge of the art of landscape gardening. Rarely was the potential of a site realized by establishing a coherent connection between house and garden.

31

27 Richard Munday: Colony House, Newport, Rhode Island, 1739.

The buildings of Newport, Rhode Island, exemplified both the achievements and the limitations of the architecture of the American colonies. First settled in 1639, Newport soon attracted a thriving merchant population because of its harbor and favorable location. Since Rhode Island had adopted in 1637 a strict separation between church and state, Quakers and Jews were among Newport's early settlers and through their cultural interests helped to give the town a breadth of outlook that was unusual in the American colonies. In 1712, when the first survey of Newport was made, the vast majority of the buildings were houses, but there were also nine churches, a building for the conduct of government, several taverns, a mill, and an array of barns, stables, sheds, and other such structures. These buildings can best be described as being in a medieval tradition. Except for a few stone houses and a mill, they were all made of a wood frame, had gable, gambrel, or hipped roofs, and generally were covered with clapboards.

Throughout the first half of the eighteenth century, Newport continued to prosper as it became a vital link in trade routes that extended between England, Europe, Africa, the West Indies, and other American colonies. The general increase in wealth and the contact with distant lands had a marked impact on Newport's architecture. Houses in city and country, churches, buildings for the conduct of public affairs, and many other structures all began to assume attributes of a style associated with Christopher Wren. Newport's most prominent builder was Richard Munday (?–1740), who described himself as a carpenter and innkeeper. Munday designed and built Trinity Church (1726) and many of the town's substantial houses, but his most accomplished work was the Colony House (1739), a building for government functions. A brick structure, eighty by forty feet in plan, the Colony House was set on a rusticated base and was elaborated with freestone beltcourses and quoins. Its focus was an ornate balcony, an intricately carved doorway, and a cupola at the center of a long pitched roof cut off for a flat deck. 27

Munday's background contrasted with that of the man who succeeded him as Newport's preeminent designer. Peter Harrison (1716–76) was born in England and began his adult life as a sea captain. When he married an American-born heiress, he settled in Newport and established himself in shipping. Only then, like other wealthy gentlemen of the period, did he begin to pursue an interest in architecture. From 1748 to 1764 Harrison designed several notable buildings, his first significant work being the Redwood Library in Newport (1748–50). On the evidence of this building, Harrison was chosen to design King's Chapel in Boston (1749–54). A decade later he supplied the drawings for Christ Church at Cambridge (1759–61) and at the same time designed a synagogue for a small congregation of Sephardic Jews in Newport (1759–63). His last substantial building was the Brick Market in Newport (1761–62). 28 29 31, 32 30

Given the colonial context, Harrison's buildings were advanced. The Redwood Library, for example, had the first temple front in the colonies; the portico on King's Chapel was one of the first on a church, and in many other ways, too, Harrison's works stood apart from other buildings in the colonies. By European standards, however, they were in no sense distinguished. Their conception and detail was mainly derived from English books and though Harrison occasionally designed them with skill and grace and was sufficiently knowledgeable not to make obvious blunders, he nevertheless usually betrayed his essentially amateur status.

It must be said, however, that Harrison's clients gave him few opportunities to extend himself. In a sense it was remarkable that they initiated buildings like the Redwood Library in the first place. But too often they did not follow through. For example, construction on King's Chapel began in 1749; the church was opened for services in 1754. But the porch with Ionic columns was not built until the late 1780s, and then was made of

28 Peter Harrison: Redwood Library, Newport, Rhode Island, 1748–50.

wood, not stone as Harrison intended. The spire, which was a vital part of the design, was never executed, and the building has always looked unfinished without it. Harrison faced similar problems on other jobs, especially in designing Christ Church. That building was finally budgeted for only about a third of what the parishioners originally pledged to subscribe for it. Harrison then had to resist efforts by the building committee to omit the tower. Typically, the spire was never built.

One way to turn this situation to advantage might have been to make a virtue of simplicity. The exterior of Harrison's Christ Church has a gaunt dignity because the tower is a straightforward volume and the siding is made of match boarding. Other colonial buildings have the same quality. To those modernist eyes that have wanted to find precursors of an architecture of unadorned white volumes, these buildings have often seemed attractive. It now appears that many were originally painted in bright colors, and it is a mistake to think that their designers considered austerity a virtue. They did

29 Peter Harrison: King's Chapel, Boston, Massachusetts, 1749–54; additions by T. Clement, 1785–87.

30 Peter Harrison: Touro Synagogue, Newport, Rhode Island, 1759–63.

31, 32 Peter Harrison: Christ Church, Cambridge, Massachusetts, 1759–61.

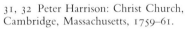

not sanction honorific gestures, but they did usually respond to the opportunity to provide a tasteful level of elaboration whenever it arose.

Another quality on which designers might have capitalized was the disjunction between those forms and details which were highly elaborated and those which were stark and seemingly unfinished. This contrast between aspiration and reality, between what was built and what was unfinished, was evident throughout the architecture of the colonies—for example, in the juxtaposition of the florid capitals and the stark vaulting of Harrison's Christ Church. But though this contrast or disjunction might be said to have been the summary quality of colonial architecture, it was not knowingly exploited for its own sake. To have done so would have presupposed a sensibility that no one at the time had.

By any standard other than a purely local or chauvinistic one, the architecture of the colonial period was at best a marginal achievement, but the great paradox of American architectural history is that this period has received more study than any other. Starting shortly before the Civil War, reaching a peak in the 1910s and 1920s, and continuing even until today, dozens of monographs on colonial buildings have been written, state and local historical societies have been established to preserve the few structures that remain, and even where buildings have disappeared, as at Williamsburg, huge efforts have sometimes been undertaken to reconstruct them. This interest has not been confined to historical studies and preservation campaigns. Its impact has also long been felt on architectural practice. In the 1870s, especially after the centennial celebration of 1876, there was a broad revival and reinterpretation of colonial architecture, and since then American architects have periodically drawn upon these venerable buildings as a source of renewal.

This enthusiasm for colonial architecture is probably more revealing about attitudes of subsequent periods than it is about the buildings of the seventeenth and eighteenth centuries. Because Americans do not have a long architectural history, those interested in their building heritage have naturally been possessive of what little they do have. Except for the architecture of native Americans, the buildings of the colonial period have a primacy because they are the oldest. But they are also attractive because they represent the nation's infancy, a seemingly untrammeled time that contrasts sharply with the more complex periods that followed. As Americans tested out the meaning of nationhood and experienced the results of industrialization, they were attracted by the stories written for them about hardy and devout settlers who lived simply, built directly, and were self-sufficient. Every American, no matter of what background, has been exposed to these themes. Thus it is probably impossible to step over the threshold of a Vermont farmhouse, to sense the cool quiet of its interior, and not to respond to the vision of the unspoiled past that this setting has come to represent. For the same reason Americans feel that Mount Vernon, the home of the first president, is their ancestral home, the nation's childhood home.

These facts raise difficult problems for the historian. On the one hand, it is important to establish the truth. Colonial architecture can be appreciated for what it tells about the lives of its inhabitants, but inevitably it is necessary to measure it against the incomparably more accomplished works of Europe and to indicate that these modest buildings were erected by settlers who at best were ambivalent about the art of architecture. On the other hand, it is important to recognize that the myths that surround buildings are also part of architectural history. In the case of colonial architecture they may be as potent as the reality, if not more so.

The only period in which there has been no enthusiasm for colonial architecture was that in which this work was most familiar—the period which began with the American Revolution. Thomas Jefferson was the most outspoken critic of the meager accomplishments of the colonists in architecture. In *Notes on the State of Virginia*, a tract published originally in France in 1785, Jefferson described the buildings at Williamsburg as a "shapeless pile of bricks" and, after surveying the few structures of merit in Virginia, concluded that the "genius of architecture has spread its malediction on this land."

Jefferson undoubtedly chafed at the quality of the architecture of the colonies even before he traveled abroad, but when he compared the buildings of Virginia to those he saw during his long stay in Europe, he was able to give special emphasis to his remarks. An amateur architect himself, even his first version of Monticello looked provincial in the light of what he saw being built in Paris. Probably anyone who made the comparison would have come to the same conclusion, but in understanding its implications Jefferson also took into account the analysis of American culture then being made in Europe.

Although many European writers were enthusiastic about the prospects of the New World, beginning in the 1750s there had been a countercurrent of opinion which doubted whether a viable civilization would ever develop there. One frequently-asked question was whether Americans could produce great works of culture or art. European critics acknowledged that Americans were a practical people. They already included eminent doctors and scientists, but their accomplishments in the arts were meager. Without the court and other prominent institutions as patrons, it seemed doubtful that they would ever transcend an emphasis on utility in their cultural and artistic output.

This criticism was made from many perspectives and often for indirect or suspect reasons. Nevertheless, Americans were sensitive to it and responding frequently dominated all other concerns. The architects and builders who matured in the first decades after the founding of the new nation were left many legacies from the colonial period. They inherited a dispersed pattern of settlement and some direct and useful knowledge about how to build in the local context, but few Americans then argued that this humble experience was to be the basis of architecture. On the contrary, stung by European doubts about whether the arts could flourish in the New World, the chief concern of American architects was to make a fresh start by transcending the conditions that had limited colonial buildings. In the spirit of independence some called for a uniquely American architecture. This appeal to national sentiment has been powerful and persistent, but even in the decades directly after the Revolutionary War the phrasing of the problem along patriotic lines seemed forced. The more telling question was whether Americans could produce buildings which were worthy of the designation "architecture"—which, in effect, could match the timeless qualities that characterized the great works of other civilizations. The posing of that self-conscious question marked the true beginning of American architecture.

CHAPTER TWO

Temples in Arcadia

The Architecture of the New Republic

In the half century after the signing of the Declaration of Independence, and well afterwards, many Americans continued to have inhibitions about architecture as a fine art. Nevertheless, during this period they had to contend with the fact that architecture had become a subject of civic and national pride. This development was a direct result of independence. In order to assess their new political system, Americans often looked to their cultural output as an index of their productivity and well-being. Since they were conspicuous, buildings attracted special attention. Newspapers were quick to publish reviews or notices of them, and travelers frequently mentioned them in letters and diaries. This scrutiny gave American architecture a new purpose. More so than ever in the colonial period, buildings were now not only frameworks in which to live and work; they were also provocative projections of what Americans wanted to be.

American architects and builders responded to the challenge implicit in this distinction. During this period there was a remarkable degree of enlightenment both as to the nature of architecture and how it could be realized in the circumstances of the new nation. Major figures emerged to produce this flowering, but equally significant was the way in which an enthusiasm for architecture was transmitted to builders and craftsmen in every city, town, or hamlet. The result was not a uniform style. Indeed, there were sharp differences of opinion about what kind of architecture suited a particular context. Nevertheless, given how little discussion there had previously been, the very existence of a debate on the subject was itself an accomplishment.

The work of Charles Bulfinch (1763–1844) is ample evidence of the new significance attached to architecture. Bulfinch came from a prominent Boston family, and his initial interest in architecture was that of a gentleman amateur. After graduating from Harvard College, he worked for a local merchant, and in his spare time designed houses for his employer, family, and friends. The chance to turn hobby into vocation came in 1785, when Bulfinch received a legacy which he used for European travel. After a year and a half in England, France, and Italy, Bulfinch returned to the United States and decided to practice architecture full-time.

Many of Bulfinch's instincts and tastes were conservative, but it is a mistake to think that he was an architect without a compelling message. A self-effacing man, Bulfinch wrote virtually nothing about his approach to architecture, but his buildings make it clear that, in addition to resolving the specific tasks at hand, he always set himself a much broader goal. His intentions were succinctly summarized in an early review of his work: Bulfinch's purpose was "to adorn his native town and country." He designed his buildings so they would serve as standards for future works.

During his career Bulfinch worked in many cities, including Washington, D.C., where from 1817 to 1830 he designed renovations and additions to the Capitol. However, he began and remained essentially an architect of Boston. Bulfinch did not produce a plan of Boston indicating that his buildings might be part of a grand scheme to transform the city, but it is not too far-fetched to think that this was his tacit aim. It is possible to imagine Boston, as Bulfinch might have, with the spaces between his buildings filled in by works based on similar principles.

33   Bulfinch's first executed public commission, a temporary triumphal arch erected in 1789 in honor of George Washington's visit to Boston, was a direct manifestation of his desire to display, even to flaunt, architecture. The Washington Arch was not a sophisticated achievement, but it had lofty ambitions. Spanning Boston's main street in front of the old State House, this simple three-arched screen was probably inspired by a similar work that Bulfinch had seen three years before in Milan. The world of culture inherent in this triumphal arch contrasted sharply with the limited sources upon which the untutored buildings that surrounded it drew. But by spanning the street, the intention of Bulfinch's arch was as much to draw the otherwise incoherent elements of the city together as it was to display a new standard to the throngs that passed under it.

Bulfinch's desire to promote architecture was revealed in the siting as well as the detail of many of his other buildings. Some were located at major intersections so that future buildings would have something positive to which to respond. But his most successful device for bringing architecture to the attention of Bostonians was to capitalize on that city's hilly terrain. In

34   1789 he began a campaign to erect a column on the summit of Beacon Hill, the highest point in the city, to commemorate Boston's role in the Revolution. The monument, as built in 1791, was a distillation of basic classical forms. It consisted of a plinth which served as a base for a simple Doric shaft, which in turn was surmounted by an eagle.

While Bulfinch was promoting and designing this monument, he was also involved with another, even more commanding, work of architecture, the

35   Massachusetts State House. Bulfinch first made a design for the State House

40

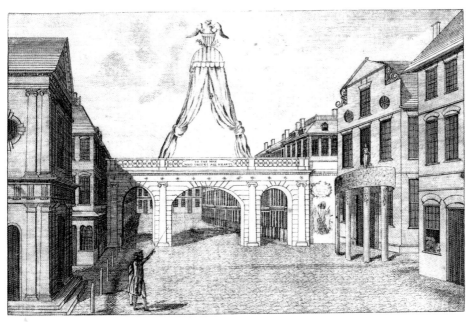

33 Charles Bulfinch:
Washington Arch, Boston,
Massachusetts, 1789.

34 Charles Bulfinch: Beacon
Hill Memorial Column,
Boston, Massachusetts, 1791.

35 Charles Bulfinch: Massachusetts State House, Boston, Massachusetts, 1795–98.

in 1787. The project was not approved until 1795 and building work was not completed until 1798. The result was a striking contrast to the pattern and character of surrounding buildings. Like most of Bulfinch's other works, the State House was based on a well-established precedent. Bulfinch used Sir William Chambers's Somerset House as a model, but he made significant departures from it. He toned down its solemnity by substituting brickwork for heavy rustication and by altering the proportions of the columns. Most important, he made the dome and belfry more vertical than that of its counterpart in London. The dome thus echoed and accentuated the siting of the State House on a hill and gave its profile unrivaled prominence in its surroundings.

The Beacon Hill Memorial Column and the Massachusetts State House were unique structures, but Bulfinch also believed that everyday buildings—the prose as well as the poetry—could contribute to the architectural life of the city. In individual residences, such as those he designed for Harrison Gray

Otis, Bulfinch tried to set a pattern that could be extended on adjacent parcels. But his most important works in this vein were projects for groups of houses in which he convincingly showed that the whole could be more than the sum of its parts. The outstanding development of this type was the Tontine Crescent, which, when it was conceived in 1793, was the most ambitious housing and urban design scheme in the United States. The project was composed of two crescents which formed an ellipse, in the center of which was a small park named in honor of Benjamin Franklin. Only one crescent of this speculative scheme was built, but this range of sixteen houses, extending 480 feet in length, stood decisively apart from its neighbors, not only in its broad scale, but also in the quality of its detailing. The wall of the crescent was made of brick, painted gray to emulate stone. The window and door openings were straightforward, even routine, but this regular wall pattern was offset by an arched passageway and attic in the middle and two projecting end pavilions.

In comparison to English works, especially the buildings of Robert Adam and Sir William Chambers, Bulfinch's architecture was austere. But it is wrong to read into the unpainted brick facade of the State House or the equal arches of the entrance porch of the Church of Christ at Lancaster, Massachusetts (1816), an intention to articulate an aesthetic based on simplicity and a desire not to differentiate parts. Bulfinch had a realistic sense

36

36 Charles Bulfinch: Tontine Crescent, Boston, Massachusetts, 1793. Elevation and plan.

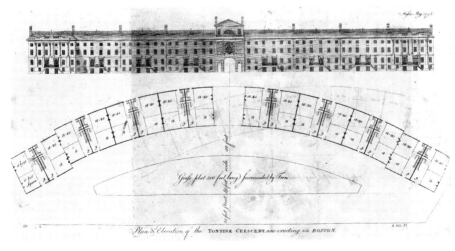

of what could be accomplished in America, but he also had aspirations for architecture which he hoped his countrymen would eventually share.

If Bulfinch was not a proto-functionalist, he was also not a sophisticated neoclassicist. When he traveled to England in 1785, both Adam and Chambers were already old men and their influence in England was waning. Nevertheless Bulfinch drew upon their work throughout his career and ignored contemporary developments in English architecture. He was even more untouched by what was happening on the Continent. When he visited Paris, he saw some of that city's recent buildings, but their progressive principles were never reflected in his own work.

The nature of Bulfinch's references is significant because some of his contemporaries claimed that Americans should shun English traditions and seek the basis of a truly republican architecture either in work then being designed in France or, more pointedly, in the primary sources—the buildings of antiquity. Thomas Jefferson (1743–1826), who as American Minister to France arranged for Bulfinch to see several important Parisian buildings, shared this point of view. When, in 1785, Jefferson wrote his scathing appraisal of the state of American architecture, he did not do so from the perspective of an outsider. He had, as a young man, developed an interest in architecture, which he furthered by collecting a library of architectural books and by finding opportunities to put his ideas into practice. The dominant interpretation has been that Jefferson's architecture was the work of a gentleman amateur who dabbled in the subject while undertaking the more serious business of politics. But his buildings cannot be taken so lightly. They were infused with a passion that went well beyond what the dilettante usually applied to architecture.

Jefferson conceived of his three major works—Monticello, the Virginia State Capitol, and the buildings at the University of Virginia—as the physical frameworks for significant institutions. The independent farm, the state government, and the university each had an important role to play in establishing the kind of society that he hoped would develop in the young nation. Others may have thought about their work in the same terms, but the intriguing fact about Jefferson's buildings is not only that he understood that novel programmatic requirements had to be treated with a fresh interpretation of forms but also, and more importantly, that he was able to achieve this. Even in his first version of Monticello, which he built well before he went to France, Jefferson was not content with the English prototypes that were most frequently used in the colonies. His initial attempt to go beyond these sources was tentative and awkward. The plan of Monticello was uninspired, as was the main elevation, which was a naive adaptation of a Palladian design. Even so, this was not the typical country

37

37 Thomas Jefferson: Monticello, drawing for the first facade, 1771–72.

house of the period. Jefferson seems to have been groping after a special relationship between his building and its context, in both its physical and cultural dimensions. Thus, Monticello's position on top of a mountain may have echoed that of Palladio's Villa Rotunda, but the landscape beyond was not cultivated and contained; it was wild and virtually without limit. Similarly, the extensions from the main building were also uncharacteristic. Instead of making a forecourt, they were turned toward the back. Most important of all, Jefferson seems to have thought that the appropriate shape for this simple country house, as distinct from its far more sophisticated counterparts in Europe, was a basic volumetric enclosure with a full-height portico to provide protected outdoor space at each of the building's two levels.

There are many possible sources for this modest building. Jefferson drew upon European examples, but it is also likely that, despite his feelings about the shortcomings of American architecture, he was intrigued by a characteristic western Virginia farmhouse. The very first building at Monticello, the Honeymoon Cottage, was clearly an interpretation of this local building type. As construction proceeded, this simple cottage was

38 Thomas Jefferson: Virginia State Capitol, Richmond, Virginia, 1785–96.

always retained as part of the overall scheme. The juxtaposition of the Honeymoon Cottage to the main house served to remind Jefferson of the architectural task that lay ahead, but it can also be understood as a statement about the origins of American architecture. Jefferson never elaborated directly upon this retrospective impulse, but it was implicit in his continuing fascination with simple volumetric enclosures.

The first version of Monticello, conceived as early as 1769, was finished in 1782. Two years later Jefferson arrived in Paris, where he remained until 1789. During this period he encountered a world of architecture which, though completely new to him, was one to which he had been predisposed by his early intuitions about what might be appropriate in the New World. The interplay between Jefferson's preconceptions and what he learned in Paris figured prominently in the evolution of the design for the Virginia State Capitol. In 1780 while still in the United States, Jefferson had made several designs for this building. All included a basic rectangular block, capped by a simple gable roof, with a portico on back and front. The architects he met in France, especially C.-L. Clérisseau, urged him to study directly the architecture of the ancient world, rather than absorbing it from the books written by many generations of Italian, French, and English interpreters. However, Jefferson did not embark on a grand tour of architecture. Instead he chose to visit a specific building, the Roman Maison Carrée, which had striking similarities with his already partially formed ideas about the Virginia State Capitol. Jefferson's famous confrontation with the Maison Carrée thus both confirmed the validity of his image of what the Capitol should be and gave him specific ideas for many of its parts and details, such as the portico and the pilasters that encircled the building's sides and back.

When Jefferson returned from France, he began the reconstruction of Monticello, a project which lasted until 1809. The way in which he transformed his house has been the subject of much discussion and conjecture. However, all Jefferson's changes and additions were toward one end: to monumentalize the building. Given his beliefs about the connection between the independent farmer and a truly democratic society, Jefferson thought it important to give to Monticello, which acted as a framework for this way of life, a special presence. He used specific devices to achieve this end. He replaced the entrance hall and doubled the amount of area on each floor. He drew all the parts of the ground floor together with a continuous horizontal cornice and balustrade that culminated in a large pedimented portico. To emphasize the increase in scale that resulted from these gestures, he repressed the second-story windows in the entrance elevation by coordinating them with the first-floor windows. In short, Jefferson did everything he could to accentuate the size of the building and thus to make as sharp a departure as possible from buildings in the English tradition.

Monticello was not simply a house; it also contained outbuildings that were coordinated with the main structure. The University of Virginia (1817–26) was an even more ambitious group of buildings. As in his other works, the significance of its architecture came from the values that Jefferson attached to the institution. To Jefferson, education was a fundamental precondition of responsible citizenship. In his scheme of schooling the university occupied the paramount position. Rather than serving an established religion, as did English universities and those already in existence in the United States, Jefferson's university was to be based on the "illimitable freedom of the human mind."

His revolutionary program needed an equally revolutionary setting. At the University of Virginia, therefore, Jefferson retained no vestige of the monastic courtyard, the traditional basis of the university plan. Instead his "academical village" was essentially three sides of a rectangle. On the closed side Jefferson placed a Pantheon-derived rotunda that contained a library, lecture room, the first planetarium in the United States, a gymnasium, and other shared facilities. Leading to the south from the rotunda were two rows of five separate pavilions, one for each professor and discipline in the

41, 42 Thomas Jefferson:
University of Virginia,
Charlottesville, Virginia,
1817–26. Aerial view, and
plan before 1822.

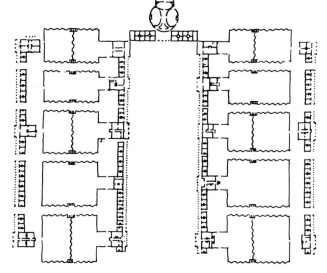

< 39, 40 Thomas Jefferson:
Monticello, near
Charlottesville, Virginia,
1772,1789–1809. Aerial
view and facade.

49

university. Each pavilion had a classroom on the first floor and two rooms for the professor above. Between the pavilions were dormitories. Each range of buildings was connected by a wide portico. Behind were additional dormitories joined to the inner ranges by gardens enclosed by serpentine walls. As originally conceived, the axis established by the rotunda led to the open, south end of the complex and then to the vast surrounding landscape. Jefferson envisaged that as the university grew, more pavilions would be added. The style of the ten pavilions and the rotunda expressed Jefferson's aspirations for the future of architecture in the United States. He intended the university's buildings to be a living example of the history of classical architecture. Each pavilion was based on a different order or Roman source.

Whether this conception was originally Jefferson's and what debt he owed to François Mansart's project for the Château de Marly, William Wilkins's Downing College at Cambridge, England, J.-J. Ramée's plan for Union College in Schenectady, New York, or European hospital designs is a matter of interest, but ultimately not one of great importance. Similarly, there is no need to mythologize the University of Virginia and say, as has often been said, that in the separation and repetition of its pavilions it presaged a uniquely American pattern of land and building development. All this may be true, but the University of Virginia is significant as a work of architecture in its own right. Its stature does not rest either on its origins or on what it promised.

In the event, Jefferson's architecture had little impact on what was to follow. Much more consequential was his suggestion to Congress in 1785 for the subdivision of land north and west of the Ohio River. On Jefferson's advice Congress authorized surveyors to establish a checkerboard grid over an area that stretched from the border between Ohio and Indiana to the West Coast. The surveyors marked out a six-mile grid and then further subdivided these townships into thirty-six one-mile-square sections. The intention was simply to provide a quick and efficient method for dividing vast tracts of land, but this surveying grid had far-reaching consequences. It encouraged the sale of large tracts of land and thus furthered the American propensity for a dispersed pattern of settlement. In addition, since roads between and within towns were usually built along the grid lines, it established the basic plan of most communities in this vast area. Because of Jefferson's seemingly innocuous directive, grids of streets became the standard context for American building.

Charles Bulfinch and Thomas Jefferson were the only American-born architects of the period who were able to see European buildings at first hand. The experience of European architecture was therefore mainly brought to bear on America by books and by European architects who worked or settled in the United States. After the Revolution, the first significant foreign architect to arrive was J. F. Mangin (*fl.* 1794–1817) who came in 1794 and, with John McComb (1761–1853), designed the new City Hall in New York in 1802. Other French architects soon followed: J.-J. Ramée (1764–1842) designed Union College, Pierre Charles L'Enfant (1754–1825) was responsible for the planning of Washington, D.C., Stephen Hallett designed the national Capitol, and Maximilian Godefroy (1765–1840?) was the first professor of architecture in the United States. Significant architects also emigrated from England and Ireland. George Hadfield (1767–1826) worked in Washington, D.C.; William Jay (1792/3–1837) in Savannah, Georgia; James Gallier (1798–1868) in New Orleans, Louisiana; and John Haviland (1792–1852) in Philadelphia, Pennsylvania.

The most important architect to settle in the United States was Benjamin Latrobe (1764–1820). Born in Yorkshire, Latrobe worked for several years for the engineer John Smeaton and in 1787 entered the office of the London architect S. P. Cockerell. Four years later he set up his own practice. In 1795, shortly after the death of his wife, Latrobe arrived in the United States to begin a new life. His technical knowledge was soon sought after in the construction of canals, but Latrobe was also asked to design buildings. This work followed along the lines he had already established in England. Inspired by the buildings of Sir John Soane, Latrobe abandoned the sophisticated forms of Robert Adam and developed an architecture based on simple, geometrical massing, undifferentiated walls, and a logical structure that derived as much from Greek as from Roman architecture.

Latrobe's first important commission in the United States was the new State Penitentiary in Richmond, Virginia (1797–98). While still in England, Latrobe had become familiar with recent discussion on prison architecture, and so was able to produce a design which was advanced in its interpretation of both penology and architectural form. It included water closets in each cell, ventilated rooms, spaces for small groups of reformed prisoners, and separate infirmaries for men and women. The entire prison was encompassed in geometrically simple shapes: a cylinder that contained the cells and several rectangular blocks. Latrobe's choice of material emphasized this straightforward geometry. The first story was made of random stonework; the levels above were of unarticulated brick. Windows were crisply pierced into otherwise undifferentiated walls.

Latrobe was as skilled an engineer as he was an architect. In 1801 he completed a project to supply Philadelphia with water from a central system. This involved moving water by steam pumps and an aqueduct from the Schuylkill River to a storage tank in the center of the city from where it

43

43 Benjamin Latrobe: Virginia State Penitentiary, Richmond, Virginia, 1797–98.

was then distributed by gravity. The main structure of the system was, like the Virginia State Penitentiary, a direct, even blunt, reflection of the functions within. It had two parts. A one-story block contained the pumping machinery and the offices. This mass was surmounted by a cylinder, which housed the storage tank and which was capped by a low dome. The spare detailing of the stonework emphasized these basic shapes.

Latrobe applied the same principles to buildings with more elevated functions and it was in these works that his skill as an architect was most evident. His Bank of Pennsylvania (1799–1801), for example, had a functionally clear plan and section. It was a temple-like building with porticoes on each end that gave access to two levels of secondary spaces, such as an entrance vestibule, stockholders' room, bank vaults, and offices. The center of the building contained a full-height circular room covered by a segmental dome and glazed cupola.

A clear organization does not guarantee a sophisticated work of architecture. The Bank of Pennsylvania's quality came as much from Latrobe's ability to give his forms expression as from the underlying diagram. The side elevation was a case in point. Instead of leaving the wall undifferentiated, Latrobe wisely projected the center volume out a few inches and then carried the mass of that room above the roof line of the front and back sections. The windows in this wall were thematically related, but they also had variations in detail to reflect the different types of rooms within. An even more telling example of Latrobe's skill was the entrance sequence which capitalized on the contrast between the vestibule and the banking room. The vaulted ceiling of the vestibule hinted at the nature of the

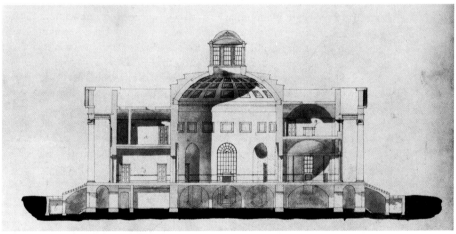

44, 45, 46 Benjamin Latrobe: Bank of Pennsylvania, Philadelphia, Pennsylvania, 1799–1801. Perspective of front, section, and ground floor plan.

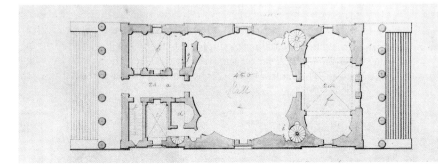

building's main space, but it did not detract from the impact of proceeding from a low area into the expansive cylinder beyond.

The Bank of Pennsylvania was the first building in the United States to be vaulted throughout in masonry. In the use of this type of construction and in the magnificence of its great domed banking room, it served as a precursor
47, 48 for Latrobe's finest work, the Baltimore Cathedral, a commission he received in 1804. Since there were no obvious precedents for this, the first monumental Roman Catholic cathedral in America, Latrobe initially presented two schemes, one Gothic and one classical. He reasoned that Gothic architecture inevitably elicited a degree of "veneration," and thus would be appropriate. His design was a competent, if uninspired, rendering of a Gothic cathedral. Fortunately, it was rejected for the "Roman" design, which went through several stages of development and was completed in 1818, with sympathetic additions to the east end in 1879 and 1890.

The Baltimore Cathedral bore the imprint of English and French late eighteenth-century neoclassicism, not only in its bold massing and subtle detailing, but also in the sequence of interlocking spaces from portico to apse and rotunda with diagonal views through hollowed-out piers to side aisles and transept. The most important space was the crossing, which covered the side aisles as well as the area at the intersection of the nave and transept. Because of this enlargement and the resulting spatial complexity, it had an unusually dynamic quality.

Equal in importance to Latrobe's buildings was his training of apprentices who eventually made a significant impact on American architecture. Chief among these was Robert Mills (1781–1855). Born in Charleston, South Carolina, Mills attended Charleston College where he studied the classics and wrote essays on architecture. He then worked for several years for the best architects he could find. After a few months with James Hoban, who designed the White House, he spent two years working for Thomas Jefferson and then helped Benjamin Latrobe with the Bank of Pennsylvania. Because of this background, Mills later claimed to have been the first native-born person purposefully trained for the profession of architecture.

Mills once advised American artists: "Study your country's tastes and requirements, and make classic ground *here* for your art. Go not to the old world for your examples. We have entered a new era in the history of the world: it is our destiny to lead, not to be led." Mills had decisive ideas about the nature and significance of his "country's tastes and requirements." His life-long interest in commemorative monuments was the most direct manifestation of his fascination with symbolic form. But just as he always tried to make his monuments simple and direct—a colossal Doric column for
49 the Washington Monument in Baltimore, Maryland (1814, completed

47, 48 Benjamin Latrobe:
Baltimore Cathedral, Baltimore,
Maryland, commissioned 1804,
dedicated 1821. Exterior, and
interior looking from the
crossing towards the choir. The
towers and portico were built
later (the towers probably not
to Latrobe's design). In 1890
a spacious choir was inserted
between the crossing and the
columned apse, as Latrobe had
originally wished.

49 Robert Mills: Washington
Monument, Baltimore, Maryland,
1814, completed 1829.

50 Robert Mills: Monumental
Church, Richmond, Virginia, 1812.

1829); an obelisk for the Washington Monument in the nation's capital
(1833, completed without the circular colonnade in 1884)—Mills's buildings
were always based on an immediate logic of plan and construction.
Commodity and utility were to be emphasized in building for such a young
and raw nation.

Mills's knowledge of construction had its most overt impact on the
County Record Office or, as it is better known, the Fireproof Building,
which was completed in 1822 in Charleston. Because the building was to
contain offices and space for record-storage, it had to be fireproof. Mills's
ability to make such a structure did not come only from his knowledge that
if timber floor framing was to be eliminated, a completely vaulted structure
was necessary. Equally important was his understanding that this technique
had important consequences for plan and expression. The building was
rigidly organized into a grid of nine squares. Eight of these contained groin-
vaulted rooms; the central one had an open stairway. Two barrel-vaulted
corridors gave access to all the rooms. Such solid construction demanded
little elaboration. Mills thus treated the Fireproof Building as an
uncompromisingly compact two-story block set on a high base and entered
through two Doric porticoes.

Mills's main innovation in plan, and a way in which he directly reflected
his "country's tastes and requirements," was in the design of churches. Mills

56

lived at a time when preaching was becoming a major force in American religion as unprecedentedly large crowds flocked to hear a new generation of popular ministers. The attenuated nave of the Gibbs-derived church did not suit these new conditions. In the Sansom Street Baptist Church, Philadelphia, Pennsylvania (1808–09); the Monumental Church, Richmond, Virginia (1812); and the Octagon Unitarian Church, Philadelphia (1813) Mills developed an auditorium-type church that had as one of its primary objectives the accommodation of the maximum number of parishioners within the shortest distance of the preacher. Each of these churches had at its center a regularly shaped auditorium that was given direct expression on the exterior. 50

Whereas Mills's buildings bore the stamp of his conscientious personality, the works of William Strickland (1788–1854), another of Benjamin Latrobe's apprentices, were the products of a more mercurial mind. The influence of the master was most obvious in Strickland's major work, the Second Bank of the United States, Philadelphia, Pennsylvania (1818–24). The plan of this building owed an obvious debt to that of the Bank of Pennsylvania, but the sequence of rooms had its own character, just as its Doric porticoes differed from Latrobe's Ionic. The distinctive feature of the plan was not merely its evident logic and efficiency—a quality which Strickland undoubtedly absorbed from Latrobe—but the varied sequence of 51

elegant rooms from the north portico, to an oval-shaped vestibule, to a
lobby, to a banking room with a barrel-vaulted ceiling supported by two
rows of freestanding columns, to another tight lobby, to a groin-vaulted
stockholders' room, and finally to the south portico.

Strickland's portico, which contemporaries described as strikingly
beautiful, has long been an ornament to Philadelphia's streetscape, but his
52 most successful work of urban architecture was the Philadelphia Exchange
(1832–34), which occupied a difficult but prominent triangular site at the
intersection of Walnut, Dock, and Third Streets. Strickland dealt with the
unusual shape of the site by placing the building's major facade on Third
Street; a rounded portico capitalized on the view down Walnut and Dock
Streets. The form of the portico was reflected in the exchange's circular
tower. The vertical organization of the building was equally suited to the
site. The building was composed of a solid full-story-high base which served
not only as an entrance to the rooms on the two stories above, but also as the
location for the many stores which lined the streets on which the exchange
was situated.

51 William Strickland: Second Bank of the United States, Philadelphia,
Pennsylvania, 1818–24.

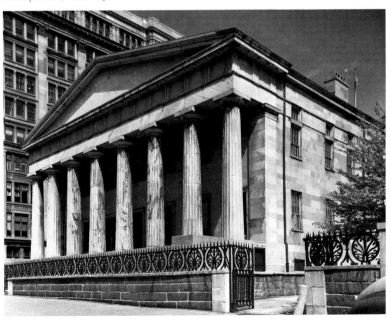

52 William Strickland: Philadelphia Exchange (Merchants' Exchange), Philadelphia, Pennsylvania, 1832–34.

By the 1820s Mills and Strickland had been joined by a considerable group of architects such as Alexander Parris (1780–1852), Ammi Young (1798–1874), Isaiah Rogers (1800–69), Gideon Shryock (1802–80), and Thomas U. Walter (1804–87), all of whom were producing work of merit. Of equal significance, however, were those practitioners who continued to describe themselves as builders. In his 1785 comments on the state of architecture, Thomas Jefferson complained that it was impossible to find a builder who knew how to draw an order. Fifty years later this was no longer the case. The education of the American builder was largely due to a new type of architecture book. Previously, not only had few books on architecture been available, but, since they were written in Europe, much of what they contained could not be applied to a context in which wood was the dominant building material. Besides, few American clients could afford or even wanted what was perceived to be the staple of the English architectural book, the large country house.

By the 1820s there were several American books on architecture. The first and foremost author of these works was Asher Benjamin (1773–1845). Benjamin had a long and distinguished building career, but he was much better known for his writing. His first book, *The Country Builder's Assistant*,

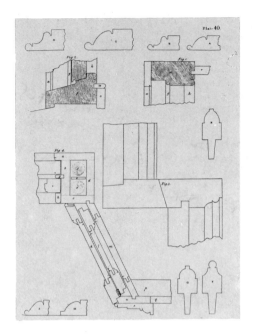

53 Asher Benjamin: Plate XL,
*The American Builder's
Companion*, 6th edition, 1827.

53

went through forty-seven frequently revised editions between 1797 and
1856. *The American Builder's Companion* followed in 1806, and Benjamin
wrote five other books, all of which were frequently republished.
Benjamin's significance, as indicated by the word "American" in the title of
his second book, was that he tailored his information to an audience of native
builders. His works were illustrated with examples of contemporary
American buildings, and he assumed throughout that his readers would
probably build in wood. Equally important, his style of writing and
presentation had a commonsensical directness that was lacking in European
books.

How the American builder used books such as Benjamin's varied. A few
were able to interpret their guidelines to create a body of consistent work.
The best known of such builders was Samuel McIntire (1757–1811), who
worked exclusively in and around Salem, Massachusetts. The key to

54, 55

McIntire's art was the narrowness of the problem he set himself. Most of his
houses were three-story rectangular solids with flat or undemonstrative
roofs. Their plans were based on a central entrance and a largely symmetrical
room arrangement. The architectural issue on the exterior was, therefore,
how to compose the facade with proper proportions and a suitable hierarchy
of detailing that focused on the entrance; and on the interior, to give each
room an appropriate character.

60

54, 55 Samuel McIntire: Pingree House, Salem, Massachusetts, 1804–05. Facade and front parlour.

McIntire's work was an exploration of these limited but fundamental themes. His earliest houses were simple to the point of austerity. The doorway, though the main feature of the facade, often consisted of no more than a pedimented portico supported by two freestanding columns. Later he began to use side-lights, an elliptical fan light, and a semicircular portico supported by florid orders. As he gave emphasis to the doors, McIntire played down the windows which never departed, except in unexecuted designs, from a rectangular format. The casings of his early houses were often elaborated with a frieze and cornice. Later, McIntire tended to simplify these elements so that they would be more continuous with the plane of the facade.

The rooms in McIntire's houses had a similar combination of straightforwardness and subtlety. Symmetrical in plan, they were organized to give emphasis to the doorway, the fireplace, and the windows. He employed themes of detailing to unify these elements, but at the same time emphasized the identity of the parts. Thus his fireplaces frequently had a frieze that could be read as composed of both one and three panels. Similarly, flanking columns were entities, but also had palpable subdivisions.

Less is known about the lives of other builders, but many of the works from this period display both the varied personalities that were brought to bear upon architecture and the shared enthusiasm for that subject. The noble portico of the Perkins House in Windham, Connecticut (1832), the elliptical arches of the facade of the Rider House in Rensselaersville, New York (1823), the intricate parapets of the Norris House in Bristol, Rhode Island (1810), and hundreds of other equally striking details all attest to the fact that builders throughout the United States were not only thinking about architecture, but were also enjoying it.

Such builders have often been criticized for not finding that elusive median between convention and invention and for being either slavishly imitative or indulgently original. This criticism has often focused on their use of the Greek temple front. On the one hand, it had become too much of a standard; it was applied indiscriminately to house, bank, tavern, or store. On the other hand, it was rarely designed according to precedent. American builders quickly learned that a wood column supporting only a light load could be much thinner than a stone member holding up a heavy pediment. Such attenuation not only seemed awkward to critics who knew the history of the orders, but it was also symptomatic of a tendency to place expediency over a concern for the culture of architecture.

Although many examples can be found to validate this criticism, the same points can also be used to illustrate the positive qualities of the period's architecture. The temple front may often have been used indiscriminately, but the flaunting of this iconic element served a purpose that was deeper than functional appropriateness. Its persistent use was a statement about republicanism; it was an affirmation of that system of government and an acknowledgment of a common set of values. Similarly, the custom adopted in this period of painting all buildings white, even older structures, has often been called an insensitive response to local circumstances and a manifestation of a worrying tendency toward conformity. But this convention also showed that architecture had become an important medium of expression, one which Americans could use to show their shared identity as citizens of a new nation.

A similar interpretation can be made of many gestures which have often been called ungainly and ungrammatical. They can be thought of as attempts to find an appropriate local or regional realization of basic classical themes. The temple front may frequently have been used unthinkingly, but it was often artfully adapted to a specific location. It could serve the narrow house lots of Charleston, South Carolina, as well as the ample frontages of the gridded towns of the Ohio valley; it was applicable equally to the hot and humid climate of the Mississippi plantation house and the cold winters of the Nantucket whaler's residence; it could be made of stone to give presence to a prominent urban building and of wood as was appropriate for a modest country house. Similarly, the formal front did not necessarily lie about what happened behind. The New England farmhouse of this period may have had a portico which led to a sequence of house, shed, barn, and outbuildings, all of which were frequently joined together and straggled into the backyard. Yet the front and the back each encapsulated a significant aspect of the life and dreams of the inhabitants of these buildings. Although different, the two can be read as complementary parts of an unaffected whole.

The new interest in architecture revealed even in these modest buildings is undeniable, but it is important to remember that American practice at this time was not free of debilitating problems and disputes. The irregular careers of those who tried to make their living as architects show how hard it was to be a professional. For example, when Charles Bulfinch went bankrupt trying to finance the Tontine Crescent, he became and for twenty years remained chairman of Boston's Board of Selectmen and superintendent of its police force. That full-time job provided him with a livelihood, but it also drained much of the energy he might have given to architecture. When Benjamin Latrobe arrived in the United States, he had high aspirations and even published a portfolio of projects that he hoped soon to build. But he quickly became disillusioned by what he perceived to be an uncaring public, was constantly in financial difficulty, and was more sought after for his engineering knowledge than for his skill as an architect. In 1813, after over a

56

63

decade of uneven practice, Robert Mills became general architect to the federal government in order to secure a regular income. Nevertheless, after twenty years of service in that position, he bitterly complained that he was penniless. Builders experienced similar vicissitudes. Asher Benjamin's career as a designer–builder was interrupted from 1810 to 1828 when he kept a paint store and worked as a mill agent in Manchester, New Hampshire.

It was easy to blame an untutored and unappreciative public for not being good patrons, but architects often did not help each other or themselves. As competition for desirable jobs increased, backbiting became common. Benjamin Latrobe's most revealing conflict was with his American apprentices Robert Mills and William Strickland. While publicly offering them encouragement, Latrobe privately (and in letters to other European architects trying to establish themselves in the United States) complained that American architects, and Mills in particular, were all too ready to compromise professional standards to get a commission. Other European architects had an equally difficult time in the United States. Maximilian Godefroy and J.-J. Ramée both eventually returned to France. Stephen Hallett, after achieving early success, lived out his years in obscurity. After J. F. Mangin designed the City Hall in New York, he had a patchy career for the next fifteen years, and then disappeared from public view.

The trying state of architectural practice had important implications for the discussion of architectural principles. For example, when Latrobe used forms based on Greek precedents in his Bank of Pennsylvania, he attached no ideological significance to these origins, beyond a general sense of appropriateness. However, by 1814 a few Americans were already claiming a special affinity between the American and Greek republics. When the Greeks went to war with the Turks in 1821, the Greek temple front became the symbol of republicanism. As the portico proliferated, architects often decried such an unthinking adaptation of form to function. Nevertheless, they also championed Greek architecture, or specific versions of it, for less than idealistic reasons. Many favored the Doric order, not out of any sense of appropriateness, but because it was easier and cheaper to build. Robert Mills, for example, emphasized commodity and firmness because he understood that these were the qualities which most directly appealed to his clients. Much to Latrobe's disgust, Mills knew all too well his country's "tastes and requirements." Probably no one understood these problems better than Thomas Jefferson. He shunned Greek architecture and remained committed to what he thought were the more complex and subtle Roman orders. But he did not make his living from architecture. Had he done so, he might have had to reflect more deeply on his experience with the Virginia State Capitol, the scope of which was drastically reduced by a recalcitrant legislature.

DESIGNS

OF BUILDINGS ERECTED OR PROPOSED TO BE BUILT

IN VIRGINIA, BY

B. Henry LATROBE Bernd.

From 1795 to 1799.

56 Benjamin Latrobe: Title
page of *Designs of Buildings
Erected or Proposed to be Built
in Virginia from 1795 to 1799.*

Both the problems and the promise of the period's architecture were
encapsulated in the experience of planning and building the nation's capital.
It was frequently charged that in the new republic, with no court as patron,
the arts would never flourish. The building of the capital was, therefore, a
conspicuous test case of whether architecture could prosper in the new
system. It also raised the compelling question: What kind of architecture is
appropriate for a democracy?

During and directly after the Revolutionary War, the Continental
Congress moved frequently. Because of disputes about its location, the site
for a new city was not chosen until 1790. Washington, D.C., was planned by
Major Pierre Charles L'Enfant, a French volunteer who had become an
officer during the Revolution. L'Enfant had trained as both an artist and
engineer. He had grown up at Versailles, where his father had been a court
painter, and was familiar with the techniques used by André Le Nôtre to
shape the grounds of the Palace. This knowledge had a direct bearing on his
ideas for the nation's capital. From the outset both he and George
Washington wanted a "grand plan." L'Enfant stipulated that the city's
avenues were to be broad, eighty feet wide with thirty feet on each side for a
sidewalk with a double row of trees. The most important aspect of the plan

57

was L'Enfant's attempt to develop the city comprehensively over time. He based the city on a series of focal squares, each one either to be developed by one of the states or to serve as the location of a major institution such as a national church or college. L'Enfant connected these points by grand boulevards, at the intersections of which were fountains. The center of this ambitious plan was a four-hundred-foot-wide mall, leading from the Capitol to the Potomac. On Washington's periphery the street system connected with the major roads leading out of the city.

Washington's growth in its first three decades was slow. Foreign visitors often mocked "The City of Magnificent Distances," calling it instead "The City of Magnificent Intentions." Indeed the long vistas interspersed with thickly overgrown woods and the private houses next to major buildings must have seemed incongruous, and it was many years before the city grew to a size that was commensurate with L'Enfant's grand plan.

The buildings of Washington had as checkered a history as the plan itself. By 1830 only two major government buildings, the Capitol and the White House, were complete. Both buildings resulted from competitions which revealed much about the state of United States architecture at this time. Competitions were held so that American architects could have a chance to design the buildings, but it soon became apparent that no native entry was suitable. Thus, the commission for the White House went to an Irish-born architect, James Hoban (1756–1821). His scheme was derived from a design by James Gibbs. As such, it was English in inspiration and detail, with little to suggest that it was the residence of the president of a new democratic nation.

The story of the Capitol competition is more complex. No scheme was deemed good enough for the award, but the French-born architect Stephen Hallett was retained to improve his design. William Thornton (1759–1828), a doctor from the Virgin Islands and a designer in the tradition of the gentleman amateur, asked to submit a design. The officials consented and awarded the prize to Thornton. In the end, however, Hallett was retained to evaluate Thornton's plan, and thus began years of acrimony in which Thornton, Hallett, and Benjamin Latrobe, who was appointed Surveyor of Public Buildings in 1803, struggled for control of the enterprise.

The conflict was resolved to an extent in 1814 when the British attacked Washington and burned both the White House and the Capitol. In the subsequent rebuilding Latrobe was responsible for much of what is fine in these buildings. Although he had to adhere to Thornton's design for the exterior of the Capitol, Latrobe suggested that the central block be capped with a dome, which Thomas U. Walter later replaced with an even higher version. Latrobe was freer to shape the Capitol's interiors. The smooth walls and vaults of the vestibule of the Senate wing were evidence of his

58, 59

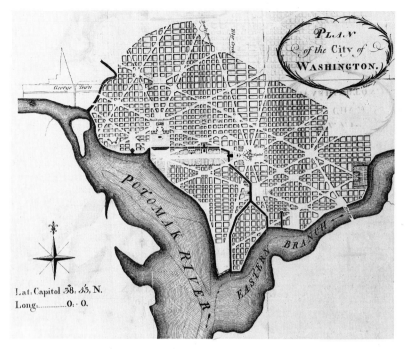

57 Andrew Ellicot: Plan of Washington, 1792. (After Pierre Charles L'Enfant)

sensibility, as were the columns in that space. These famous columns had 60
capitals decorated with corn motifs and a fluting pattern based on a stalk.
Latrobe had less influence on the rebuilding of the White House, but he did 61
design the front portico, giving the building a much more impressive
entrance than Hoban's unduly modest doorway.

By the nation's fiftieth anniversary no one could have been oblivious to
the shortcomings of American architecture epitomized in the planning and
building of Washington, D.C. But Americans were not especially reflective
about these matters. They prided themselves on the advances that had taken
place in the previous decades and looked forward to continued progress. In
the 1830s and 1840s many buildings continued to be erected which repeated
and elaborated upon the themes that had first been articulated in the years
directly after independence. Especially in the rural parts of the United
States—in the Deep South and the small towns of the Midwest—this vision
of a classical America persisted for many years. However, the anticipated

67

58 William Thornton, Benjamin Latrobe, Charles Bulfinch: United States Capitol, Washington, D. C., 1792–1830.

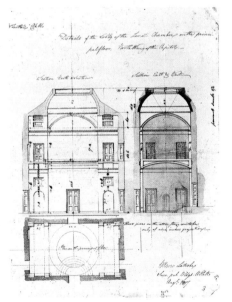

59 Benjamin Latrobe: Design for the lobby of the Senate wing, United States Capitol, Washington, D. C., 1807.

60 Benjamin Latrobe: corn cob columns in the vestibule of the Senate wing, United States Capitol, Washington, D. C., c. 1809.

68

61 James Hoban and Benjamin Latrobe: President's House (White House), Washington, D. C., 1815.

flowering never took place. Some of the temples built in what might otherwise have seemed close to an Arcadian landscape were inhabited by an increasingly criticized class of slaveholders whose chattels often had to live in squalid hovels. From a distance other temples may have looked like farmhouses, but they were in fact factories producing goods to be sold to Americans then being drawn from the countryside to rapidly growing cities. In the 1820s no one, no matter how farsighted, understood the implications of these facts. But it would soon be apparent that a new type of society, one not envisaged by the founding fathers, was taking shape. These changes were so encompassing that no aspect of the culture, especially architecture, could remain untouched by them.

CHAPTER THREE

Beauty and the Industrial Beast

Architecture for a Culture of Commerce

When Americans of the 1820s drew an analogy between their society and culture and that of ancient Greece and Rome, they were not simply indulging in fanciful rhetoric. The comparison was plausible because some basic conditions of their everyday life confirmed a sense of continuity with civilizations remote in time and distance. The nature of American cities was a significant case in point. The New York cities, Ithaca, Rome, and Syracuse, for example, did in fact share some vital characteristics with the places after which they were named. They were, first of all, small. In 1820 New York was the largest American city; 152,000 inhabitants lived in what later would become the five boroughs. Only four other cities then had more then 25,000 residents and only 7 percent of the population lived in communities with a population of 2,500 or more.

The self-contained and isolated nature of these settlements also matched that of their ancient counterparts. In the 1820s the journey even between cities as close as Hartford and New Haven was difficult. Roads were bad, navigation routes were not systematically charted, and ships and coaches did not run according to a regular schedule. Transportation remained rudimentary because few people needed to travel. Cities were largely self-sufficient. They did not produce many goods to be distributed elsewhere; their economic ties to other places resulted primarily from the warehousing and exchanging of the limited staple crops that irregularly trickled in from the hinterlands.

Within half a century these age-old conditions were quickly and irrevocably transformed. By 1870 New York's population had burgeoned to over one million inhabitants, a figure all but inconceivable a few years earlier. Five other urban centers had more than 250,000 residents, there were forty-five cities with more than 25,000 inhabitants, and 25 percent of the nation's citizens lived in communities with a population of 2,500 or more.

Even more significant than this extraordinarily swift urbanization was the change in the structure of the nation's economy. In 1820 the basic unit of production was the small isolated farm. By 1870 the mechanization of both manufacturing and agriculture, the construction of rapid and reliable transportation systems, and the establishment of efficient business techniques had all been instrumental in linking not only the expanding cities, but also the previously unsettled parts of the continent into one economically interdependent entity. The result was a quick and often painful transition from a traditional to a modern society.

This transformation had profound implications for every aspect of American life. In architecture the change was so substantial that it called into question the utility of the accumulated experience of the past. This sense that architecture had to be rethought was in part a response to what was perceived to be an enormous increase in the programmatic complexity of buildings. Previously, when architects like Benjamin Latrobe and Robert Mills had to devise a new type of prison or church, they were able to find precedents in classical architecture to guide them. But in the antebellum period architects increasingly came to the conclusion that the institutions to be housed in the buildings they were designing were both so new and so complex that such ready analogies could not plausibly be made.

Architecture was equally affected by changes in building materials and techniques. The eighteenth century was a fertile period of invention in building technology, but architects then generally were able, as with shifting programmatic requirements, to incorporate these innovations into the practices that had long served them. In the nineteenth century this was no longer so readily the case. Rapid systems of transportation now often made a type of stone quarried a thousand miles away cheaper than a local one. Stone also began to have to compete with new materials such as glass, cast iron, and steel. Faced with choices such as these and with dozens of new machines which had started to transform the way building materials were shaped both on and off the site, architects began to lose their sense of command over the making of buildings. They could no longer so easily master the expertise that had previously enabled some of them to double as engineers. Also, as the complexity of running a practice increased, they felt ever more isolated from craftsmen and laborers whose habits of work were also being transformed.

Forced to cope with such novel and demanding programmatic and technical requirements, American architects might have been expected to make these factors the foundation of a new approach to architecture. In a series of remarkable essays, written mainly in the 1840s, the American sculptor Horatio Greenough (1805–52) made this case. His theory of architecture entailed:

A scientific arrangement of spaces and forms to functions and to site; an emphasis of features proportioned to their *gradated* importance in function; color and ornament to be decided and arranged and varied by strictly organic laws, having a distinct reason for each decision; the entire and immediate banishment of all make-shift and make-believe.

Functionalism in architecture has had a varied history. Greenough's ideas resemble those of the eighteenth-century Venetian author, Carlo Lodoli. Greenough may have read interpretations of Lodoli's works when he was living in Florence, and in turn, when Greenough's essays were rediscovered in the 1940s, he was quickly championed as a precursor of modern architecture. At the time, however, except for a handful of transcendentalists centered around Concord, Massachusetts, virtually no one paid any attention to him.

Although architects and critics were quick to point out the failings of simplistic formulas drawn from precedents like the Greek temple, they still believed that a knowledge of the history of architecture was important and that a familiarity with precedents would help them come to terms with the complex conditions they now encountered. However, they had to know a much broader range of prototypes from the past than before. They had to be familiar with Gothic as well as classical architecture, and they also found it necessary to understand the principles at the root of the many minor styles derived from these two fundamental sources.

Such knowledge might indeed suggest useful ways to solve specific problems of practice, but it was not the primary reason why architects of this period studied the buildings of the past. They did so because they thought these sources had an important role to play in the development of the expressive qualities of architecture. Unlike Horatio Greenough, most architects believed that beauty in architecture was at least in part independent of utility. They did not simply acknowledge this fact. They embraced it. At a time when material concerns were thought to be dominating every aspect of American life, it became almost a matter of national urgency to assert the existence of spiritual values by emphasizing the independent nature of beauty in architecture.

Beauty in this sense was defined in two ways. Abstract properties such as proportion and harmony were important, and there was much discussion about the nature and source of the rules that governed such principles. But buildings were also attractive because of their associations. Precisely because they were aware of the drastic changes taking place around them, architects of this period tried to establish in their buildings visible links with the past. Some, especially those influenced by the widely read English authors A. W. N. Pugin (1812–52) and John Ruskin (1819–1900), favored the revival of a specific style or period of architecture which they believed had flourished during and thus epitomized a high state of civilization. Most, however, were

72

not so adamant in their condemnation of the present. They felt that it was important to affirm a sense of continuity with the past, but they were also committed to progress. They based their buildings on precedents, but adapted new functions and techniques to them, transforming the images they drew from the history of architecture.

Even the designers of the period's great engineering works heeded the call of independent beauty. The structures associated with the new transportation routes that did so much to create a national economy were the period's most explicit and dramatic examples of advances in civil engineering. Accounts and illustrations of these structures were frequently included not just in the technical journals of the day, but also in the popular press. Some of these works, such as the five pairs of locks at Lockport, New York (1825–44), were associated with the construction of canals. But the most celebrated engineering works were for railroads. When the Starrucca Viaduct, a 110-foot-high and 1200-foot-long structure of eighteen stone arches, was completed near Susquehanna, Pennsylvania, by the New York and Erie Railroad in 1848, it was considered one of the great achievements of the age. The Hoosac Tunnel (1851–75) in western Massachusetts was notorious, rather than famous; it took over twenty years and the invention of a new digging technology to complete. Nevertheless, it too was celebrated as a significant achievement.

These works may have been classified as civil engineering projects, but parts of all of them, especially major sections in masonry, were designed with architectural intentions in mind. The interaction of these two sets of values was especially apparent in bridges. These structures received a great deal of attention because of the drama with which they spanned ever greater distances. In the first two decades of the nineteenth century the span of bridges increased because of innovations in timber farming. Despite these advances, the very fact that bridges were of wood made them obsolete. Those which were more directly identified as expressive of the progressive tendencies of the era were made of iron or steel. Of these, the suspension bridge was the most breathtaking. This type of structure had many predecessors. When it was first used in the United States by James Foley, it was based on chains of wrought-iron links. Wire cable was employed as early as 1816, but the collapse of a four-hundred-foot-long span across the Schuylkill River deterred further experimentation until James Ellet (1810–62), an American-born engineer who had been trained at the Ecole Polytechnique in Paris, proposed a cable-supported suspension bridge in 1832.

A decade passed before Ellet was able to erect such a bridge. By the early 1840s his chief rival was John Roebling. Born in Germany in 1806, Roebling was educated at the Royal Polytechnic School in Berlin and came to the United States in 1831. He was no ordinary engineer. Part of his education included the study of philosophy under Hegel, and he always conceived his projects in both practical and idealistic terms. For Roebling, designing a bridge was not simply a matter of understanding physical forces. Since a bridge joined previously unconnected parts of the landscape and thus facilitated human communication, it had for him a larger, almost metaphysical, purpose.

Roebling's first suspension structure was not a bridge but an aqueduct. In order to avoid a difficult intersection between the Delaware River and a canal from the Lackawanna coal fields, Roebling elevated the canal above the river with a suspension structure which was built in only nine months, between August 1844 and May 1845. In the next five years Roebling constructed five other such aqueducts, but by this time his primary preoccupation was suspension bridges. His outstanding achievement, the

62 Brooklyn Bridge, was begun in 1867, and, when Roebling died in 1869 after an accident that occurred when inspecting the site, supervision of the work was undertaken by his son Washington (1837–1926) until the bridge was completed in 1882.

Critics have often interpreted the Brooklyn Bridge in terms of a contrast between the forward-looking web of cables and the retrospective masonry piers. However, to conclude that this contrast should have been resolved in favor of the engineering is to mistake Roebling's intention and, more importantly, to misunderstand the emotive force not only of the bridge, but of much of nineteenth-century building. The bridge's power surely does not stem only from its metal members. Rather, the structure continues to attract us because of the essentially unending dialogue—sometimes discordant, sometimes harmonious—between its web of wire cables and its Gothic piers.

Each of the characteristic building types that evolved in the fifty years before the Civil War participated in varying degrees in this conversation between past and future. The buildings that marked the termination of vital transportation routes were an important case in point. Of these, the railroad station quickly became the most significant. Railroads were first constructed in the early 1830s, and it soon became obvious that a depot building was necessary. But how these structures should be designed was not immediately apparent. Until 1850 most stations, whether in large cities or small towns, were encompassed under one roof. The trains and the volume of business and passengers were both still so small that there was no need to differentiate train shed, waiting room, ticket office, and baggage handling area. In the

63 1830s and 1840s the typical train station took the form of a pedimented Greek temple or large barn. The train entered the structure through a pair of

62 John Roebling and Washington A. Roebling: Brooklyn Bridge, East River, Brooklyn, New York, 1867–82.

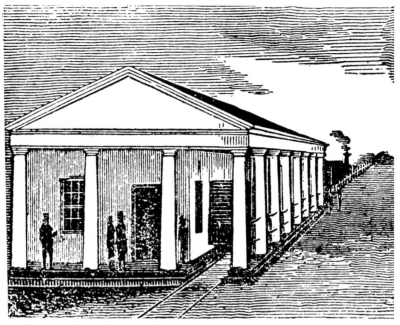

63 Boston and Lowell Railroad "Car House", Lowell, Massachusetts, 1835.

columns or on one side of a pitched roof, and then stopped at a platform. Another model was a simple, house-like building, usually identified as a station only by large overhanging eaves to shelter waiting passengers, and perhaps by a belfry or clock tower.

Attempts to keep all the functions of the station under one roof persisted for many years. The station of the Atlantic and Great Western Railroad at Meadville, Pennsylvania, constructed in 1862, measured 120 by 300 feet in plan and was housed under a high gable roof. One side contained the waiting room and railroad offices, the other had a dining room, and the trains were located in the middle. However, the unitary structure was not the model of the future. Eventually, the diverse functions of the railroad station were seen to be too complex to be packaged in one volume, and by 1850 it was also clear that this building type was inherently too large to be casually incorporated into the urban landscape. Instead, the railroad station became the city's major gateway. As such, trains could not properly pass through it; they arrived at the back through a train shed which abutted a building that

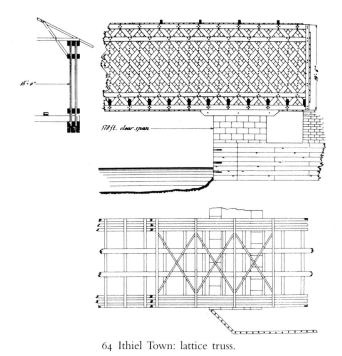

64 Ithiel Town: lattice truss.

contained not only a waiting room, ticket office, and restaurant, but perhaps also the offices of the railroad company and even a hotel for travelers.

At the time of the Civil War, structural steel was still too scarce to be used to roof train sheds. But designers of railroad stations were able to span surprisingly large distances with timber trusses. The more taxing problem, however, was how to give expression to the structure in the front of the shed, the building that presented a face to the city. Here, certain functional requirements had to be met. It was important, for example, to have a clock tower that could be seen from a distance and an entrance to accommodate the requisite flow of passengers. The station had to work in many other ways, but it often seemed that the most important issue was to give it a distinctive character, one which spoke to the romance of travel through the associations of its architecture. Thus, Italianate towers, Egyptian pylons, Swiss chalet roof details, and dozens of other such motifs found their way into American stations. Perhaps the most exotic was Henry Austin's New Haven station (1848–49). One end of the front of this building had a

64

65

65 Henry Austin: New Haven Railroad Station, Connecticut, 1848–49.

campanile with clock. A squat pagoda announced the central entrance, and the other end was marked by a tower which combined both Italian and Chinese motifs. The roof was supported by exaggerated Italianate brackets to which were added Chinese and Indian details.

The process of evolution that took place in the railroad station, from a small, simple structure with a limited and well-understood range of references to a large, complex building with diverse and often exotic iconography, was shared by other types of buildings, including those which housed the manufacturing of the mass-produced goods that were so central to the period's changing economy. The siting of the first factories was determined by proximity to a source of water power. Because they were located in the countryside, the first English mills were adaptations of traditional barns and sheds and their simple and well-known forms were used for factories well into the nineteenth century. However, as machines became bigger and more demanding of their immediate environment, these simple structures were gradually supplanted by building envelopes that were more directly related to the functions within.

The American textile industry developed later than the English, thus giving Americans the opportunity to observe and profit from the English experience. At the outset, factory owners understood that a simple, well-built enclosure was necessary. Thus, the first American factory, the Old Slater Mill, constructed in Pawtucket, Rhode Island, in 1793, had two stories, interrupted only by a line of columns, and a storage attic. The entire structure was supported by heavy post-and-beam framing. Its walls, unlike those of English factories, were clad in wood, not stone or brick. Although this building was designed with a specific purpose in mind, it could still be seen as essentially similar to the other buildings that then dotted the New England landscape. As a two-story box with a pitched roof, it followed the format of house and church; it was still small enough to be conceived of, and if necessary decorated, within the classical language of architecture.

By 1809 twenty-seven mills were operating in New England, most of which were similar to the Old Slater Mill. It was only after the War of 1812 that mill construction started to assume new properties and dimensions. Factories became taller and larger, but it was not only sheer size that

66

66 Samuel Slater: Old Slater Mill, Pawtucket, Rhode Island, 1793.

differentiated them from the other structures nearby. They also had certain distinctive characteristics, the most important of which was the clerestory monitor window, which replaced the pitched roof because it admitted more light and made the attic another usable story. Another feature of the mill was the vertical circulation tower which was sometimes attached to the exterior of the building so that a clear space would be left on the interior.

Materials and methods of construction also began to separate factories from other buildings. In an attempt to make these structures fireproof, masonry walls, usually of brick, were used instead of the customary clapboard on wood frame. It was all but impossible to use masonry throughout, since vaulting was both impractical and prohibitively expensive, but by the 1820s several enlightened mill owners had experimented with techniques to prevent the spread of fire and to enhance the safety of the workers. The stair tower, in combination with fire doors, was used to isolate a means of exit from the main body of the building, and by the 1830s sprinkler systems had been installed in factories. But the most effective way to control fires was to use a special type of construction. Instead of a structure of many small joists, which was easily consumed by fire and thus caused a quick collapse, mill owners began to favor heavy beams with two layers of floor boards. Since it took longer for this more substantial construction to burn through, there was more time to bring fires under control and to evacuate the workers.

67   Another important feature of the mill building that emerged in the 1820s and 1830s was its overt decoration. As early as the 1780s, when Thomas Jefferson and Alexander Hamilton debated the advisability of promoting manufacturing in the United States, Americans began to have doubts about the consequences of the factory system. However, since the early factories were small, it was still possible to incorporate them not only into the New England landscape but also into an image of a society based on self-sufficient individuals. When mills became larger, this was more difficult. Their size and the repetitiveness of their construction meant that factories were seen as symbols of a new social order that few people unreservedly welcomed. Thus, though economic considerations argued for the stark treatment of mills, factory owners often insisted on decoration. The extraneous nature of these embellishments was crucial because it demonstrated to public view that money was not the measure of all things—that, in effect, the corporation was not heartless. The decoration occurred mainly around doors and windows, but was also often used to articulate the outline of the roof. Given that the depth as well as the height and length of the mill building had increased, it probably would have been most practical to use a flat roof. Nevertheless, other profiles were favored. Cornices were sometimes crenellated, but the

67 Boston Manufacturing Company, Waltham, Massachusetts, 1826–30.

most common device was the mansard roof surmounted by a distinctive cupola. This element served both to fit the factory into a landscape of similarly featured structures and at the same time to advertise the mill.

The uncertainty that underlay the quest for an appropriate image of a factory was also instrumental in determining the appearance of the large department store. European stores of this kind were often planned around spacious covered courtyards, but this format was not used in the United States. Instead, the large store was customarily a three-, four-, or five-story structure with as much undivided space on each level as possible. These buildings, in effect, were similar to warehouses or factories and are noteworthy only because of their facades. The owners and designers of these stores understood that it was important to display goods in first-floor windows and to let light into the spaces above through large windows. Nevertheless, the determining factor in the design of a facade was usually the need to evoke an aura of sumptuousness that would identify the store and, in so doing, attract customers.

The separation of the image of these buildings from technique and function was most clearly underlined by the fact that the facades of many of

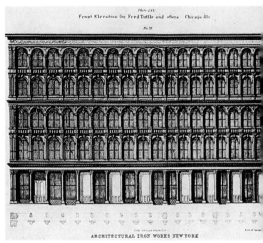

ARCHITECTURAL IRON WORKS, NEW YORK

68 Daniel D. Badger: Elevations and sections of cast-iron columns and capitals, 1865.

69 Daniel D. Badger: Front Elevation of a Building in Chicago, 1865.

70 John Kellum & Son: A. T. Stewart Store (Wanamaker's), New York City, 1859–60.

the largest and most stylish stores were made of cast-iron sections that were fabricated in factories, sold through catalogs, and shipped to building sites for quick assembly. Manufacturers of cast-iron elements were not precursors of modern architecture. They attached no significance to cast iron's structural capabilities and made no attempt to capitalize on the fact that cast iron could render an external wall non-load-bearing. Nor did they extend the logic of a facade made of modular elements straight through the building to include a structural and floor framing system. In fact, the buildings covered with these facades were usually supported by wood columns and joists. A cast-iron frame was thought appropriate only for structures of an essentially utilitarian nature, such as the two shot-towers that James Bogardus (1800–74), a manufacturer of cast-iron elements, built in Brooklyn. For a building which housed a significant institution, cast iron was used because it was an inexpensive way to emulate, and therefore perpetuate, some of the characteristics of traditional architecture. In fact, Bogardus wrote that he conceived of the idea of cast-iron facade elements when he was traveling in Italy, and his subsequent designs can probably best be described as Venetian. Another manufacturer, Daniel Badger (1806–?),

82

displayed an array of styles in his catalog. His desire to emulate traditional   *68, 69*
architecture was so strong that many of his designs even mimicked the
mottled surface and deep rustication of stone work.

However, Badger and Bogardus were not architects, and they did not
understand the difference in scale between the old buildings they admired
and the new stores they were helping to erect. The problem was probably
most pronounced in the A. T. Stewart Store (later Wanamaker's), erected on   *70*
Broadway, New York, between 9th and 10th Streets in 1859–60. The
building was two hundred feet long, five stories high and contained 325,000
square feet of space.

The question such a vast building posed was whether to subdivide the
facade and if so, how? Should the base and top as well as the middle and
corners be emphasized, as in Renaissance palaces? Or should the logic of the
repetitive unit take over and establish a new aesthetic order? John Kellum
(1807–71), the building's architect, could provide no clear answer. The elevator then was only in its infancy, but in the next half century, when it forced
the issue by making it possible to build above five or six stories, architects
began knowingly to cope with this matter.

In an age increasingly dominated by manufacturing and commerce, one of the primary functions of a building was to advertise the institution it housed. This fact posed special problems for clients and architects. A vivid and memorable image, one which incorporated materials or textures with up-to-date associations, was desirable. Yet it was equally important for buildings to give the appearance of dignity and tradition, especially since critics of industrial society often pointed to garish architecture as a sad manifestation of troubled times.

Many types of buildings were caught in this dilemma, but the hotel was probably the extreme case. Before 1800 few buildings were sufficiently large and varied in their facilities to transcend the status of inn. The hotel as it is now known largely evolved in the course of the nineteenth century as traveling became more frequent. Between 1825 and 1835 large hotels were built in Baltimore and New York, but the most significant building of this type was in Boston. The Tremont House, designed by Isaiah Rogers in 1827, was probably conceived in response to some of the shortcomings of the Boston Exchange Coffee House, which Asher Benjamin designed in 1809 and which burned down in 1818. That building was planned around a domed central space that on the first floor served as an exchange hall for local businessmen. Galleries ringed the floors above and gave access to the hotel's two hundred rooms. This mixing of uses never worked, and Rogers in the Tremont House set the pattern for future hotels by understanding that the diverse functions of such a building, especially those public activities customarily located on the first floors, had to be carefully segregated. The complexity of the resulting internal organization was compounded by the need for direct routes to escape the fires which occurred all too frequently in early hotels.

71, 72

One quality which the Tremont House shared with the Boston Exchange Coffee House and other large hotels of the period was the blatant sumptuousness of its interior. A Doric portico announced the entrance. Then began a sequence up a flight of stairs, through a domed rotunda which gave access to six grand public rooms that fronted on Tremont Street and ultimately to a dining room for two hundred. This substantial rectangular space had two apse-like areas at its ends and was dominated by fourteen freestanding Ionic columns on its perimeter. The four-story facade of the Tremont House marched for 150 feet along Tremont Street. The building was considered colossal. Charles Dickens called it "a trifle smaller than Bedford Square," but Rogers was still able to compose its facade within the conventions of classical architecture.

A few years later such formulas seemed less useful. Beginning in the 1830s in every major city and throughout the nation the builders of hotels

71, 72 Isaiah Rogers: Tremont House, Boston, Massachusetts, 1827–29. Facade and plan.

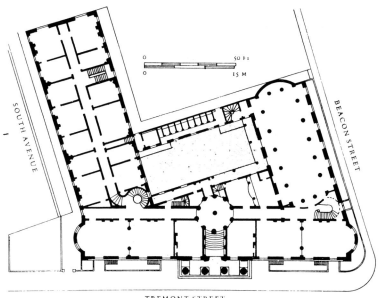

73 Mount Vernon Hotel, Cape May, New Jersey, 1853.

competed to surpass their predecessors. Thus, when the Astor House was built in New York in 1843, it was considered the last word, but it was soon topped in size by the Metropolitan, which was then superseded by the St. Nicholas and the Fifth Avenue. The same phenomenon occurred in resort hotels, of which the Mount Vernon in Cape May, New Jersey, was the largest. When that building was opened in 1853, it was only half completed but it already housed 2,100 guests. Full capacity was never reached, as the Mount Vernon was destroyed by fire in 1854.

73

As these structures grew to six stories and stretched along streets for over three hundred feet, the question of how to give expression to a seemingly endless number of essentially similar rooms became increasingly pointed. Many forced attempts to enliven an essentially repetitious facade were made, but the more prescient solution was to make a blunt distinction between the public floors and the many levels of private rooms above. The first were sumptuously articulated, especially at the entrance, to impress guests and pedestrians; the second were treated in a frankly utilitarian and serial manner. If a guest needed any compensation for the fact that his room was like hundreds of others, he found it in the lobby and public rooms. By the 1840s any sense that the style of such spaces had to be consistent with the exterior of the building had been abandoned. It was common practice by this time to decorate public rooms to conform to different periods of architecture.

In reaction to the seemingly irresistible attraction of the commercial culture housed in factories, railroad stations, office buildings, department stores, and hotels, many Americans felt it important to assert the primacy of more permanent values. To do this, they often focused on the church and tried to make both its rituals and its architecture more appropriate to the needs of the age. A search began for an ecclesiastical style which conformed more accurately than the habitual classical design to deeply rooted images of what a church should look like. This search inevitably led to an interest in Gothic architecture.

A few Gothic churches had been built in the United States throughout the eighteenth and early nineteenth centuries, their designers motivated by a lingering belief that Gothic was the correct style for a church. But these buildings were Gothic only in the most superficial sense. In a quest for picturesqueness, their architects simply grafted a few Gothic details onto a building generated from a symmetrical and static plan. The result was a classical building dressed up as Gothic. Because of their essentially superficial nature, such churches were attractive at best because of their naïveté. One of the few exceptions was William Strickland's St. Stephen's Episcopal   74
Church, built in Philadelphia in 1822–23. Its octagonal towers, lancet windows, and crenellated walls all identified it as Gothic, but St. Stephen's

74 William
Strickland: St.
Stephen's Episcopal
Church, Philadelphia,
Pennsylvania,
1822–23.

75 Richard Upjohn:
Trinity Church, New
York City, 1839–46.

76 Richard Upjohn: St.
Paul's Episcopal
Church, Brookline,
Massachusetts, 1851–52.

was more than a caricature of earlier churches because Strickland knowingly abstracted these forms and incorporated them into a larger compositional order.

The Gothic churches constructed in the 1830s and afterwards marked a fundamental departure from earlier buildings. This change was brought about by a new sense that much more was at stake in ecclesiastical architecture than a desire to achieve a picturesque effect. It was felt that because Christianity had flourished when the Gothic style was in its prime, it was not enough for churches to be just Gothic, they must be a correct version of Gothic. In making this argument, Americans echoed a group of English clergymen and architects who, beginning in the early 1830s, had been writing about the debasement of religious architecture. What came to be known as the Ecclesiological Movement originated in Cambridge and Oxford, but the architect A. W. N. Pugin soon became its chief spokesman. He believed not only that Gothic was the only Christian architecture, but also that a church had to be shaped to accommodate specific rituals that had been integral to the practice of Christianity in its prime.

The Gothic revival in the United States had many advocates, including a group of British-born architects. Of these, the most prominent was Richard

Upjohn (1802–78). Trained as a cabinetmaker and carpenter, Upjohn came
to the United States in 1829. In the following decade he designed several
churches, but his most important commission, for Trinity Church in New   75
York, came in 1839. Dedicated in 1846, Trinity Church was remarkable
because, with its soaring spire, vaulted chancel, timber ceiling over the nave,
and carefully elaborated stone detailing, it was the first building in the
United States that could be described as truly Gothic. Upjohn's design
resembled a drawing for an Ideal Church published by Pugin in 1841, but
Trinity Church was all the more noteworthy because its basic outlines were
probably established before that scheme was known in the United States.
    Trinity was emphatically an urban church; its siting was reflected in its
symmetrical plan. But within a few years Upjohn was pioneering another
type of ecclesiastical structure, the small parish church. His buildings of this
type included the Church of the Holy Communion (1846) in what was then
a residential part of Manhattan, St. Mary's in Burlington, New Jersey
(1846–48), and St. Paul's in Brookline, Massachusetts (1851–52). Upjohn   76
tried to emulate the unpretentious quality of the churches found in small
English villages by using highly evocative elements such as steeply pitched
roofs, articulated transepts, bold buttresses, soaring spires, and austere

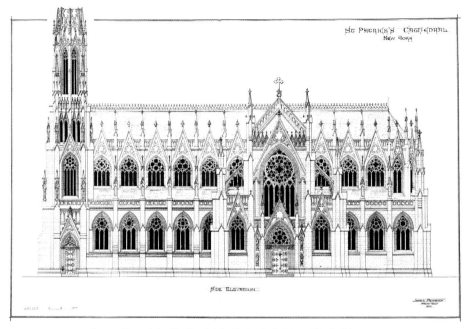

ST PATRICK'S CATHEDRAL
New York

SIDE ELEVATION

JAMES RENWICK
ARCHITECT
N.Y.

77 James Renwick: St. Patrick's Cathedral, New York City, 1853–89.
Composite reconstruction of the original side elevation.

interiors covered by roofs of exposed beams and trusses. All these features
further separated Upjohn's churches from their colonial predecessors, but his
main innovation in this direction was an asymmetrical plan and irregular
massing which he usually created by placing the entrance and tower off-
center.

In the same period Roman Catholics also felt the inadequacy of the
classical language and turned to Gothic architecture. But unlike Protestants
influenced by the Ecclesiological Movement, American Catholics were
attracted more to the great Gothic cathedrals of the Continent than to the
quaint English parish church. In submitting designs for Baltimore
Cathedral, Benjamin Latrobe had sensed that a Gothic building might be
appropriate, but his design in that style was essentially a classical building
elaborated with Gothic details. In the first decades of the nineteenth century,
several Catholic churches along these lines were built, but by the 1830s the
word "cathedral" conjured up a more specific and compelling image.

77   The most important Roman Catholic cathedral of this period was St.
Patrick's in New York. Designed in various stages in the years 1853–57, its
construction was frequently delayed for lack of funds. It was finally opened

90

in 1879, though its spires were not completed until 1889. The result of the delays was that the original design was often compromised. But the final building was still astonishing, especially considering that its architect, James Renwick (1818–95), had previously only designed much smaller churches. Renwick was able to transcend his limited background by a trip he took to France in 1855. During this visit he not only saw some of the great works of the French Gothic revival, but also probably came into contact with architects who were using cast iron to form the structure of buildings that were not exclusively utilitarian in nature. When Renwick returned to the United States and resumed work on St. Patrick's, he produced a design for a church that was to be 385 feet long, with a nave that rose to 112 feet. He intended the church's facade to have two 330-foot-high towers and the crossing to have been celebrated with an octagonal spire, rising 135 feet above the ridge of the roof. This vivid design, which one contemporary called a combination of Cologne Cathedral and the Crystal Palace, was not fully realized, but it provided the most striking American example of what a living Gothic architecture might be.

In seeking an appropriate image for a place of worship, every religion and denomination had to engage in a self-conscious search for an architecture that was not only identified with its history but also allowed for a fresh and compelling interpretation. This task was probably most difficult for American Jews. Their attempt to find an appropriate image for the synagogue epitomized a condition that was general to all nineteenth-century architecture in that they had no obvious precedent to which to turn. Until the early nineteenth century, Jewish congregations were content to build classical synagogues that were not stylistically different from Protestant and Catholic churches. Thus when William Strickland used vaguely Egyptian motifs on the exterior of Temple Mikvah Israel, which he designed in Philadelphia in 1818, he possibly thought these exotic references suited the congregation that had hired him, but he composed the rest of the building, especially the oval-shaped interior, in a manner that would have suited many other buildings of the period.

Although in the 1830s several synagogues were modeled after Greek temples, by the end of that decade spokesmen for various congregations often expressed the desire to have a structure that was not only specifically calculated "to turn the mind to the sublime, and to spiritualize the feeling," but was also one which in style was associated with the Jewish past. Since Jews had never been rooted in one place, this search resulted in buildings in a variety of styles, including Byzantine, Egyptian, and Romanesque. One solution was to build in the style that had prevailed in the area of Europe from which a congregation's members had emigrated. Thus, it was not

78 Alexander Saeltzer:
Anshe Chesed
Synagogue, New
York City, 1850.

78 uncommon for a synagogue to be Gothic, with details copied from sources such as Cologne Cathedral.

Throughout the antebellum period all religions and denominations mounted huge campaigns to build places of worship that were compatible with their changing needs. Discussion arose too about those institutions that had begun to undertake aspects of the work traditionally performed by the church. Some Americans, aware of the deep, though elusive, influence of schooling, became interested in educational reform and in the process wrote about the architecture of schoolhouses. School buildings at this time were rudimentary, and the appropriate image for a schoolhouse was not the subject of any deep scrutiny; usually it was simply indicated by a drawing of a "model" structure. More frequent were discussions about functional considerations, such as heating, ventilation, and the design of comfortable desks. Occasionally, it was pointed out that a specific theory of education had implications for the design, construction, and layout of the building, but this connection was largely left to be established after the Civil War.

Both school and church were seen as alternatives to several other institutions. In these decades, attention was often drawn to the ever-increasing demand for prisons, asylums, and hospitals in which to house the period's outcasts and casualties. Although considerable thought was given to the design of these buildings, most authors and architects basically felt that if the home was satisfactory, there would be less need for such institutions. Domestic architecture therefore received an unprecedented amount of attention. As with the discussion of school buildings, much that was written about domestic architecture focused on how to make a more healthy and sound physical environment. Doctors at this time were postulating new theories about the origin of diseases, and it was increasingly assumed that the immediate environment was an important agent in contagion. The fact that research was still in the preliminary stages only served to draw more attention to this subject and to increase the demand for central heating systems, indoor sanitary facilities, and many other conveniences.

Builders and architects were also making new demands on domestic architecture. They argued for a more rational method of construction, especially in newly settled areas where skilled labor was scarce. One manifestation of this desire to do away with old practices was the invention and popularization of the balloon frame, a type of construction that was easy to erect, mainly because it was based on the use of light pieces of wood which were joined by nails instead of the time-consuming mortise and tenon. This was an important development, but it was only one of the many ways in which construction was rationalized in this period. The invention and refinement of many hand tools and machines also played a significant role in this process, as did the manufacture and mass availability of a broad range of building products from asphalt shingles to prehung windows and doors.

Although these practical developments were usually welcomed as signs of progress, it was often charged that there was a danger that the house would become routinized and subject to the same business-oriented values that dominated other types of buildings. Because the rise of industrial society was seen by many as a threat to the family, architects tried to find an image for domestic architecture which would encapsulate an ideal of family life. In this quest they followed a lead established by authors of the period who were trying to define the appropriate context for the romantic novel and short story. The houses these authors admired were those which echoed in their architecture the rugged and irregular countryside in which they were located rather than the refined classical buildings that appealed to the generation of Bulfinch and Jefferson.

The novelist Washington Irving was probably the first American to build in response to these impulses. He renovated and added a picturesque wing onto an old farmhouse in Tarrytown, New York (1835–36). The first significant architect to translate these notions into a body of substantial work was Alexander Jackson Davis (1803–92). His career in architecture was long and diverse. It began with the design of buildings based on Greek precedents, a style he continued to favor for public structures. But Davis's reputation came primarily from the villas that, starting in the early 1830s, he designed for wealthy clients in romantic settings such as on the banks of the Hudson River. In these buildings Davis attempted to achieve everything that the classical residence was not. In plan and massing his villas were irregular so that they could respond to the varied landscape in which they were set. Equally important, crenellated roof lines, pinnacles, pointed arches, ogee windows, and dozens of other similar motifs associated these buildings with a place and culture that was compatible with romantic ideas about what a country house should be.

The person who did most to popularize houses based on these ideas was Andrew Jackson Downing (1815–52). He made his reputation primarily as a writer of several important and widely read books on landscape gardening

79

79 Alexander Jackson Davis: Knoll, Tarrytown, New York, 1840.

80, 81 Andrew Jackson Downing: "A House Without Feeling" and "A House
With Feeling".

and architecture. These books gave instructions on planning and building a
house, and Downing was especially interested in the relation of a building to
its setting. But his most important message was that beauty in architecture   *80, 81*
grew out of, but ultimately transcended, the useful. He felt it was vital for
Americans to understand and appreciate this kind of beauty because he
believed that such qualities had "a powerful civilizing force." At a time
when so much seemed to be determined only by material concerns, it was
essential to assert the existence of transcendent values.

Downing's message was a subtle one. Although beauty had to transcend
utility, the two nevertheless had to be sufficiently connected so that a
building would still appear truthful to purpose and technique. This applied
especially to the use of forms with historical associations. Downing believed
that a Swiss chalet or an Italian villa was pleasing because of the associations it
evoked, but he recommended the use of such evocative forms only if they
also made sense in terms of siting, planning, and construction. Inevitably, it
was easy to overlook such distinctions and to conclude that anything that did
not look specifically useful was beautiful. This misconception led to the   *82, 83, 84*
construction of an extraordinary array of idiosyncratic houses based on
exotic styles of architecture drawn from sources as far-flung as Persia and
China. At the time of the Civil War most architects still considered the
colonial farmhouse too humble a source for domestic architecture.
Nevertheless, authors, artists, and many other Americans had begun to
succumb to the charms of these buildings, and it would not be long before a
demand for their revival would be heard.

82 Samuel Sloan: Longwood ("Nutt's Folly"), Natchez, Mississippi, 1860. Facade.

83 Samuel Sloan: A Picturesque Gothic Cottage, 1861.

84 Samuel Sloan: Villa in the Italian Style, 1861.

Downing's influence extended well beyond the scale of the individual building. Although he recognized that there was no equivalent to the English aristocracy in the United States, he knew that many Americans wanted and could afford country estates. Downing included designs for such establishments in his books and because of this was frequently accused of being haughty and aristocratic. Yet he was equally interested in farm buildings and it was primarily through his urging that by 1850 the American agricultural press began to encourage its readers to build more than strictly utilitarian structures.

Downing hoped that those attracted to the period's burgeoning cities would all be able to live in the suburban districts that by the late 1840s were already being connected to urban centers by commuter railroad lines. In 1853 his friend Alexander Jackson Davis designed one of the first and most exemplary suburbs, Llewellyn Park in West Orange, New Jersey. This 85 extensive tract of land was subdivided into house lots of 3–10 acres fronting on parkland. But by the 1850s it was clear that most Americans could not afford to live in anything like so spacious a setting. In New York, for example, though row houses for single families continued to be constructed, there was already discussion of the need to build a type of multiple dwelling

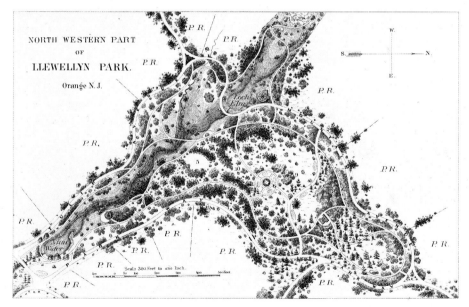

85 Alexander Jackson Davis: Llewellyn Park, West Orange, New Jersey, 1853.

86 Lowell, Massachusetts, *c.* 1833, as seen from across the Merrimack River.

to accommodate not just the laboring population which largely lived in subdivided houses, but also wealthier people who either did not have the means to maintain a separate house or did not want to make the effort to do so.

Defining the characteristics of the model tenement and apartment house was a task that was largely undertaken after the Civil War. But by 1860 important questions had already been raised about the context in which such structures might be built. Throughout the antebellum period many communities in the United States continued to grow in an orderly fashion. For example, sects such as the Shakers were often able to control the planning and the design of their buildings and the resulting communities have long been admired for their order and quiet urbanity. But such places retained their cohesive quality because they were not composed of diverse and often conflicting population groups. Nor did they participate fully in a rapidly expanding economy. Appealing as these communities may have been, their closed nature made them necessarily a part of the past.

The same is true of the handful of communities which were founded on the utopian principles of Robert Owen, Charles Fourier, and others. Some interesting buildings were constructed in a few of them, but the far more intriguing developments in architecture and urban design were taking place in quite different communities which in the broader scope of history were more truly experimental: the dynamic cities to which thousands of people from rural America and the peasant villages of Europe were gravitating. The founders of some of the first mill towns had hoped that the buildings of an industrializing society could be contained within a simply ordered context. For example, the proprietors of the first factory in Lowell, *86* Massachusetts, built coordinated rows of dormitories for its workers that led down to the Merrimack River, where they faced a group of symmetrical mills. But as the company expanded, it abandoned this unifying plan. If that was the case in Lowell, which originally was largely controlled by one company, it was many more times so in the rapidly expanding and diverse cities not only of the East Coast but also of the Midwest. Confronted by the burgeoning, unpredictable, and often hostile nature of these cities, some Americans started to long for a return to a simpler village-like context. In extreme reaction, others for the first time even began to admire the rituals and architecture of native Americans and the rural populations of other countries. But the more compelling challenge was to define an aesthetic that *87* could respond to the dynamic, diverse, and often contradictory nature of the great metropolis, one that could do justice to the "high growths of iron" in "numberless crowded streets" that in 1860 Walt Whitman presciently celebrated in his poem "Mannahatta" and which were then already dwarfing nearby buildings constructed only a few years before.

87 *Panic of 1857, Wall Street. Half past 2 o'clock, Oct. 13, 1857.* Painting by James H. Cafferty and Charles G. Rosenberg.

Toward New Types

Romanesque for an Industrial Society

One view of the postbellum period is that it was a Gilded Age, a time when a handful of nouveau-riche millionaires unabashedly displayed their wealth while hundreds of thousands of workers sank to unprecedented levels of poverty. According to this interpretation, the period had little of architectural quality. Its characteristic buildings were either ostentatious mansions and degrading tenements, or the armories constructed in most major cities to quell labor uprisings.

There is much to justify this interpretation. Huge expenditures often produced only outlandish exercises in bad taste and local governments usually took no more than grudging steps to improve the buildings in which the urban working population lived and was employed. Even so, this was also a constructive age, a time when the first concerted efforts were made to establish an appropriate institutional basis for a modern society. This had been hardly possible in the antebellum period because the changes that occurred then were too new and sudden to be assimilated in a meaningful way. Those who lived through the decades after the Civil War were often as bewildered as their parents and grandparents had been by the upheavals that continued to disturb American life. Nevertheless, by the time of the Civil War, these changes had already been taking place for half a century. Americans were beginning to put them into perspective, and were thus better able to establish the kinds of organizations and institutions that were crucial to the successful functioning of a modern society.

In the period before the Civil War, most architects found it difficult to transcend the mere assimilation of the new programmatic and technical requirements they were called upon to incorporate into their buildings. The questions their work raised were more interesting than their answers. One index of this fact is that although Americans were in touch with the discourse on architecture that was taking place in Europe, virtually no one produced work that contributed to it. If American architecture was known at all in Europe, it was usually for what seemed to be an emphasis on simplicity or utility. Some critics found this quality refreshing, but most saw it as opportunistic, a manifestation of an increasingly commercial mentality which had little appreciation of culture.

In the postbellum era programmatic and technical developments continued to tax the skill of architects. But by this time some designers were ready to give expression to these new conditions by articulating a language of architecture that could do justice to the emerging institutions they were called upon to accommodate. Not only did some of these architects achieve a stature that enabled them to speak on behalf of the profession in the United States, but they also started to have a significant impact on European architecture. For the first time a handful of architects even became generally known to the American public and were considered important cultural figures.

The nature and quality of the works designed by these architects reflected the sources upon which they drew. From the late 1820s to the Civil War, most of the important developments in American architecture were in large part responses to what was happening in England. American architects read the works of A. W. N. Pugin, John Ruskin, and many other British authors on architecture and landscape gardening. They looked for guidance not only to what was built in England, but also to the works of an influential group of British architects who had recently settled in the United States. Even the American use of cast iron and glass in the 1840s and 1850s fed upon the English innovations that culminated in the construction of the Crystal Palace in 1851.

Ruskin's books continued to be widely read in the United States well after the Civil War. His theories were reflected in significant works such as Peter B. Wight's (1838–1925) polychrome, Venetian Gothic building, the National Academy of Design, New York (1862–65), and Ware & Van Brunt's Memorial Hall at Harvard University, Cambridge, Massachusetts (1876–80). Such devoted allegiance to a single authority, especially a remote one, was rare, but American architects continued to consider English precedents relevant to their practice, especially for houses, churches, and university buildings. Many subscribed to British magazines such as the *Builder* to find out what William Butterfield, J. L. Pearson, Norman Shaw, and their contemporaries were designing. A handful of English architects were even asked to build in the United States. Unfortunately, what might have been the most impressive imported project, William Burges's scheme for Trinity College in Hartford, Connecticut (1873–82), was only partially built. Nevertheless, by the 1870s many American architects could turn out capable designs which, though based on English ideas and sources, were suited to local circumstances and institutions.

Although Americans continued to feel a special attachment to England, the Continent had a much more significant impact on the architecture of the postbellum period. In the 1850s, Leopold Eidlitz (1823–1908), Detlef Lienau

88
89

90

88 Peter B. Wight: National Academy of Design, New York City, 1862–65.

89 Ware & Van Brunt: Memorial Hall, Harvard University, Cambridge, Massachusetts, 1876–80.

90 William Burges: Trinity College, Hartford, Connecticut, 1873–82.

(1818–87) and other German- and Austrian-born and trained architects had already begun to bring a different educational background to bear upon American practice. This influence was long felt in American architecture, especially in Midwestern cities such as Chicago, Cincinnati, and Detroit. But the more significant developments were French in origin or inspiration. Most of the important American architects of the period either attended the Ecole des Beaux-Arts in Paris or came under its influence through contact with those who had studied there.

The impact of the Ecole des Beaux-Arts began with the work and career of Richard Morris Hunt (1827–95), its first American graduate. Born in Brattleboro, Vermont, Hunt traveled extensively in Europe after the death of his father, a prominent congressman. He enrolled at the Ecole in 1848. Although Hunt was not a brilliant student, one of his teachers, Hector Lefuel, offered him the opportunity to work on the extensions to the Louvre that were then being designed. Hunt's efforts focused chiefly on the Pavillon de la Bibliothèque. Through that work he was able, more directly than any other American, to become familiar with the sophisticated architecture of the Second Empire. That style had little to do with earlier Palladian and neoclassical revivals. Nor did it resemble the austere language of the so-called neo-Grec buildings that had recently been so popular in France. Instead the extensions to the Louvre were characterized by a profusion of balconies, columns, caryatids, acroteria, and patterned rustication, a palette of lush forms and motifs that by 1860 had no precedent in the United States.

Although Hunt might have had a successful career in France, he had always intended to return to the United States and did so in 1855. In 1856 he worked for a short period on the extensions to the Capitol in Washington, D.C., but he spent most of the late 1850s in New York. Building opportunities were scarce during the Civil War; Hunt's practice therefore started to flourish only in the late 1860s. From then until his death in 1895, he designed a body of work which was one of the first and most concerted attempts to articulate a language of architecture that could give suitable expression to the institutions of a modern society, especially those located in a great metropolis.

Hunt's most significant urban projects were for New York. Taken together, they can be seen as an endeavour to respond to the various building contexts presented by the street system of that city. One of the most demanding of these situations was the transition from streetscape to Central Park. In their prize-winning design, Frederick Law Olmsted (1822–1903) and Calvert Vaux (1824–95) had assumed that Central Park would be surrounded only by a low wall and simple iron gates. These minimal barriers were probably an expression of the designers' desire to allow the influence of the park's landscape to extend outwards and infuse the buildings that were then engulfing Manhattan. However, by the early 1860s, discussion arose as to whether a more pronounced and urbane barrier was necessary to mark the transition between a city which would soon contain millions of inhabitants and this vast area of greenery. In 1863 Hunt responded to this challenge by 91 supplying designs for the entrances to the southern end of the park. There was nothing understated about his plans; he used plazas with fountains and monumental sculpture to mark these important points of transition.

Most New Yorkers still wanted to believe they were living in a village and were not ready for such grand gestures. However, Central Park also figured 92 prominently in Hunt's design for the Lenox Library (1870–77). This building housed the book and art collections of James Lenox, a philanthropist and one of New York's wealthiest citizens. It faced Fifth Avenue, stretched between 70th and 71st Streets, and extended 114 feet down those blocks. The Lenox Library gave New Yorkers who had been accustomed to the Italianate facades and Ruskinian designs of the 1850s a

91 Richard Morris Hunt: Design for the Central Park Gateway at Fifth Avenue
and 59th Street, New York City, 1863. Rear view of terrace.

92 Richard Morris Hunt: Lenox Library, New York City, 1870–77.

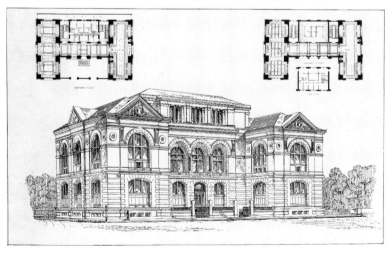

taste of a new type of monumental architecture. To acknowledge the fact that the Library faced Central Park, Hunt provided a small courtyard between the two wings of the building. This space gave access to a large vestibule, which in turn led to two reading rooms, each 108 feet long, 30 feet wide, and 24 feet high. Reading rooms on the second floor had vaulted ceilings that rose to 40 feet.

Hunt designed the exterior of the building to emphasize its monumentality. The walls, which were faced with gray limestone, were treated with flat classical elements. The carefully controlled rustication and belt courses that demarcated the various levels were countered by a vertical emphasis on the two wings facing Central Park and at the center of the elevations on 70th and 71st Streets. These points were each marked by substantial pediments with elaborately carved tympana.

Given the prominence of the institution and its site, the Lenox Library deserved to stand apart from other buildings. The more typical problem, however, was how to put a far less monumental building into a segment of the New York street system. Hunt addressed this issue in designs for row houses that occupied minimal frontages; in the first block of apartments in New York; and in several large houses for millionaires like W. K. Vanderbilt. Hunt tried to give distinction to buildings in this often

93 Richard Morris Hunt: William K. Vanderbilt Mansion, New York City, 1882.

94 Richard Morris Hunt: "Stevens House", New York City, 1872

95 Richard Morris Hunt: Tribune Building, New York City, 1875.

unyielding context by devising a strategy for treating street facades. In the
W. K. Vanderbilt house (1882), for example, he set the structure back a few   *93*
feet from the sidewalk, and was thus able to project from this datum a series
of elaborately detailed bay windows and turrets that in their intricacy
countered the solidity of the wall. Hunt also enlivened the walls of urban
buildings by exaggerating the proportions of stone heads and sills and by
providing a definite center to a structure stretching over several city lots.

   Equally important was Hunt's treatment of roofs. He understood that the
conditions that governed the growth of American cities would never be met
by the uniform cornice and roof lines then being imposed in Paris. Although
most buildings in New York would be constructed to the street line, their
heights would probably vary, and this lack of uniformity might be put to
picturesque advantage. Thus, Hunt designed varied roofs, based on French   *94*
fifteenth- and sixteenth-century architecture, which ascended in mansards
and dormers. In addition to being quaint, these roofs accommodated the
mechanical equipment that at this time increasingly found its way onto the
tops of such buildings. Hunt's most provocative use of such roofs was in the
Tribune Building, New York (1875), an eight-story structure with a two-   *95*
story attic and a tower capped by a spire that rose to 260 feet above the
sidewalk. Whether the Tribune Building was the first skyscraper is a matter

107

96 Richard Morris Hunt: Ochre Court, Newport, Rhode Island, 1892.

of definition, but when it was completed in 1875 it was certainly the tallest commercial structure in the nation. As such, it forcefully raised the question of whether such exotic roof forms would be meaningful in the even higher buildings that some architects were already envisaging.

Hunt's ability to conceive such roof forms also served him in his country house designs. He had a summer home in Newport, Rhode Island, and so was well situated to attract clients from among the many millionaires who settled there. In his early houses, Hunt drew on a variety of English, French and German sources to develop a highly romantic architecture. What distinguished a work such as his Thomas G. Appleton house, Newport (1871), from many similar structures designed by less capable contemporaries was Hunt's ability to respond to complex programmatic requirements and a varied landscape while still maintaining a basic distinction between base, middle, and top to differentiate the levels of the house. In his later houses, Hunt was increasingly attracted to the chateaux of the Loire as a point of departure. Biltmore House (1895), which was set in 125,000 acres of land near Asheville, North Carolina, was certainly the most elaborate country house ever built in the United States. In that building and also in Ochre Court, a Newport mansion of 1892, Hunt achieved roof silhouettes that were unrivalled as picturesque compositions.

96

Hunt's primary contribution to American architecture was the standard of design that he set in such buildings, but he was also important because he helped to establish an organization of architects. In common with leaders of other professions, Hunt saw that such organizations were a necessary part of the complex society that was developing in the United States. In the first half of the nineteenth century, several short-lived professional and fraternal organizations had been formed by small groups of architects, builders, and carpenters, but it was not until 1857 that the American Institute of Architects was founded. Hunt was one of the original members and served as secretary until the organization was disbanded during the Civil War. When it was revived in 1864 and established on a national basis in 1867, Hunt became the first president of the New York chapter and later the third president of the parent organization.

Hunt also played an important role in architectural education. When he returned to the United States, he recognized that aspiring American architects could not obtain an education equivalent to that at the Ecole des Beaux-Arts without going to France, so he established his own atelier on the Parisian model. In 1866 one of his students, William R. Ware (1832–1915), began to organize the first architectural program in the United States—based on the system at the Ecole—at the Massachusetts Institute of Technology. Ware established a similar program at Columbia in 1881, and by the turn of the century it was possible to study architecture at twelve other American universities.

One test of the importance of Hunt's atelier was the quality of the architecture designed by its graduates. George B. Post (1837–1913), upon leaving Hunt's atelier in 1860, soon established himself in practice and quickly became one of the nation's leading architects. In buildings such as the Troy Savings Bank, Troy, New York (1872), the Williamsburg Savings Bank in Brooklyn, New York (1875), and Chickering Hall in New York (1874–75), Post demonstrated some of the same sensibility that informed Hunt's work. Perhaps because Post's initial training was in civil engineering, he never fully matched Hunt's self-assurance. But his engineering background did help him deal with the period's most notable architectural problem: the tall building.

From the late 1860s, Post designed a succession of elevator-based buildings that both reflected, and contributed to, the discussion of the development of the skyscraper. One issue Post came to grips with was the planning of these structures. Most early skyscrapers were built by a single client. Because their basic volumes, bay spacing, and column grids were planned to accommodate that client's needs, there was little consideration of a general rental market or of the possibility that, with a shift of tenants, major

97 George B. Post: Western Union
Building, New York City, 1873–76.

98 George B. Post: New York Produce
Exchange, New York City, 1881–85.

alterations might be necessary. Post was probably the first architect to try to
come to terms with these factors. In planning the Post Building, New York
(1880–81), around a deep court, he determined the shape of this office
structure by implicitly making a calculation based on a trade-off between
more space buried deep in a building and naturally lit and ventilated rooms.
In trying to balance what would be both physically and financially viable,
Post, in effect, initiated the quasi-science that has been one of the most
significant factors in determining the bulk of skyscrapers.

97
95

Post also contributed to the debate about the profile of the skyscraper. His
Western Union Building, New York (1873–76), was similar to Hunt's
Tribune Building in that it terminated with a picturesque assortment of
mansard roofs, dormers, and clock tower. In subsequent works, as
skyscrapers rose to new heights, Post seems to have sensed that such
architectural gymnastics at the rarely seen roof line were a waste. Thus, by
the early 1880s his tall buildings usually ended with a continuous cornice and
a flat roof. Like other architects of the period, Post was not sure how to
divide a skyscraper's wall. No one at this time simply expressed the basic fact
that most of the stories of such a building were essentially the same. Instead,
they all tried to differentiate their structures by giving emphasis to various

horizontal levels. Post's most assured effort in this vein was the Produce *98* Exchange, New York (1881–85). This enormous building had a trading room of thirty-seven thousand square feet and three hundred offices. Its elevation was made up of a ground floor surmounted by a four-story arcade, which in turn supported two more linked stories. The composition was finished with a single story and an attic. As the building rose the window spacing decreased, producing a progression from bottom to top.

The composition of the wall continued to be a problem partly because architects were tentative about how to support buildings. The Produce Exchange had an internal iron structure, but its exterior walls were load bearing. In one sense, Post had yet to understand that if the external wall was supported by a metal frame, it could have larger window openings. However, it can be argued that Post's hesitancy was deliberate. He may have recognized that the skin of a building, which mediates between outside and inside, is fundamentally different from the interior and has to have its own character.

Post had one of the first of the many huge architectural practices that would later be such a dominant force in the profession. Consequently, he was able to tackle some of the period's newest and most significant building

problems. However, he was by no means an inspired architect. His contemporary, Frank Furness (1839–1912), was far more original and even though he did not deal with the range of buildings that Post designed, was certainly the most important architect to emerge from Richard Morris Hunt's atelier. Furness worked for Hunt from 1855 until the outbreak of the Civil War. After a distinguished career in the cavalry, for which he was awarded a Congressional Medal of Honor, Furness returned to Hunt's atelier late in 1864. In 1866 he went back to Philadelphia, where he had been brought up, and, with a succession of partners, conducted a practice which flourished in the 1870s and 1880s, petered out in the 1890s, and was all but inactive by the time of his death in 1912.

Many of the details of Furness's buildings are reminiscent of English work and recall the highly articulate and colorful motifs of George Edmund Street, William Butterfield, and William Burges. Furness may also have drawn upon Christopher Dresser's books about ornament. But the sensibility that suffused his buildings had little to do with these sources. It may have been shaped by Furness's exposure to neo-Grec works in Hunt's atelier, but in the end Furness's buildings were entirely his own.

At first glance they appear to be agglomerations of unrelated incidents— expressions, but not resolutions, of the multiplicity and variety of forces that then played upon architectural design. There is much evidence to support this interpretation, yet the power of Furness's work does not come from a wilful randomness. He had a definite method of design, one which capitalized on the tension that was produced by first making a coherent composition and then distorting it to the point of decomposition. For example, many of his facades were ostensibly symmetrical, but were so elaborated that they had none of the repose associated with symmetry. This

99 quality was fundamental to Furness's Pennsylvania Academy of the Fine Arts, Philadelphia (1871–76), one of his earliest and, because it still survives, probably his best-known building. But it was even more pronounced in

100 other works, such as the National Bank of the Republic, Philadelphia (1883–84). There, Furness used a stair tower with an exaggerated conical roof—an element which customarily was only a minor accent on a facade— as the major focus of the front elevation. Having established this uncharacteristic tower at the center of his facade, Furness was able to dispose of the other elements of the building in a free and dynamic way.

The same attitude informed the design of many of the parts of Furness's buildings. The customary way to make an opening for a window or a door was either not to subdivide the space under an arch or lintel or to compose it in an odd number of parts so that there would be a distinct center. Furness deliberately flouted this convention. He often divided his openings into two

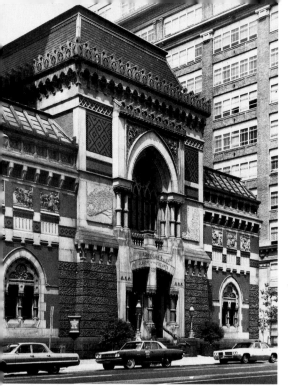

99 Frank Furness: Pennsylvania Academy of the Fine Arts, Philadelphia, Pennsylvania, 1871–76.

100 Frank Furness: National Bank of the Republic, Philadelphia, Pennsylvania, 1883–84.

parts so that at doorways there was an ambivalence about which was the preferred entrance. This quality was accentuated by making the division between the two parts more than just infill. Furness often established his opening with a substantial arch or lintel but then introduced in the middle a pier or a column that was stout enough to support them.

Furness's window heads, sills, and related belt courses stressed this contradictory or eccentric quality. Like Hunt, many of the period's architects gave emphasis to these elements by making them of stone and thus contrasting them with brick walls. The result was a decorative facade pattern, but usually with a clear distinction between the primary wall and the secondary accents around the openings. Furness often reversed this order. In his building for the Provident Life and Trust Company, Philadelphia (1876–79; 1888–90; 1902), for example, he so exaggerated the lintels and sills *101*

101 Frank Furness: Provident Life
and Trust Company, Philadelphia,
Pennsylvania, 1876–79; 1888–90;
1902.

that it was difficult to tell what was primary and what secondary. Furness
sometimes further subverted the identity of these stone elements by making
them assume the shapes of machine parts.

He used structure for the same ends. Although, like other architects of the
period, he usually took explicit steps to demonstrate how his buildings were
made and supported, just as often he seems to have wanted to produce the
appearance of a state of instability. Elements of his facades were often
corbelled or projected outward toward the sidewalk, so that, especially for
those entering, the building seemed almost threatening. Furness designed his
chimneys for the same effect, frequently making them larger at the top than
at the bottom so that they appeared to be teetering.

Furness wrote little about his work, and in the absence of any statement
about his intentions, it is easy to dismiss his buildings as coy or mannered. It
can be argued that since he was a talented caricaturist, his works were simply
parodies of other buildings. But there is much more to his architecture than
that. It can be read as a frank reflection of the often dissonant nature of life in
the latter half of the nineteenth century. In this respect, his buildings on

corner sites are especially revealing. Because of their strategic locations, they typically had to respond to two different conditions: a major thoroughfare built up with a continuous wall of separate buildings, and a side street that straggled into a sparsely developed area. Such sites, in effect, encapsulated the unpredictable nature not just of American urban development, but of American life itself. That was why Furness often made the passage through the front doors of his buildings so full of consequence. His interiors accentuated this message. Resolved and regular, they were a haven for those seeking refuge from the seemingly anarchic world outside. Ultimately, however, there was no real escape. The fact that so many of Furness's buildings have been demolished to allow for new development is a sad but eerily appropriate conclusion to his attempt to make the flux of American life the currency of architecture.

Furness's work is a telling contrast to that of his contemporary, Henry Hobson Richardson (1838–86). Born and brought up in Louisiana, Richardson graduated from Harvard College in 1859. During the Civil War he enrolled at the Ecole des Beaux-Arts, was a member of Jules André's atelier, and received a diploma in 1865. Later that year he returned to the United States, set up a practice in New York, and soon won a competition for the Church of the Unity in Springfield, Massachusetts (1866–69). That building led to another job, the Brattle Square (now First Baptist) Church in Boston (1870–72), which in turn brought him his most widely publicized commission, Trinity Church, Boston (1873–77). With the completion of *102*

102 Henry Hobson Richardson:
Trinity Church, Boston,
Massachusetts, 1873–77.

that building, Richardson began a decade of productive work that was terminated by his untimely death in 1886. During these years he designed over sixty buildings ranging from a small bridge in a public park in Boston to a scheme for a monumental Episcopal cathedral in Albany, New York. It is hard to overestimate the impact of these works. By the mid-1880s there was probably no sizable city in the United States that did not have at least a few prominent buildings which imitated Richardson's style. It had taken him no more than ten years to gain the complete respect and admiration of his fellow practitioners, and he was one of the few architects to be known outside the immediate circle of the profession.

The key to understanding not only Richardson's artistry, but also why he was so widely imitated is his use of Romanesque precedents as the point of departure for much of his work. When Richardson began to practice, Romanesque was usually seen as a transitional style between Roman and Gothic architecture. Richardson reversed this interpretation. For him, Romanesque synthesized the best qualities of both. Like the Roman vault and the Gothic arch, the rounded Romanesque arch was the basis of a consistent structure. But unlike Roman architecture, Romanesque buildings were not based on an armature of cheap materials covered by a coat of applied and often highly refined decoration. Nor did they depend for their quality on a high degree of elaboration, as was true of Gothic architecture. Instead, Romanesque was direct and simple, characteristics which Richardson thought reflected the American approach to building construction as it had developed by the end of the nineteenth century. Romanesque also had great programmatic advantages. Unlike Gothic, its use was not restricted primarily to churches, nor did it presuppose the rigid planning compositions then associated with Roman architecture. Romanesque forms could be deployed more freely, and Richardson was attracted to them because they could be used to accommodate the complex institutions that were vital parts of the emerging city and suburban society in which he lived.

The quality of the many buildings produced in a busy practice varied, but the remarkable fact about Richardson's work was that though it encompassed a vast range of buildings—large and small, city and suburban, East Coast and Midwest, functional and symbolic, private and public—it was all recognizably part of a coherent oeuvre. In effect, Richardson was able to elaborate a language of architecture which he could unaffectedly apply to any job. The development of this language can best be understood by comparing the five libraries Richardson designed. These buildings show a remarkable working out of common themes to suit the particular circumstances of each commission. The most striking contrast was between what Richardson called the "pyrotechnic" quality of the buildings of his early career, as exemplified by the Winn Memorial Library, Woburn, *103* Massachusetts (1877–78), and the quiet assuredness of his later period, which is best represented by the Crane Memorial Library, Quincy, Massachusetts *104* (1880–83). The Woburn library had the remarkable strength of Richardson's best work, but he did not achieve in it those subtle effects that later distinguished his buildings from those of his imitators. Its parts were much more assertive than the whole. Episodes such as the entrance portal and the patterned stone worked against the assertion of basic volumes. By contrast, in the Quincy library Richardson was able to posit one dominant idea and to subordinate all elements to it, but without compromising their integrity. The subtlety with which he alternately joined and separated the stair tower, reading room, vestibule, and roof gable was a profound essay on the relationship between the part and the whole.

Richardson's greatest project, his Episcopal Cathedral in Albany, New *105, 106* York (1882–83), was designed for a competition he did not win. Of his own works, the building he most admired was the Allegheny County Court *107, 108* House, Pittsburgh, Pennsylvania (1884–88). The plans of both works were based on a simple axial organization that differentiated the major and minor elements of these highly complex institutions. In both projects Richardson was able to combine Romanesque forms with modern requirements. In the cathedral he transformed the apsidal chapels of the great French churches into vestries. The courtyard of the court house served to give light from two sides to all rooms, and the tower acted as a fresh-air intake for the building's mechanical system. Both works did justice to the sources on which they drew, but in neither was there a single detail that was forced in its application, mainly because from the solid base to the varied roof line, one theme governed the pyramidal compositions of these master works.

For the cathedral and the court house, plausible analogies could be made with earlier works of architecture. When Richardson received the *109* commission to design the Marshall Field Warehouse, Chicago (1885–87), he had no equivalent guide. To be economical, this building had to cover a site that measured 325 by 190 feet, and it had to be 125 feet high. Richardson did not express the seven stories of this building by repeating the same window. Instead, he differentiated its facades by grouping several levels together and varying the stonework from one group to the next. Nevertheless, Richardson saw no need for elaborate detail. The warehouse's entrance was understated; round-headed arches were simply expressed; and the cornice was not highly articulated. What mattered most was a sense of mass; all details were subservient to this larger purpose.

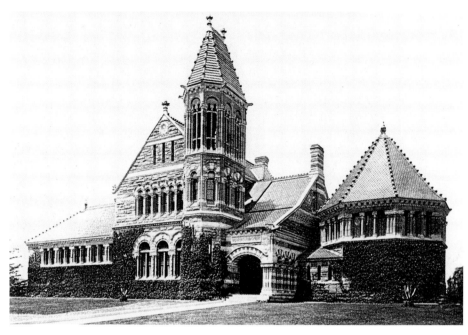

103 Henry Hobson Richardson: Winn Memorial Library, Woburn, Massachusetts, 1877–78.

104 Henry Hobson Richardson: Crane Memorial Library, Quincy, Massachusetts, 1880–83.

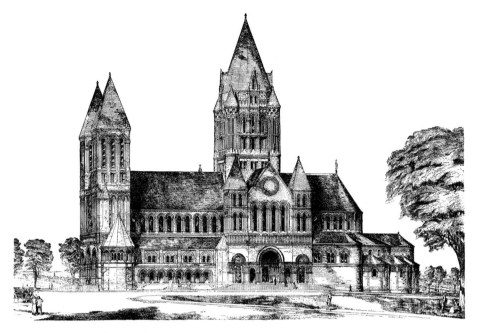

105, 106 Henry Hobson Richardson:
Episcopal Cathedral, Albany, New York,
1882–83. Perspective and plan.

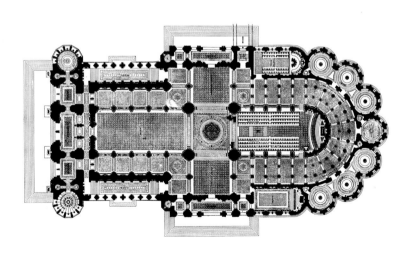

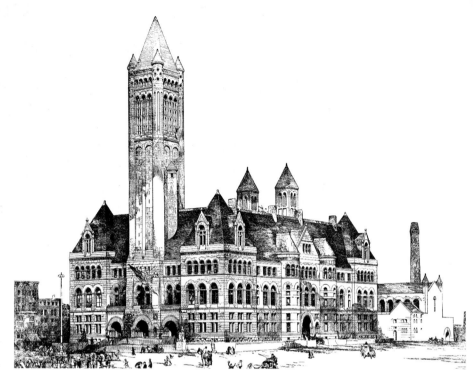

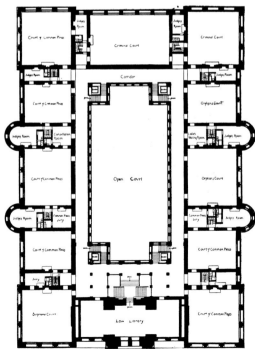

107, 108 Henry Hobson Richardson:
Allegheny County Court House,
Pittsburgh, Pennsylvania, 1884–88.
Perspective and second-floor plan.

109 Henry Hobson Richardson:
Marshall Field Warehouse, Chicago,
Illinois, 1885–87.

Toward the end of his career, Richardson increasingly tried to subsume all the parts of his buildings under one all-encompassing principle. Perhaps he pressed this quality to an extreme in the Marshall Field Warehouse because of the tight boundaries of the site and the building's utilitarian function. But Richardson probably also thought that the direct, even blunt, solution was appropriate because he was building in Chicago. Chicago had risen rapidly to prominence. In 1860 it was no more than one of several Midwestern boom towns. It left cities like St. Louis, Cincinnati, and Kansas City behind when railroad traffic was diverted northward during the Civil War. Its population increased from 109,000 in 1860 to 380,000 in 1873, when half its downtown area was leveled by fire. Even before the conflagration was out, new buildings were being constructed, but that boom was dampened by a depression. Nevertheless, in the late 1870s business picked up and building resumed in earnest.

By the 1880s, Chicago was widely thought to be the world's most characteristically modern city, and it was often claimed that there even existed a Chicago school of architecture. This subject was discussed in the magazine *Inland Architect*, first issued in 1883, and it arose frequently in meetings of the Western Association of Architects, founded in 1884. Although this organization was consolidated with the American Institute of Architects in 1889, its existence and rapid growth in membership testified that architects in the Midwest, particularly in Chicago, felt there was something special about the nature of practice in that part of the country.

Contemporary observers, like many historians since, frequently mentioned the role of expediency in the development of Chicago's architecture. Because architects had to build quickly and efficiently in Chicago, advances in building technology, especially for the tall office building, have dominated accounts of that city's architecture. Of course, it is important to chart the developments in building technology and to establish, for example, whether William Le Baron Jenney's (1832–1907) Home Insurance Building, Chicago (1884), was the first to be supported entirely by a steel frame or whether Leroy Buffington (1847–1931), a Minneapolis architect, described the basic outlines of such a structure earlier. And, indeed, the significant architects of that city were themselves all concerned with how their buildings were supported, and with questions about heating, ventilation, fireproofing, foundations, and so on. Some of them were even well read in the works of Eugène Viollet-le-Duc and Gottfried Semper, European theorists who were interested in the role of function in the development of architectural form. But such discussions miss the central fact about Chicago architecture. Even William Le Baron Jenney, who was trained as an engineer, considered technical issues subservient to the issue of primary concern: the matter of expression. It is this issue which continues to make the architecture of Chicago significant.

No architect was more articulate about what was at stake in the buildings of Chicago than John Wellborn Root (1850–91). Root grew up in Georgia and at the age of fourteen was sent to England to study. When he returned to the United States in 1866, he enrolled at New York University and received a degree in science and civil engineering in 1869. He then worked for several architects in New York, and when one of his employers, Peter B. Wight, went to Chicago in 1872, Root followed. Shortly after, Root met Daniel Burnham (1846–1912), and the two started a practice. The depression that followed the Chicago fire was a difficult time for Burnham and Root, as it was for many other architects, and it was only at the end of the 1870s that the firm received a steady stream of respectable work. Root died early in 1891, so he had only a decade of productive practice, but in that time he produced not only some remarkable buildings, but also a substantial body of essays which contained lucid statements about the state of architecture in Chicago in these vital years.

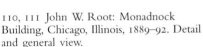
110, 111 John W. Root: Monadnock
Building, Chicago, Illinois, 1889–92. Detail
and general view.

Everything Root built and wrote was a reflection of his perception that he was living through a special time in history. He understood that great works of art were coherent because they adhered to a type. However, by the end of the nineteenth century the traditional types were, in many instances, no longer viable. Like all manifestations of civilization, architecture was moving from "homogeneity to heterogeneity." Since the Renaissance, but, more specifically, since the beginning of the nineteenth century, human needs had become more complex. Buildings had to respond to this fact. The architect's task was therefore to make "the frankest possible acceptance of every requirement of modern life in all of its conditions, without regret for the past or idle longing for a future and more fortunate day."

Even so, the simple expression of heterogeneity was not enough. Architecture also had to aspire to the production of new types—those suitable to the modern age. Thus, Root's work can be seen as an attempt to re-establish for a far more complex society the sense of coherence and unity that had characterized earlier styles of architecture. This search motivated all of Root's work, but it was most pronounced in his designs for the tall office building, which by the 1880s had been identified as the period's most characteristic structure. Root's most successful attempt to establish a type of the office building was the Monadnock, Chicago (1889–92). One of the *110, 111* reasons why this building was Root's exemplary achievement was that he

123

did not resort to meaningless belt courses, extraneous tourelles, a tenuously bowed central bay and an arbitrarily interrupted cornice—devices he had used earlier in the Rookery, Chicago (1885–88)—to differentiate its facade. Instead, he accepted a basic division of the two-story base, thirteen similar floors of offices, and one more level of an attic and cornice. Having made this frank differentiation of levels, Root then drew the parts of the building together into a coherent entity. He achieved this effect largely through the suppleness of his brick detailing, which allowed a protruding base, the flaring cornice, and the assertive bays imperceptibly to move into and out of the building's wall. The result combined both the vitality and the repose that Root knew were characteristic of all great works of architecture.

Root's increasing emphasis on the need for unity was a response both to his own more idiosyncratic earlier work and to his distaste for much of the work of his contemporaries. He frequently complained about the abuse of the supposed freedom offered by "Queen Anne" architecture, which he dubbed the "Tubercular Style," because of its many unattractive eruptions, both external and internal. The Queen Anne style was never so specific as to have a distinct set of characteristics. Instead, it contained a broad range of forms and historical references, some combinations of which have been characterized as Italianate, Second Empire, Eastlake Style, Stick Style, Shingle Style, and Chateauesque. Queen Anne architecture, as such, could be manifested in all building types, in urban, suburban, and rural locations, and in any material. However, it was probably made most vivid and memorable in suburban or country houses built primarily of wood.

The houses of the 1870s and 1880s were and probably forever will remain problematical. Their "tubercular" exteriors made them look as though great emphasis had been put upon the articulation of a plan, one shaped to accommodate particular and highly diverse functions within. Yet these houses were often impractically organized. Despite the many books printed in this period on how to plan and care for a house, the domestic architecture of the 1870s and 1880s frequently had large halls, small living rooms, and bedrooms that were hard to furnish. Kitchens were especially contorted and difficult to maintain. As servants were expected to preside over them, little thought was given to their arrangement, a fact which quickly became apparent to subsequent owners, especially those who did their own cooking. An illogical interior makes an eccentric exterior seem even more bizarre, because a picturesque assemblage of forms and details is usually only achieved by violating basic principles about how best to shed snow and rain from roof surfaces. Roofs with many peaks and valleys are generally only bought at the expense of damp attics, rotting eaves, deteriorating gutters, and stained and peeling paint, all of which tax the patience and pocketbook

112

113

112 Hall and staircase in Jacobean style from Henry Hudson Holly, *Modern Dwellings*, 1878.

of the owner. This fact in part explains why so many of these houses, especially the more effusive ones, have been taken down.

Even so, such houses continue to be attractive. There was a time, of course, when anything "Victorian" was considered fussy and old-fashioned, but, given the perceived sterility of modern architecture, the individuality of these houses stands out. This quality is all the more remarkable because the houses of the 1870s and 1880s were often constructed, not individually, but in groups by builders who used pattern books and stock doors, windows, moldings, gutters, cabinets, mantelpieces, lighting fixtures, and other such elements.

A contemporary French writer summarized the ambivalence created by these houses. Writing about a house in St. Paul, Minnesota, he stated:

Observe the plan, the facade of this dwelling; could anything be imagined more ignorant or worse studied! Yet notice, in the midst of all this carelessness, the detail of the entrance porch, how pretty, interesting and useful. Look also at the little balcony overlooking the water, and see

114

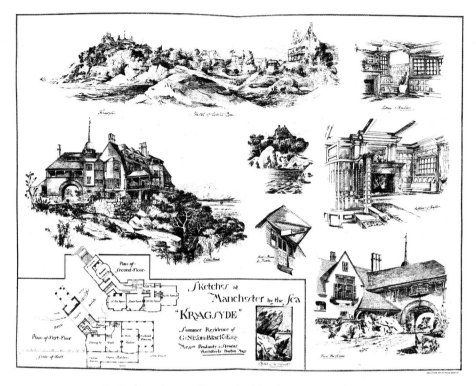

113 Peabody & Stearns: Kragsyde, Manchester, Massachusetts, 1885.

114 W. W. Boyington: Residence of Benjamin Franklin Allen, Des Moines, Iowa, 1869.

how pleasant life must be in that house; yet with all this—what gables on top of gables; what strange openings and curious balustrades! How an architect must have to torture his mind to invent such things.

It is clear that by the late 1880s John Wellborn Root had lost patience with this architecture. He lashed out at builders who erected "hideous nightmares." But they were only "unconscious assimilators" of the works of architects who too often indulged in fanciful flights of self-expression at the expense of the discipline that should have been the basis of the profession.

One of these "individual personalities," a man who, Root felt, was often too exuberant, was Louis Sullivan (1856–1929). Sullivan had an unconventional upbringing. Born in Boston, he lived for much of his childhood with his grandparents. His grandfather, a follower of the transcendentalist George Ripley, nurtured in Sullivan a love of nature and encouraged him to be a freethinker. From the age of thirteen Sullivan knew he wanted to be an architect, but he was repelled by the education that he had to undergo in order to become one. In 1873 he enrolled in the architecture program at the Massachusetts Institute of Technology, but left after only one term. Sullivan then went to Philadelphia, found employment with the eccentric Frank Furness, but gave up that job for reasons which are still unclear. He next moved to Chicago, where his parents were then living, and worked with William Le Baron Jenney. After nine months Sullivan decided to enroll at the Ecole des Beaux-Arts. Studying at that most academic of architectural institutions convinced him of the uselessness of formal education. He described his atelier as a "damned pigsty" and was able to escape the insufferable atmosphere of Paris only by traveling to Rome where he exulted in the work of Michelangelo, one of history's most intuitive and individual architects.

When Sullivan returned to the United States, he settled in Chicago, where he soon established a partnership with Dankmar Adler (1844–1900), who largely handled the business and technical aspects of the practice. The partnership flourished, and in addition to designing buildings, Sullivan found time to write about his approach to architecture. The essence of his philosophy was the belief that in order to have an architecture commensurate with the society he hoped would develop in the United States, it was necessary to supersede outmoded traditions and rules made for other eras and societies. For Sullivan the United States version of democracy was a unique development in the history of mankind because it promised the full realization of the individual. In several lectures and articles, but expecially in his essay "Inspiration" which he read at the 1886 convention of the Western Association of Architects, Sullivan pinpointed nature, not books or buildings, as the most fertile source of inspiration, and he frequently spoke of the need for architects to return to the child's uncorrupted state. He reiterated these ideas in a symposium on the vital subject, "What is the Just Subordination, in Architectural Design, of Detail to Mass?" Sullivan refused to commit himself to any position. Claiming that he valued "spiritual results" only, his ideal was a truly organic architecture, "an expansive and rhythmic growth," which was incompatible with such artificial ideas as a distinction between detail and mass.

Sullivan was soon identified with this iconoclastic point of view. However, it was one thing to state such ideas and another to show how they could be put into practice, especially since buildings are characteristically thought to be static and finite, not growing and expansive. Certainly, by the late 1880s Sullivan's buildings had not yet matched his words. Far from being individual and original creations, they were all too obviously derivative of two sources: Frank Furness and Henry Hobson Richardson. Sullivan's earliest works were highly idiosyncratic, much in the manner of Furness. His domestic architecture of the late 1870s and early 1880s indulged

115

115 Louis Sullivan: Three Houses for Dankmar Adler, Dila Kohn, and Eli Felsenthal, Chicago, Illinois, 1885–86.

116 Adler & Sullivan: Auditorium Building, Chicago, Illinois, 1886–90.

in oriel windows, a picturesque skyline, and highly individualistic detailing. Even the facades of his office buildings were obsessively complex and cranky.

By the mid-1880s the influence of Richardson's work, particularly the Marshall Field Warehouse, was evident in the designs of Adler & Sullivan. The connection was most overt in the Auditorium Building, Chicago *116, 117* (1886–90). The very fact that such a young firm received this important commission was remarkable, especially since it was given on the recommendation of the normally conservative William Ware, who acted as advisor to the client. The building posed highly complex technical and programmatic problems. It had to contain not only an auditorium for an audience of 4,200, but also a hotel and office building, which served to finance the space after which the building was named. All these requirements had to be packaged into a neat envelope that took maximum advantage of the valuable real estate on which the building stood. To achieve this, not only did difficult foundation conditions have to be overcome, but structural problems that resulted from the need for a large, column-free space also had to be solved.

117 Adler & Sullivan: Auditorium Building, Chicago, Illinois, 1886–90. Interior.

109 The Auditorium Building dealt with these matters admirably, but its two main facades were equivocal. Inspired by the Marshall Field Warehouse, it can be similarly faulted because floors with essentially the same functions were treated in arbitrarily different ways. But the more important criticism concerns Sullivan's inability to draw all the parts of the elevation into a coherent and forceful composition. The continuous cornice of the final design was an improvement over earlier studies, but the end result had neither the cohesiveness of Richardson nor Furness's tantalizing sense of decomposition.

There were only two aspects of the Auditorium Building which came close to achieving an ideal of an "expansive and rhythmic growth." Sullivan's ornament, which remains the most enticing feature of his work, was based on studies of patterns from nature, rather than on the historical sources that served most architects of the period. These flowing and effusive decorative panels give the best sense of what Sullivan's work promised, but the auditorium itself also offered telling insights into the vision of this remarkable man. That space was truly expansive because it had a number of complex devices that could alter its shape to suit both the size of the audience and different types of productions. But its Sullivanian quality came mainly from its rippling parabolic ceiling, its pulsating ivory and gold leaf decorative patterns, and its hundreds of bright incandescent lights. Over the proscenium was a painting of a processional; at the back of the auditorium were two huge murals. All three were illustrations of passages from Sullivan's essay "Inspiration." Though the result was a dazzling performance, Sullivan was not able to relate the auditorium in a hierarchically meaningful way to the other spaces of the building. Perhaps he considered that kind of order antithetical to his concept of an expansive and growing architecture.

By the late 1880s other American architects were already looking for an antidote to an architecture fostered by "individual personalities." Furness's work was more subdued, and when he died in 1886, Richardson had long since given up his "pyrotechnic" manner. At the same time, Root was criticizing architects for speaking so many languages that the result was as coherent as a "chattering chimpanzee." This desire for order and unity was consonant with, and reinforced by, events outside the immediate concerns of the profession. The labor difficulties of the late 1880s and the influx into the United States of an increasingly diverse population were only two manifestations of what many perceived to be a general state of divisiveness and disintegration. In 1890 the census bureau announced that the frontier was closed; stark confirmation that a critical turning point had been reached. These diverse facts seemed all to have one message: If the United States was to avoid dissolving into anarchy and self-destruction, a new phase of development would have to begin. Shared values, based on the highest cultural standards, were necessary. Because of its high visibility, Americans once again looked to architecture to express and inspire the renewal they hoped would take place. The new direction—a return to classical principles—was as alluring as it was obvious.

CHAPTER FIVE

The Cause Conservative

The Architecture of the American Renaissance

No building was more pivotal in hastening the transformation that occurred in American architecture in the early 1890s than McKim, Mead & White's *118, 119* Boston Public Library (1888–95) which faces Henry Hobson Richardson's Trinity Church across Copley Square. Charles Follen McKim (1847–1909) and Stanford White (1853–1906) both worked in Richardson's office prior to founding their own firm; White had even helped with the drawings for Trinity Church. Yet it is hard to conceive of two more different buildings. The church is medieval in spirit and detail, effusive in coloring, and pictur-esque in massing. The library derives from buildings of the Italian Renaissance and of the French nineteenth century influenced by the Renaissance, and presents itself through its largely monochromatic, symmetrical, planar facade.

The architecture of antiquity and the Italian Renaissance had never been completely forgotten during the nineteenth century. In the 1840s and 1850s Greek and Roman sources were still deemed appropriate for public buildings, and in the same period Italian architecture inspired the many storefronts that lined the streets of major American cities. By the 1860s a few architects were also beginning to argue that the only suitable style for a church was the one used by the builders of colonial America.

Of course, every American who attended the Ecole des Beaux-Arts studied classical architecture. But the architects of Richard Morris Hunt's generation differed sharply from those who went to Paris at the turn of the century in their interpretation of the meaning of that education. Although Hunt and, even more so, Richardson knew their precedents, neither felt compelled to replicate those sources in any literal sense. McKim, Mead & White put a much higher premium not just on an adherence to precedents, but on an adherence to particular precedents—to those from antiquity (e.g. *131, 132* at Pennsylvania Station) and the Italian Renaissance. As Joseph Wells (1853–90)—McKim, Mead & White's chief designer in the late 1880s—put the matter: "The classical ideal suggests clearness, simplicity, grandeur, order and philosophical calm—consequently it delights my soul. The medieval ideal suggests superstition, ignorance, vulgarity, restlessness, cruelty and religion—all of which fill my soul with horror and loathing."

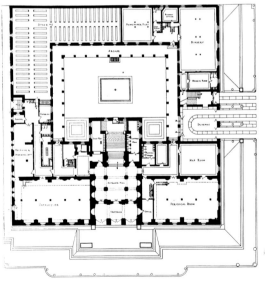

118, 119 McKim, Mead & White:
Boston Public Library, Boston,
Massachusetts, 1888–95. Facade and
first-floor plan.

133

These values caught on quickly. The founding in 1894 of the American School of Architecture, which in 1897 was transformed into the American Academy of Fine Arts in Rome, was one important way in which ties to the classical world were strengthened. But the most visible demonstration of a 120 commitment to classical principles occurred at the World's Columbian Exposition in Chicago in 1893. To lend coherence to the site of the Fair, Daniel Burnham, the architect in charge, persuaded the designers of the major buildings to adopt white, classical facades. Because the uniformity and serenity of this ensemble stood in such sharp contrast to the chaos and restlessness that seemed to have been the inevitable outcome of the architectural values of the previous decades, leaders of the profession found it all but irresistible to argue that the classical language could be put to productive use in turn-of-the-century America in the same way that it had served many other cultures and periods.

The only dissenter at the World's Columbian Exposition was Louis Sullivan. His Transportation Building, if not completely original in conception, was at least derived from an eccentric source, Saracenic architecture. Its major feature was an arched portal surrounded by polychromatic ornament that was accented by a symbol of the modern age: hundreds of glistening incandescent light bulbs. The exuberance of Sullivan's portal stood out from the sobriety of the white buildings that surrounded it; the contrast summarized a fundamental disagreement in architectural values.

Most of the architectural histories of this period have concentrated on this division between conservative and progressive, East Coast and Midwest, and the conflicting ideals of beauty and truth. These distinctions did exist, but their importance has usually been overstated. Just as a closer examination reveals that the Boston Public Library was not a direct copy of any precedent and in fact had many subtle medievalisms that echoed details of the church it faced, the two sides of the period's architecture had more in common than has generally been acknowledged. What makes this period all the more fascinating is the fact that academically inclined architects were often highly innovative, whereas the best of the progressive practitioners achieved their originality by making a fresh interpretation of the meaning of architectural tradition. This complex interplay of values resulted in the most significant architecture in American history.

One way to understand the buildings that were shaped by Beaux-Arts principles is to come to terms with the criticism that has been made of them. The prominent critic Montgomery Schuyler (1843–1914) never fully endorsed the architecture of what has been called the American Renaissance. He thought its ready adoption due to important changes in the nature of

120 World's Columbian Exposition, Chicago, Illinois, 1893. The Court of
Honor, looking west to the Administration Building.

architectural practice that had taken place in the preceding quarter century.
To take one specific case, Henry Hobson Richardson had been extremely
busy in the last decade of his life, but was still able to conduct his practice in
the informal atmosphere of an annex to his home in Brookline,
Massachusetts. According to Schuyler, this relatively leisurely approach
would not have been feasible in the 1890s. By then the pressures on the
practice of architecture had increased radically. Architects no longer had the
time to design every building and detail afresh. If they wanted their practices
to succeed as businesses, they needed a system to make architecture easy. The
classical language, especially as codified and distilled by the many handbooks
then available, answered such a need.

By the 1890s a few American architectural practices had grown to an
unprecedented size. Such offices were structured like factories for the
production of buildings. Daniel Burnham's was probably the most
notorious. It had hundreds of employees, organized into designers,
draughtsmen, engineers, specification writers, superintendents, and

executives—a division of labor that facilitated the design and construction of large buildings of previously unequaled technical complexity. To expedite the work, such offices may have adopted the classical language as an easily accessible and repeatable medium of expression. Yet it can hardly be argued that Americans were attracted to the Ecole des Beaux-Arts because that institution espoused, and helped to train students to produce, an architecture of expediency. For it to have been adopted so enthusiastically, classical architecture must have had a far deeper appeal.

In *Sticks and Stones*, a pioneering study of American architecture published in 1924, Lewis Mumford offered a penetrating criticism of this architecture. In a chapter entitled "The Imperial Facade," Mumford raised two issues. First, he implied by his disdainful use of the word "facade" that there was something dishonest about classical architecture. Mumford presupposed that a building should be truthful; its exterior should reveal what is happening inside, and it should honestly represent the way it is made. Second, Mumford found the message expressed by these buildings offensive. The facades celebrated the imperial nature of the institutions for which they acted as a framework. Mumford claimed that the adoption of this architecture went hand in hand with the closing of the frontier, the growth of monopolies, and the rise of a class of robber barons with ambitions to become a new aristocracy. In effect, Mumford despised this architecture because it seemed to be based on and project an image of imperial Rome, the antithesis to his ideal of American society.

Mumford's first criticism would not have concerned architects like Daniel Burnham and Stanford White because they placed a much higher premium on beauty than on truth. They would have argued that well planned and constructed buildings are not automatically beautiful and that every building has a facade in the sense that the exterior can never be a direct translation of what happens inside. Because the exterior is public in nature and has to deal with the special conditions posed by the outdoor environment, some degree of independent expression is inevitable.

Even so, it is still important to assess the extent to which the architecture of the American Renaissance was untruthful. For example, were the planning techniques taught at the Ecole des Beaux-Arts inappropriate to the complexity of the modern building program? The answer is not clearcut. Contrary to what has usually been written about them, American architects trained at the Ecole did not deal only with a narrow and exclusive range of buildings. Their practices included works of civil engineering, and some of them were interested in designing for people who lived in other than owner-occupied houses. Drawing on his French experience, Richard Morris Hunt designed the first American apartment house. Other American architects

136

trained at, or in schools influenced by, the Ecole des Beaux-Arts made significant contributions to the development of this emerging building type, and they also tried to solve one of the great problems of the day: the housing of the American working population in large cities. Ernest Flagg's (1857–1947) work toward this end was the most significant. In 1894 Flagg demonstrated an alternative to the standard New York City dumbbell   *121, 122* tenement by showing the advantages to be gained by joining several building lots. He later invented several inexpensive construction techniques. Other Beaux-Arts-trained architects had similar interests. The eminent city planner George Ford (1879–1930) spent four years at the Ecole and wrote a

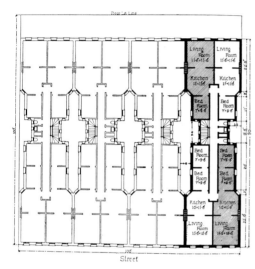

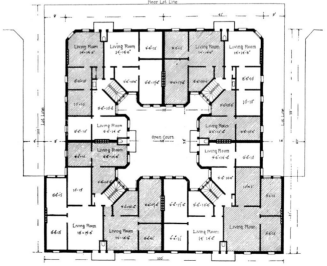

121, 122 Ernest Flagg: dumbbell apartment plan, and plan for a 200-foot by 200-foot building lot in New York City, 1894.

thesis entitled "A Tenement in a Large City." Isaac N. P. Stokes
(1867–1944), after three years in Paris, returned to the United States to
establish an architectural practice which produced important buildings for
major institutions, but at the same time he took an active role in tenement
house reform and was instrumental in forming the New York State
Tenement House Commission.

Architects like Flagg thought that the techniques they learned at the Ecole
enabled them to solve any planning problem. But like practitioners of any
period or background, they were better able to handle small,
programmatically simple buildings than large, complex ones. McKim,
Mead & White's Knickerbocker Trust Company, New York (1904), was a
telling case in point. This bank, which was demolished only two decades
after it was built, had many masterful qualities. The difference and transition
between the Fifth Avenue and 34th Street facades demonstrated a
responsiveness to context of which few architects then or since have been
capable. The main banking hall was a magnificent space, generous in
dimensions and sumptuous in details. But the most impressive aspect of the
Knickerbocker Trust Company was its colossal orders. These four-story
columns and pilasters were awesome in scale, as suited a bank, but they also
indicated the structural order of the building and served as a framework
which encompassed the four separate floors. The different functions of these

123

123 McKim, Mead &
White: Knickerbocker
Trust Company, New
York City, 1904.

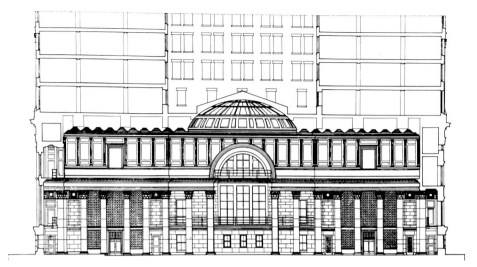

124 McKim, Mead & White: National City Bank, New York City, 1909.
Section.

floors were demonstrated through different types of windows, but these variations were subsumed by the colossal orders.

When architects trained in this tradition had to build higher than four or
five stories, they found that they could not stretch the colossal order any
further. They then had to resort to other devices, none of which in retrospect
was successful. The Knickerbocker Trust Company was originally meant to
have thirteen stories. McKim, Mead & White's solution, which can be
deduced from their National City Bank Building, New York (1909), would   *124*
have been simply to superimpose an additional nine-story element, perhaps
with an articulated cornice, on the four-story bank. This additive approach
was at best a simplistic solution to the problem of the tall building, for which
there was no obvious precedent in classical architecture.

When buildings spread out horizontally, architects trained at the Ecole
were more successful, as is amply demonstrated by Grand Central Station,   *125*
New York (1903–13). This was not only the world's largest station,
processing seventy thousand passengers and two hundred trains per hour,
but it was also a facility of unprecedented complexity. In addition to long-
distance and suburban trains, the station acted as an intersection through
which passed a steady stream of pedestrians, taxis, automobiles, several
subway lines, and special trains that transferred baggage to other stations.
The architects, Reed & Stem and Warren & Wetmore, developed an
ingenious solution to this problem. Because of the conversion from smoke-

139

125 Reed & Stem and Warren & Wetmore: Grand Central Station,
New York City, 1903–13. Section.

producing steam engines to electrically powered trains, the high shed that
had been an integral part of earlier stations was unnecessary. Instead, the
trains arrived on three underground levels, and swung around in a loop to a
marshalling yard from where they were called back when departures were
imminent. The station blocked Park Avenue so it was necessary to bridge
42nd Street and to make an upper level road on either side of the station that
eventually deposited cars down at grade past 45th Street.

Because movement was essential to the very nature of a railroad station,
architects trained in the Beaux-Arts tradition, with all its emphasis on grand
axes and a *promenade architecturale*, were well suited to deal with it. However,
the same techniques were not as relevant to other buildings, especially
126   libraries. For example, McKim, Mead & White tried to base the design of the
Boston Public Library around a monumental staircase that led up to the
main reading room. This resulted in a staircase which jutted out into and thus
compromised the interior court. Even so, the staircase remained almost
domestic in scale and did not fulfill what the approach to it promised. The
arrival at the landing and the transition into the main reading room were
equally problematical. In order for the gesture to be meaningful, much more
127, 128   space and a grander entrance were necessary. In the New York Public
Library, which opened in 1911, Carrère & Hastings addressed some of these
problems. Their approach to the library's main rooms was a sustained and
magnificent sequence. But it can be argued that this end was ruthlessly

140

126 McKim, Mead & White: Boston Public Library, Boston, Massachusetts, 1888–95. Stairhall from landing.

127, 128 Carrère & Hastings: New York Public Library, New York City, completed 1911. 42nd Street entrance hall and facade.

129 Charles Platt:
Villa at Lake Forest,
Illinois, 1908–18.

130 Charles Platt:
Woodston, Mt.
Kisco, New York,
1905–08.

pursued at the expense of the reading rooms, which seem small and have always been overcrowded.

Although such libraries were often called palaces for the people, they were not just magnificent set pieces. They also had to be efficient places for the storage and distribution of books. No library built at the turn of the century succeeded in coming to terms with this task. By 1890 it was evident that none of the traditional models for a library was useful in coping with the nineteenth-century explosion of knowledge. The single space, ringed by layer after layer of book-lined balconies, became taller and more well-like as the number of volumes increased. The large room with alcoves designated by subject similarly could not deal with a collection that expanded rapidly and in unpredictable areas, nor could a library composed of a sequence of rooms, one for each subject. Clearly some form of book stack was necessary, but incorporating this highly specialized space into the rest of the library was a task that no architect was able to handle effectively. The floor to ceiling height of an efficient book stack did not accord well with the other spaces of the library, and too often these vast storage areas were obstacles in the library's overall circulation plan.

Architects of the American Renaissance had similar successes and failures in dealing with the planning and construction of other new building types. But even though they demonstrated more skill in these matters than they have usually been given credit for, their primary concern was still the range of expression that could be achieved through the common medium of the classical language. Many firms had a recognizable style. The severity of John

Russell Pope's (1874–1937) work was immediately distinguishable from the baroque luxuriance of Ernest Flagg's buildings. But even within a firm, vast differences of interpretation were possible, depending on the nature of the job and the partner in charge. McKim, Mead & White's Interborough Rapid Transit Company Power House, New York (1903), was not only different in expression from the many buildings that firm designed for major cultural institutions, but would have been different again had Charles Follen McKim been the partner in charge instead of Stanford White. Similarly, the eight branch libraries that McKim, Mead & White designed in New York (1903–07) had essentially the same program, but each had a strikingly different facade.

Domestic architecture probably offered the designer the most latitude in interpretation. Although architects like McKim, Mead & White increasingly designed houses in recognizable styles, the choice of a particular style was neither automatic nor arbitrary. It depended, as did its interpretation in detail, on the nature of the program and the site. Thus, Charles Platt (1861–1933), one of the period's most sensitive architects, could vary his designs from the unprepossessing restraint of his villa at Lake Forest, *129* Illinois (1908–18), to the vine and trellis covered Woodston at Mt. Kisco, *130* New York (1905–08), to the stately portico of the Manor House in Glen Cove, New York (1909–11). Platt and other American architects did not restrict themselves to Roman or Italian sources. At the same time that houses modeled on classical villas became popular, there was a revival of interest in American vernacular buildings, such as the clapboard houses of New

England, the stone farmhouses of Pennsylvania, and the adobe churches and missions of the Southwest. Inevitably this revival was accompanied by many saccharine statements about the nature of vernacular architecture, but it did result in the recording and preservation of significant buildings and it also inspired a few architects to create exemplary works of their own.

Architects like Charles Platt were of course interested in more than facades. The development of the interior of a building was also important. In the period's public architecture there was no better example of the manipulation of a range of expression from exterior to interior than McKim, Mead & White's Pennsylvania Station, New York (1906–10). Its facade, stretching along Seventh Avenue from 31st to 33rd Streets, was unsurpassed as monumental architecture. Its cornice was continuous, except for slightly projecting bays at the center and ends, and was supported by thirty-two freestanding unfluted Doric columns, each sixty-eight feet high. The monumentality of this set piece was emphasized by the station's austere side elevations which were relieved only by flat pilasters and a series of small office windows.

131, 132, 133

The spaces inside complemented the character of the exterior. The main entrance on Seventh Avenue gave access to a long arcade which led to a flight of stairs that emptied into the waiting room. The inspiration for this space came from Viollet-le-Duc's restoration of the great hall of the Baths of Caracalla, but McKim surpassed even the vast dimensions of that room. To get to the trains, passengers proceeded from the waiting room to the concourse where another shift in architectural language took place. The glass roof of this space was supported by a series of intersecting arched trusses, an enticing mixture of the engineer's aesthetic that had characterized roofs of earlier train sheds and an architecture of greenhouses and garden structures.

It is easy to admire the way in which architects of the American Renaissance manipulated the classical language as a medium of expression. *What* they were expressing, however, is not always clear. Daniel Burnham and many of his contemporaries unabashedly made comparisons between their buildings and those of Rome, but the imperial nature of their work is not unambiguous. Many of the most significant works of the classical revival were not paid for or promoted by millionaires or large corporations, but by the local, state, or federal government, all of which presumably acted in the name of the people.

Of course it is possible to argue that the people were not represented in any genuine sense in the process of deciding what shape such buildings should take. Nevertheless, it is hard to deny the enduring popularity of some of this architecture. Take, for example, the Lincoln Memorial, which was designed by Henry Bacon (1866–1924) in 1912 and completed in 1922. Standing on

134

131, 132, 133 McKim, Mead &
White: Pennsylvania Station, New
York City, 1906–10. General view,
main waiting room, and concourse.

the banks of the Potomac at the end of the long axis that begins with the Capitol, travels over a mile to the obelisk of the Washington Monument and then carries past a large reflecting pool, the Lincoln Memorial is an unequivocal masterpiece of site planning. But there have always been questions about the appropriateness of the memorial itself. Some critics have expressed these reservations by excusing, and thus dismissing, the memorial as primarily a backdrop for Daniel Chester French's statue of Lincoln. The building and the statue do work well together, but Henry Bacon clearly did not intend his building to play a subservient role. He wanted the memorial to project an image, and it is important to ask whether and in what sense the image is appropriate.

This issue is inextricably involved with the architectural language of the Lincoln Memorial. Specific criticisms have often been made of Bacon's interpretation of classical precedents. Was it correct to combine a Greek temple with a Roman attic, to enter such a temple on the side, not the end, and to use Doric columns without bases on such an important monument? Other criticisms have focused on the austerity of the rooms flanking Lincoln's statue and the blandness of the steps leading up to the memorial.

The more important question, though, is why Bacon used the classical language and such a rendering of it in the first place. In 1924 Lewis Mumford put the matter in terms of Lincoln's background. He claimed that "the America that Lincoln was bred in, the homespun and humane and humorous America that he wished to preserve" had nothing in common with this "sedulous classic monument." Clearly the memorial is no homespun log cabin, but Henry Bacon would have answered Mumford by claiming that the classical language was a universal mode of expression and that his stark rendering of the Doric order was consonant with both those homespun qualities and American aspirations for culture, a valid and vital impulse with which Mumford did not come to terms.

The subsequent history of the Lincoln Memorial makes these issues even more complex, and richer. One undeniable tribute to the memorial is that it has a presence which has made it an appropriate background for significant events. In the process it has become inseparable from the memory of those events. Thus, an entire generation's perception of the Lincoln Memorial was fixed on 19 August 1963, when the March on Washington was broadcast on television. Ever since then it has been all but impossible to look at the Lincoln Memorial without associating it with the aspirations expressed that day by Martin Luther King and the devastating events of the subsequent decade.

Civic design was as problematical in these terms as architecture. In the quarter century after 1893 many American architects tried to expand and put into practice the principles that had been used at the World's Columbian

134 Henry Bacon: Lincoln Memorial, Washington, D. C., 1912–22.

Exposition. Chief among these was Daniel Burnham. In 1901, as a member
of the Senate Park Commission, he was instrumental in showing how the
center of Washington, D.C., could be improved. In the century after
L'Enfant had outlined his ideas for Washington, little had been done to carry
out his magnificent plan. The land between the Capitol and the Potomac
was largely an open pasture, a line of the Baltimore and Potomac Railroad
had been allowed to cross this area on grade, and a railroad station had been
built on the Mall near 6th Street. The commission's "great consistent
scheme" did away with the railroad and its station, strengthened the
definition of the Mall, established the vital cross axes and thus set the
guidelines that have been used ever since to locate key monuments and
buildings.

The World's Columbian Exposition was a group of temporary buildings
for a special purpose; the Senate Park Commission's plan outlined a scheme   *135*
for essentially a single, though increasingly large and never faction-free,
client. By the turn of the century it was still an open question whether these

147

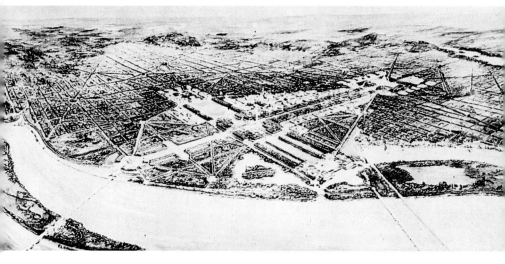

135 The Senate Park
Commission proposal for
central Washington, D. C.,
1901.

136 Daniel H. Burnham and
Edward H. Bennett: *Plan of
Chicago*, The Business Center
of the City, 1909.

137 The Midway Plaisance,
World's Columbian Exposition,
Chicago, Illinois, 1893.

principles could or should be applied to an entire city. Burnham tried to expand the range of this work in plans for Manilla, San Francisco, and Cleveland, but his most significant project of this type was for Chicago. In 1909 he presented the *Plan of Chicago*, a beautifully produced and comprehensive volume, the scope of which was breathtaking. Burnham reworked the center of the city so that major institutions were coordinated on an axis that led from a great harbor to a monumental civic center. He also designed a vast network of radial streets that knit together the various sectors of Chicago, and which were all encompassed within a circumferential highway that, anticipating the impact of the automobile traffic, joined the distant suburbs on the North and South sides. These streets and roads were not simply traffic arteries but were coordinated with a vast park system which stretched out along the lake front, throughout Chicago, and into extensive nature preserves on the as yet undeveloped perimeter of the city. 136

The difficulty with such plans was that their authors tried to impose an order on the American city that was simplistic, unrealistic, and undesirable. The gap between the ideal and the real was epitomized in the contrast between the main exhibitions at the Chicago World's Fair and the unofficial section located on the Midway Plaisance. This unofficial area contained a broad array of foreign restaurants, amusement rides, and other carnival-like attractions. In effect it encapsulated the world of commerce and everyday life that was then so much a part of the American city. The urban vision 137

projected in subsequent world's fairs made no allowance for this diversity. Nor did the ensuing plans of the City Beautiful movement. In the *Plan of Chicago*, for example, there were no skyscrapers, billboards, one-story buildings, or elevated railways. A narrow and rigid definition of order was established and anything that did not fit was ruthlessly banished.

The World's Columbian Exposition was frequently called the Dream City. Its designers and the many others who contributed to the American Renaissance have always been open to the criticism that they were out of touch with reality. Charles Follen McKim once told students at Columbia University that "the thing of the first importance in architecture is—beauty." As such, he was, of course, correct. But too often he and many other architects acted as if the *only* thing of importance in architecture was beauty. In response to what they perceived to be an uncultured, materialistic clientele, they projected themselves as artists who were too refined to soil their hands by becoming involved with any of the down-to-earth issues that are inevitably a part of architecture. In doing so they too easily allowed themselves to be content with a stereotyped version of beauty and only rarely risked trying to find something more fundamental.

Clearly the best way to criticize the architecture of the American Renaissance was to build a convincing alternative. That was the task that *138* Louis Sullivan set himself. Sullivan conceived of his Transportation Building

138 Louis Sullivan: "Golden Door," Transportation Building, World's Columbian Exposition, Chicago, Illinois, 1893.

139 Louis Sullivan: Wainwright Building, St. Louis, Missouri, 1890–91.

at the World's Columbian Exposition as an alternative to the adjacent classical facades. But like the other structures at the Fair, the Transportation Building was ephemeral; it was torn down soon after the Exposition was closed. Sullivan had, therefore, to realize his ambitious agenda in other works, especially several tall office buildings, which he considered the period's archetypical architecture problem. In an essay entitled "The Tall Office Building Artistically Considered" (1896) he argued that this building type had to be a truthful reflection of its essential functions. Like other structures, it had distinctly different parts. The first story had to have an eye-catching entrance and a generally expansive, even sumptuous treatment. The second story, which in effect was a mezzanine, followed the pattern of the first. Above that there was an indefinite number of essentially similar floors of offices, the width of one of which defined the window spacing. Finally, the top floor had to contain mechanical equipment.

In his three masterpieces of this period—the Wainwright Building in St.   *139* Louis, Missouri (1890–91), the Prudential (now Guaranty) Building in Buffalo, New York (1894–95), and the Condict (now Bayard) Building in New York (1897–98)—Sullivan put his principles into practice. These works are enduring testaments to both his vision and his cause. Yet, without at all diminishing Sullivan's achievement, it can still legitimately be asked whether the undeniable success of these buildings resulted exclusively from his having been able to solve the high-rise problem, or whether it came from other sources.

Sullivan provided a partial answer to this question in his essay. In addition to fulfilling functions it was necessary for a builder to heed the "imperative voice of emotion." The tall office building had to be lofty. "It must be tall, every inch of it tall. The force and power of altitude must be in it, the glory and pride of exaltation must be in it." It is this emotive quality which makes Sullivan's best buildings still vital. But if we ask how Sullivan achieved this result—how in effect his buildings of the 1890s departed from his earlier work—it is difficult not to conclude that Sullivan drew upon the classical principles to which he had been exposed at the Ecole des Beaux-Arts and which other American architects were then increasingly finding attractive.

Several aspects of Sullivan's works can be labelled classical in spirit, if not in detail. In the 1880s Sullivan's buildings overtly celebrated the act of construction. He used rough, seemingly hand-hewn stone to emphasize the organic quality of his architecture, and for the same purpose his ornament grew out from one part of the building to another and thus was not decisively contained within rigid boundaries. Sullivan's work after 1890 departed from these principles. His buildings did not so obviously make a statement about the process of construction. Their piers were flat and virtually undifferentiated, and their ornament was usually restricted to spandrel panels or other clearly defined zones.

Sullivan also drew upon classical architecture in the organization of his elevations, a matter that had been problematical in earlier works like the Chicago Auditorium. The basic divisions may have been dictated by the functions of the different levels, but by the 1890s Sullivan's buildings all began to have a distinctly tripartite reading, one which echoed the fundamental columnar division into base, shaft, and capital. Sullivan took many specific steps to emphasize this arrangement. He unified the office part of his skyscrapers by treating all the piers equally, even though every other one was not structural. In fact, the plans of his tall buildings contributed little to their character. By and large they were unmemorable. There is no evidence to demonstrate that their column grids or elevator locations were chosen to inform either the organization of space or the articulation of the exterior.

116

139

For an architect who frequently proclaimed that "form follows function," this lack of interest in the internal arrangement of buildings was telling. It was characteristic not only of Sullivan's skyscrapers, but even more so of the rest of his work. In addition to the tall office building, there were in the 1890s other emerging building types, but Sullivan addressed none of them in more than a perfunctory manner. He failed to do so partly because

140 Louis Sullivan: National Farmers' Bank, Owatonna, Minnesota, 1907–08.

the right commissions did not come his way. As he became more disillusioned with a society that refused to acknowledge his genius, Sullivan became more cranky, drank too much, and in 1895 separated from the steadying influence of his partner Dankmar Adler. But the tragedy of Louis Sullivan is also that he probably understood that he was not fully capable of the task he had set himself. His later years were all the more poignant because in the few buildings he did design, especially several banks in small Midwestern cities, he came to depend more and more on people who had once been apprentices in his office. George Grant Elmslie faithfully assisted Sullivan until 1909 and was responsible for much of the detail of these buildings. In conception, however, Sullivan's buildings increasingly owed a debt to the work of his most famous student, Frank Lloyd Wright (1867–1959)

140

Later in his life Wright frequently proclaimed himself the greatest architect that ever lived. Such pronouncements inevitably won him few friends, and his work has always been more appreciated in Europe than in the

United States. However, now that it is more than half a century after his death, it is time to reevaluate Wright's achievement. From this vantage point his claim does not appear far from the mark.

Wright's reputation derives in part from the epic quality of his life. The child of a ne'er-do-well father and a strong mother, Wright grew up primarily in Wisconsin. After one semester of an engineering course at the University of Wisconsin, he went to Chicago where he soon found employment with Louis Sullivan. He worked with Sullivan until he started his own practice in 1893. Wright soon married, raised a family in suburban Oak Park, and had a prosperous practice. Acclaim for his work came quickly, not just from sources in the Midwest but also from prominent East Coast periodicals and from progressive architects in Europe.

The first sharp break in Wright's career came in 1909 when, to the scandal of everyone he knew, he left his family and traveled to Europe with the wife of a neighbor. When Wright returned to the United States, he was *persona non grata* in Chicago, so he established his practice at Taliesin, his summer home in Spring Green, Wisconsin. Whether Wright could have continued to practice within the orbit of Chicago is debatable, but in any case the question was settled for him in the summer of 1914, when a crazed cook at Taliesin set fire to the building and killed most of the inhabitants, including the woman with whom Wright was living. Wright, who was traveling at the time of the fire, was then forty-seven. At that age most people would not have been able to come to terms with such a tragedy. Yet Wright was to live for another equally productive forty-five years. When he died in 1959, he had been a practicing architect for seventy-five years and had lived for over half the period of the Republic. In American architecture Wright was, and continues to be, the vital link between the past and the future.

The phrase which probably reveals the most about Wright's early work is the opening sentence of the first significant article he wrote about his architecture. The essay, "In the Cause of Architecture," appeared in 1908 in the *Architectural Record* and began: "Radical though it may be, the work here illustrated is dedicated to a cause conservative in the best sense of the word." The best way to come to terms with Wright's architecture is to understand what he meant by a "cause conservative."

At its broadest level, the cause conservative entailed a particular stance toward society and the institutions for which its buildings acted as a framework. Wright inherited from Louis Sullivan an overriding faith in democracy, but the important difference between the two men and between Wright's early and late career was that at least until 1909 Wright had no fundamental qualm about the course of democracy in the United States. This is not to say that he agreed with whatever took place. Improvement was always necessary, but strong foundations already existed. Wright's early work did not presuppose or try to nurture any new or radical institutions. He accepted and gave an architectural interpretation to the conventions of the society in which he lived. Nothing more exemplified this attitude than Wright's opinions about the family. Perhaps because he had an unsettled childhood, he embraced an ideal of family togetherness that was then shared by the majority of Americans.

Wright was also radical and conservative in his attitude toward the landscape, whether natural or man-made. In the years when he came into his own as an architect, many of Wright's contemporaries looked to European precedents as a guide to help them locate their buildings in the landscape and conceive of a broader context for architectural groupings. Wright was not unaware of ideas from Europe; indeed, he probably absorbed them more thoroughly than any of his contemporaries, but he himself did not find anything inherently unsatisfactory in the American landscape, especially in the gridded cities of the Midwest. Whereas many of his contemporaries found the horizontal ground plane and the standard street grid monotonous and tried to contrive devices to counter their effect, Wright simply accepted these conditions. All his buildings of the early period were based on plan grids which usually extended outside the external walls into the landscape immediately around the building and then eventually to the lines of the sidewalks and streets beyond. No work more exemplified Wright's attitude toward this issue than his "Non-competitive" entry in 1913 to a competition *141* for the development of a quarter section of vacant level land on the outskirts of Chicago. Whereas every other entrant tried to deflect the grid of streets that surrounded the site, Wright ran that pattern through the site.

Just as Wright accepted the characteristic nature of the landscape of the Midwest, he also intuited a fundamental relationship between public and private in the American city. Wright's buildings were essentially of two types. His public buildings, such as the Larkin Building in Buffalo, New *142, 143, 144* York (1904), Unity Temple in Oak Park, Illinois (1906), and his apartment projects were usually oriented as much as possible toward the perimeter of the site. They sometimes presented imposing facades to the street, but there were few spaces between the sidewalk and the building other than necessary transitional areas. The buildings, in effect, were enclaves planned around an interior court to which the general public did not have access.

Wright's other type of building was rooted within the landscape. His suburban houses, for example, were anchored down at the core by a fireplace and then extended outward into a landscape which was carefully zoned to contain outdoor spaces for family use and wide lawns which, though private property, were part of a continuous public realm.

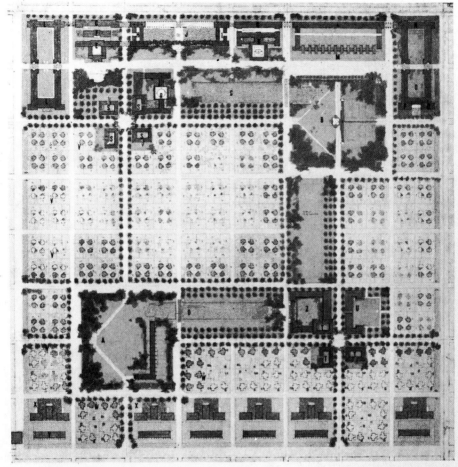

PLAN BY FRANK LLOYD WRIGHT

KEY TO PLAN

A. Park for children and adults. Zoölog-
    ical gardens.
B. Park for young people. Bandstand,
    refectory, etc. Athletic field.
C. Lagoon for aquatic sports.
D. Lagoon for skating and swimming.
E. Theater.
F. Heating, lighting, and garbage reduc-
    tion plant. Fire department.
G. Stores, 3 and 4 room apartments over.
H. Gymnasium.
I. Natatorium.

J. Produce market.
K. Universal temple of worship, non-
    sectarian.
L. Apartment building.
M. Workmen's semi-detached dwellings.
N. Four and five room apartments.
O. Stores with arcade.
P. Post Office branch.
Q. Bank branch.
R. Branch library, art galleries, museum,
    and moving picture building.

S. Two and three room apartments for
    men.
T. Two and three room apartments for
    women.
U. Public school.
V. Seven and eight room houses, better
    class.
W. Two-flat buildings.
X. Two-family houses.
Y. Workmen's house groups.
Z. Domestic science group.   Kinder-
    garten.

STATISTICAL DATA

304 Seven and eight room houses.
120 Two-flat buildings, five and six rooms.
 18 Four-flat buildings, four and five rooms.
  6 Fourteen-family workmen's house groups.
 12 Seven-room semi-detached workmen's houses.

 6 Apartment buildings, accommodating 320 families in all.
 4 Two and three room apartment buildings for women, accom-
    modating 250 to 300.
    Total, 1032 families and 1550 individuals (minimum).

141 Frank Lloyd Wright: Non-competitive Plan for the Development of a
Quarter Section of Land in the Outskirts of Chicago, 1913.

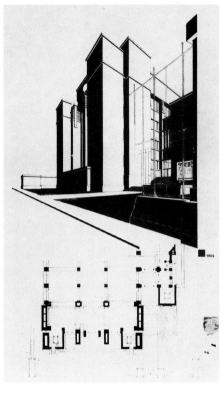

142, 143, 144 Frank Lloyd Wright: Larkin
Building, Buffalo, New York, 1904.
Exterior, interior, perspective, and plan of
the entrance.

145 Frank Lloyd Wright: Frederick C. Robie House, Chicago, Illinois, 1909.

      Wright outlined the generic pattern for this kind of suburban development in several of his so-called quadruple block plans, and he adapted this ideal configuration to particular situations, such as the difficult *145*   corner site on which the F. C. Robie House, Chicago (1909) was situated.

      Wright formulated his language of architectural elements along similar lines. His 1908 "In the Cause of Architecture" article acknowledged his method of design. The plans of his buildings used techniques that were akin *146*   to those taught at the Ecole des Beaux-Arts. All the parts of his buildings were located on a basic grid, the module of which was usually determined by the size of a window, a smaller unit than that used by graduates of the Ecole and which enabled Wright to make more "articulate" plans. With this supple device Wright planned a full range of houses from his design for a $5000 house that appeared in the *Ladies' Home Journal* in 1907 to huge mansions with complex entrance sequences and numerous wings that spread out to take advantage of particular aspects of the landscape.

      It has frequently been said that the projection of Wright's buildings into three dimensions was inspired by the exercises that he did as a child with the set of blocks devised by the Swiss educator Friedrich Froebel. Doubtless these blocks made a profound impression on Wright, but it is also important to understand that every one of his buildings was organized into three zones,

158

a division he found inherent in all organisms and also in classical, if not all, architecture. Wright's buildings rested on a distinct watertable that flared out from the wall line. Above this "stylobate" his building usually rose to the sill of the windows on the top story. From that datum he elaborated three types of roofs. Some buildings had flat roofs; others were capped by low hipped roofs either "heaped together in pyramidal fashion" or "presenting quiet unbroken skylines." Still others had low roofs that ended in "simple pediments." This essential grammar was most overt in Wright's smaller and more block-like buildings. In other structures he countered the horizontal bands that marked these basic datum levels with other lines, such as those established by the copings of garden walls and by planters. The result, therefore, varied from a simple mass to a complex play of planes in three dimensions.

Wright once described the attraction of a totally undecorated architecture, but he also admitted that there was an "ingrained human love

147

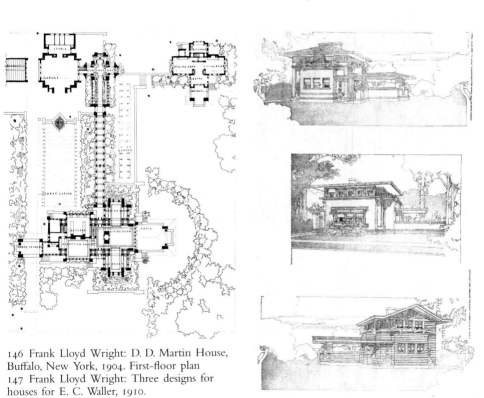

146 Frank Lloyd Wright: D. D. Martin House, Buffalo, New York, 1904. First-floor plan
147 Frank Lloyd Wright: Three designs for houses for E. C. Waller, 1910.

148 Frank Lloyd Wright: Susan L. Dana House, Springfield, Illinois, 1903. Dining room.

of ornament." Buildings were not only composed of masses and planes, they also had to "effloresce." Wright drew upon nature to make his buildings flower. Most included planters that were integral to the architecture. In addition, he often covered parts of his buildings, such as the "frieze above the second-story sill line," with patterns derived from nature and used similar designs in his leaded windows.

148   The other source of Wright's ornament was the history of architecture. In designing the capitals of columns Wright drew upon but never directly copied Romanesque, classical, and even pre-Columbian sources. His diamond-paned casement windows suggested English Tudor architecture, and the wood boarding in many of his houses was inspired by Japanese buildings. Elements of an American Palladian tradition also appeared in Wright's houses. Indeed, it is hard to think of a strain of architecture that Wright did not make use of at some level.

By manipulating these sources and organizational devices, Wright arrived at something for which other architects of the period were looking but which in their adherence to a narrow interpretation of the classical language they were never able to achieve: a grammar applicable to the complete array of buildings demanded by his society. These structures included public and private buildings ranging from office skyscrapers to churches, from houses for Chicago millionaires to small country cabins. They constitute the most substantial body of architectural work any American has ever produced, and it is not an exaggeration to say that Wright did for the United States at the turn of the century what Palladio did for the Veneto in his day.

By 1900 some progressive European architects were beginning to look to Wright's work for inspiration. His visibility in Europe was enhanced by the publication in Berlin in 1910 of a portfolio of his drawings—a catalytic event in the development of modern architecture in Europe. Given the European response, it is important to ask why Wright did not have a more consequential influence in the United States. The answer in part has to do with his untidy private life, the consequent negative publicity in the local press, and a falling off of important commissions. But more important was Wright's belief that architecture was a matter of personal creation. He was convinced that the only true style was an individual style; that is why he constantly distanced himself from other architects.

This issue came to a head in 1914 when he wrote his second "In the Cause of Architecture" article. Earlier he had criticized American graduates of the Ecole des Beaux-Arts, but in 1914 the focus of his attack was a group of architects practicing in and around Chicago, known as the Chicago or Prairie School. Many of these architects—for example, Walter Burley Griffin (1876–1937), Marion Mahoney Griffin (1871–1962), Barry Byrne (1883–1967), George Grant Elmslie (1871–1953) and William Drummond (1876–1946)—had worked for Sullivan or Wright. By 1914 they were producing substantial work, but it mostly seemed to Wright to be derivative of his own buildings. Just as he had broken away from Louis Sullivan, he expected other architects, especially those who had worked for him, to find their own individuality.

Wright's position had an undeniable integrity, but by defining "style" so narrowly he cut himself off from his contemporaries. It is possible that had he established and exerted his leadership in the profession more forcefully, the members of the so-called Prairie School might have become even more reliant on his architecture. But it is just as likely that if Wright had used his growing prominence to help to establish a climate of discourse, individuality in architecture might have flourished. Certainly Henry Hobson Richardson had seen no conflict between his own architectural development and a forceful role in the profession. Given that Wright was essentially at ease with the society for which he was building, he might have done more for the architectural profession, then still an emerging institution.

Wright's progressive view of his society's prospects differed from that of a small group of practitioners who also championed truth in architecture. At the turn of the century in many American cities there was a handful of architects who in their perhaps limited way were trying to break new ground. They often did this by associating themselves with and contributing to an informal movement that located its origins and beliefs in the ideas of John Ruskin and William Morris. This Arts and Crafts Movement was given a voice in magazines such as the *Craftsman* which was founded and edited by the furniture designer and manufacturer Gustav Stickley (1858–1942). The social vision of the Arts and Crafts Movement varied, but it was essentially regressive, usually based on a critique of machine production and an idealization of a preindustrial order.

The most noteworthy Arts and Crafts architects worked in California. As elsewhere in the United States, the architecture of California was largely a response to two divergent points of view about the legacy of the past. Because the settlement of that state had been so recent, most architects felt it was their mission to establish continuity with the great works of the history of architecture, even if that meant producing only diluted likenesses of them. Other architects, always a minority, drew the opposite meaning from California's rawness. They saw themselves as refugees from the stifling conventions of the East Coast and, by extension, Europe. To emphasize this point they often praised the seemingly indigenous and unaffected buildings that remained from the Spanish presence and sometimes even took these buildings as a point of departure for their own work.

Only a few of these architects were able to come to terms with these sources in a way that allowed their own work to achieve a vital and independent life. It took Irving Gill (1870–1936) many years in practice to do so. The son of a Syracuse, New York contractor, Gill somehow while still a teenager heard of Louis Sullivan and in 1890 went to Chicago to seek employment with him. After two years in Sullivan's office Gill moved to San Diego where he largely spent the rest of his life. Gill's first decade of practice was undistinguished. Most of his work was representative of the better architecture of the period, but it could hardly have been called his own. However, Gill soon began to put his personal stamp on his work. From the missions nearby he extracted not only a vocabulary of cubical forms with simple rectangular and semicircular openings for windows and doors, but also some basic planning rules that were at the root of the classical architecture from which these eighteenth-century buildings, however distantly, were derived. Equally important was Gill's perception that the distinctive qualities of the local landscape and plant life could inform and enrich his architecture. These sources were reflected in projects that ranged

149 Irving Gill: Walter Luther Dodge House, Hollywood, California, 1914–16.

from Bella Vista Terrace, a group of low cost houses in Sierra Madre, California (1910), to the 6,500-square-foot Walter Luther Dodge House in Los Angeles (1914–16). The Dodge House commission was especially important to Gill because it allowed him to demonstrate fully two hallmarks of his architecture—a compositional skill that could combine a symmetrical front with a varied but balanced back leading to a garden and an approach to   *149* the design of interiors that featured unadorned walls, the flush detailing of fittings, and no ornament except for necessary hardware.

Irving Gill had no formal architectural training, but a lack of education was not a prerequisite for individuality in design. Bernard Maybeck (1862–1955) luxuriated in the elaboration of idiosyncratic architectural details. He was the son of a wood-carver, but when sent to Paris to learn his father's trade, he enrolled instead at the Ecole des Beaux-Arts. On returning to the United States, Maybeck worked with Carrère & Hastings and was

163

150 Bernard Maybeck: First Church of Christ Scientist, Berkeley, California, 1909–11.

largely responsible for the design of the exotic Ponce de Leon Hotel in St. Augustine, Florida (1885–87). Maybeck eventually settled in Berkeley, California, where he remained for the rest of his life. When he was rediscovered in the 1940s architectural critics often depicted him as a rebel from convention, but in fact Maybeck always spoke with reverence about the Ecole des Beaux-Arts. He had a deep respect for Greek and Roman buildings, which he considered the seminal works of architecture, and this knowledge informed everything he designed. It was most obvious in his self-consciously theatrical stage set, the Palace of Fine Arts at the Panama-Pacific Exposition in San Francisco, California (1915). But it was also evident in his many simple homes and his marvellously eccentric First Church of Christ Scientist in Berkeley, California (1909–11). However, precedents, whether historical or local, were a point of departure rather than a standard only to be copied. Maybeck drew this distinction most overtly in his efforts to make a fresh if often idiosyncratic interpretation of a building's construction and detailing. His inquiring attitude about this matter allowed him to bring

150

151 Greene & Greene: David B. Gamble House, Pasadena, California, 1907–08.

together what usually were thought to be incompatible materials such as the metal factory windows, asbestos boarding, carved wooden brackets, and clay roof tiles of the First Church of Christ Scientist.

Charles Sumner Greene (1868–1957) and Henry Mather Greene (1870–1954) produced an architecture of equal originality with a similar fusion of classical and vernacular styles. The two brothers were trained in the late 1880s at M.I.T.'s School of Architecture, which was then based on the curriculum and methods of the Ecole des Beaux-Arts. However, equally important to them was their previous education at the Manual Training High School in St. Louis, Missouri, where they learned how to use hand tools and machines to shape wood and metal. In the early 1890s they settled in California and for a decade, like Irving Gill, produced buildings which were at best good interpretations of period styles. However, by immersing themselves in the architecture of Japan, Scandinavia, and even Tibet they gradually evolved an interpretation of the relationship between craft and form and were soon producing works like the David B. Gamble House in *151*

Pasadena, California (1907–08). Many aspects of this house clearly echoed Japanese architecture; others were reminiscent of the bungalows that, largely due to Gustav Stickley's publications, sprang up in American suburbs during the first decade of the twentieth century. Nevertheless, the Gamble House was not just another bungalow, in part because of its size, but mainly because throughout the building Greene and Greene transformed conventional elements and motifs in a fresh and seemingly unaffected manner.

By 1915 Gill, Maybeck, and the Greenes had all produced buildings which were unequivocal masterworks. But thereafter they received few significant commissions. Why this was so had on one level to do with circumstances particular to each, but on another it was a consequence of their vision of the kind of society for which their architecture was intended to serve as a setting. Gill, Maybeck, and the Greenes had moved to California to seek a simple life. Once there they chose to live in sheltered communities like Pasadena and Berkeley. For a short time they were able to find clients who shared or were willing to indulge their views. But the simple life could not continue forever. For many Americans some version of it seemed to end during the First World War. Unwilling or unable to adjust to the changing conditions of their times, the four architects all quickly faded into obscurity. That fact makes Frank Lloyd Wright's work both before and after the First World War all the more remarkable.

CHAPTER SIX

The Lost Momentum

The Architecture of the 1920s

One immediate effect of the American entrance into the First World War was the need for new buildings for the war effort. To expedite the sending of supplies to Europe, major port facilities along the East Coast had to be upgraded. The terminals and supply depots constructed in Brooklyn, Charleston, Philadelphia, Norfolk, and New Orleans were impressive primarily because of their enormous scale. The United States Army Supply Base in Brooklyn, for example, monopolized a site a half mile square. Its two eight-story warehouses contained almost four million square feet of space.

152

Cass Gilbert (1859–1934), the consulting architect for this project, understood the implications of its vast scale. Architectural interest came not from ornament, but from the mass of the building, which in turn was a direct expression of the functions within. Similarly, the quality of the complex's primary space, a glass-roofed court between the two parallel warehouses, was a by-product of what happened inside. Two railroad tracks passed through this vast area. Traveling cranes lifted freight from the trains onto projecting balconies from where it was transported out onto the warehouse floors. No one could fail to be impressed by the concentration of activity and the dynamism of the machinery in this space, which suggested one of Piranesi's prison interiors.

The war effort also called for the construction in a short time of an unprecedented amount of housing. For example, the two thousand buildings to service the fifty thousand soldiers at Camp Lewis, near Tacoma, Washington, were erected in eight weeks. The rapidity and scale of this effort were impressive, but the architecture was not, as a few standard plans were monotonously repeated with no acknowledgment of the lush landscape in which the camp was set.

The housing built for the workers who flocked to the cities in which munitions plants and port facilities were located was a different story. Prior to 1917, state and local governments had only infrequently tried to finance the construction of housing; nothing of this nature had been taken on at the federal level. Thus, the fact that in 1917 the United States Shipping Board's Emergency Fleet Corporation and the Department of Labor's United States

152 Cass Gilbert: United States Army
Supply Base, Brooklyn, New York,
1918.

Housing Corporation were created to build housing was significant in itself.

153 But even more admirable were the projects these organizations built in the
following two years.

Unlike later federally sponsored housing, there was nothing in the design
of these projects that stigmatized their inhabitants. These communities were
based on the best of the period's prevailing principles of suburban design.
Architects and landscape architects achieved this high standard by
differentiating houses that had to be made essentially from the same plan; at
the same time they provided continuity from house to house so that the total
was more than the sum of its parts. They varied houses not only by painting
them different colors, but also by adding a wide variety of porches, shutters,
and other elements. Continuity was established by the careful layout of
roads, the planting of trees, and the control exercised over the design and
placement of fences and outbuildings between dwellings. Equally
important, they tried to harmonize the new community with the
surrounding area. Thus, the houses in a project at Port Jefferson, Long Island,
imitated the buildings of an old Long Island fishing village through the use of
long shingles and low eaves and a project at Bath, Maine, was organized

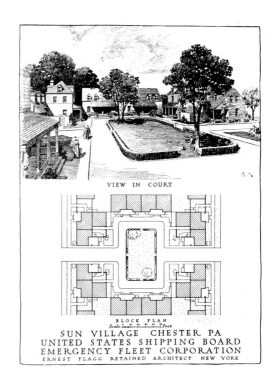

VIEW IN COURT

BLOCK PLAN
Scale ⌐———————⌐ Feet

SUN VILLAGE CHESTER PA
UNITED STATES SHIPPING BOARD
EMERGENCY FLEET CORPORATION
ERNEST FLAGG RETAINED ARCHITECT NEW YORK

153 Ernest Flagg: Sun Village,
Chester, Pennsylvania, 1917–19.

around and took its architectural language from an old mansion situated in the center of the project which was converted into a community center and apartment house.

The important question raised by the building that took place during the First World War was whether this experience was exceptional, or whether it contained clues to a new direction for architecture. Even before the war some European architects had become interested in industrial architecture and housing because they understood that it was through the exploration of such buildings that they could break from outdated and inhibiting architectural practices. The devastating experience of the war convinced them all the more that a new era had arrived and that it was essential to rethink the basis of architecture.

In the 1920s a significant group of American poets, novelists, painters, and sculptors went to Europe and, with varying degrees of success, participated in the avant-garde movements of the period. Some of them may later have been called the Lost Generation, but when they returned to the United States, attracted and often converted to modernism, they had a profound impact on their fields and ultimately on all of American culture. However,

169

few if any architects followed their lead. Although some European practitioners found American grain elevators, warehouses, and factories suggestive of a new architecture, American architects ignored these sources. The lesson they drew from the cataclysm of the First World War was not that a new path had to be taken, but that it was all the more necessary to preserve traditions.

The profession, therefore, ostensibly rededicated itself to principles it had embraced since the turn of the century. Yet there was a difference. Although the unapologetic exuberance and diversity of the imagery of the architecture of the 1920s can be seen as a telling contrast to the sober language of modernism articulated in Europe at the same time, to claim that this work represented a vital development is to misunderstand both its essential nature and how it differed from the buildings of the previous period.

Fiske Kimball (1888–1955), the historian who was most familiar with the architecture of the 1920s, characterized the change as a "loss of momentum." Before the First World War the leaders of the profession may have thought that the culture of architecture was at odds with the culture at large, yet they firmly and enthusiastically believed that they would eventually be successful in their crusade not just to establish the primacy of beauty in architecture, but in the process also to revitalize the culture. This optimistic state of mind was reflected in the grand, or grandiose, scope of their best designs. After the war this conviction started to weaken. The "loss of momentum" was due in part to the fact that the members of the generation that had rediscovered classical principles were older and in some cases tired and even burned out. Equally, younger architects, no matter how attached they were to the ethos of the Ecole des Beaux-Arts, could not have been expected to be as idealistic as those who had been to Paris earlier. But external events also played a part in weakening the resolve of the profession. As radios, automobiles, airplanes, movies, and dozens of other manifestations of a modern culture became ever more prominent, it was harder to make the case that the source of architecture was still Greece, Rome, the medieval world, and Renaissance Italy. Some architects continued to try to do so, but their efforts were undermined by the fact that they no longer were confident they would succeed. Others attempted to align themselves with their conception of the emerging culture, but they did not have enough conviction about it to create a consonant architecture.

The "loss of momentum," which often led to self-doubt and in some cases despair, was reflected in all types of structures, but it was most clearly manifested in public commissions—memorials, museums, libraries, and government buildings. Many of these were characteristically designed in a version of the classical language that was more sober, subdued, and aloof

154 Paul Cret and Albert Kelsey: Pan American Union, Washington, D. C., 1907–13.

than its counterpart of the previous period. The exemplar of this architecture was Paul Cret (1876–1945). Born in France, Cret was an outstanding student at the Ecole des Beaux-Arts and came to the United States in 1903 to teach at the University of Pennsylvania. Cret influenced American architecture not only through the students that he trained during his extended career at Pennsylvania, but also through his buildings. He received his first important commission in 1907 when, in association with Albert Kelsey, he won a competition for the headquarters of the International Bureau of American *154* Republics (later called the Pan American Union), Washington, D.C. After five years in France during the First World War, Cret returned to the United States and designed many works, including the Detroit Institute of Arts (1922), the Barnes Foundation, Merion, Pennsylvania (1923), the Hartford *155* County Building, Hartford, Connecticut (1926), the Folger Shakespeare Library, Washington, D.C. (1932), and the Federal Reserve Board Building, Washington, D.C. (1935).

Cret's approach to architecture was based on the assumption that design is a discipline that begins with a rational assessment of a building's program and the available construction techniques. Cret used metal windows, air

171

155 Paul Cret: Hartford
County Building,
Hartford, Connecticut,
1926.

conditioning, and many other contemporary materials and devices in his work, but he never wavered in his conviction that program and technique had to find expression in the classical language. The rules implicit in the orders and axial planning were fundamental to the discipline of architecture. Cret's unswerving appreciation of this discipline and his consequent disdain for the introduction of an architect's personality into a design was reflected in the evolution of his own work. During the 1920s his buildings, at least on the exterior, became increasingly austere, or, as some critics have claimed, starved. Cret gradually distilled the articulate language of the Pan American Union into one of flat piers, columns without bases or capitals, minimal moldings, and unassertive cornices.

As a reaction to buildings which indulged in personality—to the effusive Baroque-inspired classicism of the prewar period—this lack of expression was occasionally refreshing. It was used most effectively in the design of memorials to commemorate the dead of the First World War. Fearful of repeating what were then considered the banalities of Civil War monuments, many communities bypassed a predominantly symbolic statement by promoting useful projects. Some planted memorial trees. Others built community centers. Usually containing an assembly hall and sometimes an art center, the majority of these buildings were architecturally

172

undistinguished, but there were exceptions: the Club Building (1919) at Morgan Park in Duluth, Michigan, by Dean & Dean, for example, and the Scripps Playground Building (1919) at La Jolla, California, by Irving and Louis J. Gill.

However, purely symbolic memorials were occasionally built throughout the United States and on battlefields and cemeteries in Europe. Cret himself designed memorials both in France and the United States, but probably the most effective memorial, the one which used this austere classicism to the greatest effect was the Liberty Memorial in Kansas City. *156* Designed by Harold Van Buren Magonigle (1867–1935) for a competition in 1921 and dedicated in 1926, its outstanding quality was its simplicity. The focus of the memorial was a great shaft, over two hundred feet high, culminating in four statues—the spirits of Hope, Courage, Patriotism, and Sacrifice—which in turn supported a censer that at night billowed out steam to signify the Flame of Inspiration.

One problem with this spartan rendering of classical themes was that in the 1920s it was used for buildings—especially those housing a burgeoning government bureaucracy—that seemed inexorably to increase in size. At a distance, these buildings sometimes had striking profiles. But because of their spare detailing, they had little to offer at other scales. To a pedestrian walking

156 Harold Van Buren Magonigle: Liberty Memorial, Kansas City, Missouri, 1921–26.

immediately adjacent to their base, they appeared increasingly to be an interminable pile of stone.

The growth in the administrative and bureaucratic functions of government caused other architectural problems. The need to accommodate a seemingly endless number of offices upset a sense of balance between large, unique public spaces and small, repetitive rooms. Bland administrative wings were thus frequently built as separate entities and then attached with no convincing relationship to structures that contained the spaces for the public and ceremonial functions of government.

The most blatant example of this kind of architecture occurred in the Federal Triangle in Washington, D.C. Some critics had hoped that the government's major buildings would be dispersed at key locations throughout Washington, but the Public Building Act of 1926–28 staked out the area between Pennsylvania Avenue and the Mall exclusively for federal buildings. In a few years the space was covered by a network of anonymous structures. Because of the configuration of the buildings, most of the rooms in them did not face onto major streets or spaces. Instead they looked out over bleak side streets, blank light wells, or a semicircular plaza that has been used since as early as 1935 for parking.

The architect who made the most forthright attempt to develop a language of abstract classicism was Bertram Goodhue (1869–1924). In 1891, he and Ralph Adams Cram (1863–1942) had begun a productive partnership in Boston. But the two always differed in architectural values. In 1903 Goodhue set up a branch office in New York. The two offices then became progressively more independent, and in 1914 a formal separation was made. Goodhue had for many years been intrigued by the possibility of developing a language of architecture that was not overtly tied to specific, well-established precedents. This interest crystallized in his fascination with stucco and adobe construction, which he discovered in trips to Cuba and Mexico and used in several buildings in the Southwest and California.

157 Goodhue tried to use this experience in the design of his major work, the Nebraska State Capitol (1920–32). The exterior of that building had the precision of Gothic and the flatness of a stucco-faced structure. The two-story base, which marked the height of the surrounding buildings, measured 432 feet square. It was made of precise stone work and had no ornament except for modest moldings around the windows and some sculpture that emanated from the stonework at the entrance. At the middle of this base was a 350-foot stone tower, which acted as a platform for a 70-foot-high lantern.

158 On top of the lantern was a hemispherical dome covered in gold tiles which in turn served as the base for Lee Lawrie's statue, *The Sower*, which beckoned to the prairie beyond.

174

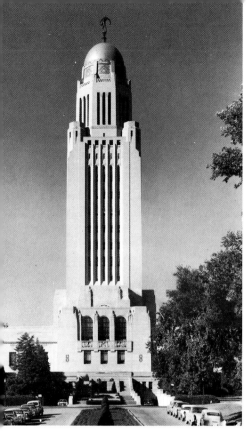

157, 158 Bertram Goodhue: Nebraska State Capitol, Lincoln, Nebraska, 1920–32. Facade, and view of the dome and *The Sower*.

Goodhue contrasted the starkness of the exterior with effusive detailing on the interior. The base of the building had a Greek cross plan, set within an outer square of offices, thus leaving four interior courts. The arms of the cross contained the principal rooms for the Nebraska government. The ceilings of these spaces were covered with multicolored mosaics with patterns based on American Indian motifs. The vaulted ceiling along the central axis leading from the entrance to the base of the tower was supported by imported green marble columns, the brilliance of which contrasted with the black and white mosaic floors.

Through such gestures Goodhue passionately tried to fuse the values of the official and the popular. Nevertheless, the Capitol was still an interpretation of what a building in the heart of America should be by an East Coast architect, one who, it was noted at the time of construction, only had a "car-window acquaintance" with the prairie and the life of the farmer.

If some of the architecture of the 1920s groped, however timidly, toward abstraction, other work attempted exactly the opposite. Many buildings of

159 H. Halsey Wood: Competitive Design for the Cathedral of St. John the Divine, 1887. Perspective.

160 Ralph Adams Cram: Design for the Cathedral of St. John the Divine, New York City, 1926. Northeast view.

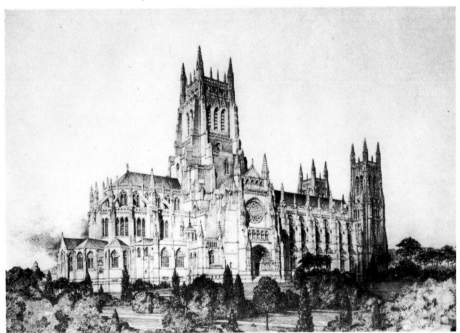

that decade were designed with an almost archaeological precision more reminiscent of the 1840s and 1850s than of any subsequent period. The architecture of Ralph Adams Cram, Bertram Goodhue's former partner, typified this reverence for an immediate correspondence between old buildings and new. Disillusioned by the First World War, not only because it destroyed so much of the architecture that he loved, but also because its conclusion seemed to produce no positive result, Cram grew progressively more disgusted with all manifestations of modern life during the 1920s. He responded to the insidious tendencies of modern architecture, which in ecclesiastical buildings he thought were epitomized by Auguste Perret's reinforced concrete churches, by making his postwar work follow known precedents much more directly than anything he had designed before the war. Nevertheless, in doing so he readily acknowledged that a return to the values of the Middle Ages, the yardstick he used to measure everything else, was increasingly unlikely. With no conviction about the present or the future, Cram may have resorted to an archaeological approach to design as much because he simply did not know what else to do as because he wanted to demonstrate what the great works of the past had been about.

No project better summarized Cram's approach to architecture in the 1920s than the work he did for the Cathedral Church of St. John the Divine, New York. A competition for the Cathedral had been held in 1887. Cram submitted two designs: one in the manner of Henry Hobson Richardson, the other more decisively Gothic. The outstanding scheme was a highly original design, an authentic vision submitted by Halsey Wood entitled "Jerusalem the Golden." The competition, however, was won by Heins & La Farge with a vaguely Romanesque or Norman design on a monumental scale. Work proceeded on the building for twenty-five years, and when the last of the partners of the firm in charge died, Cram was given the job. His response was simply to convert the scheme into a Gothic cathedral. Cram was skilled, even inventive, in doing this. He accepted the original plan, but created a new vaulting system for the nave, high side aisles with dramatic clerestory windows, novel double buttresses to receive the thrusts of the vaults, and a dramatic roof to cover the unprecedentedly large crossing. Nevertheless, all these decisions were taken within a narrow definition of what was possible. The result was a competent, but uninspired church—especially compared to "Jerusalem the Golden."

The same can be said of the buildings that Cram and his contemporaries designed for American universities in the 1920s. Harvard, Yale, Princeton, Duke, and many other universities no longer used Gothic and Georgian with any deep conviction about the appropriateness of these styles in creating a collegiate ambience. These conventions instead were drawn upon mainly to

161 James Gamble Rogers: The Harkness Memorial Tower and Quadrangle, Yale University, New Haven, Connecticut, 1931.

please alumni and to enable the architect to proceed quickly with his work. In retrospect one has to admire, however grudgingly, the fact that so much tracery and so many carved pediments were turned out in so short a time, but with only a few notable exceptions the detailing of this work was simply copied from standard books. There was also no sustained attempt to respond in the language of these buildings to the often unique sites they occupied or to the changes in scale that occurred when Georgian was extended to five stories or Gothic spread out over several acres.

Direct use of precedents was most assertive in the architecture of the period's big houses. The 1920s was the last decade in which an individual could build a house of enormous, if tasteless, magnificence. There were still a few clients who had a vague image of what a grand house should be and the money and lack of inhibitions to turn dream into reality. Of these houses, the least engaging were on the East Coast, especially on Long Island, which was much too close to centers of taste for the creation of a true architectural fantasy. In California the most lavish and famous of these houses was the castle William Randolph Hearst built for himself at San Simeon. Designed by Julia Morgan (1872–1958), who had studied at the Ecole des Beaux-Arts, Hearst's castle was actually a complex of three guest cottages surrounding the main house, La Casa Grande. This building was planned in a setting of 123 acres of gardens, terraces, and pools. Its main facade was flanked by two Spanish campaniles containing thirty-six carillon bells. These towers marked

162, 163

178

162, 163 Julia Morgan: Casa Grande, Hearst Castle, San Simeon, California, begun mid-1920s. Main house, and view of the dining room.

the entrance to the house and to a sequence of rooms which were extraordinary not only for their scale—the assembly hall measured one hundred by forty-two feet—but also for their interior decoration. Europe was Hearst's source not only for furniture, such as Cardinal Richelieu's bed, but also for entire ceilings from sixteenth-century Italian palaces and extensive mosaic floors from Pompeii.

Architects of big houses in Florida often tried to elaborate upon images of Mediterranean architecture, but the most spectacular home there was Vizcaya, an adaptation of the Villa Rezzonico in Bassano del Grappa near Venice. Built by James Deering, chairman of the board of International Harvester, the major manufacturer of agricultural equipment, Vizcaya was sited in one direction toward Biscayne Bay. Another axis of the house ran over an intricate series of parterres that culminated at a casino on a hill. Two paths fanned out on either side of the casino to an artificial lake in which visitors could paddle Venetian gondolas. The house itself was a repository for an extraordinary art collection and is now the Dade County Art Museum.

Images drawn from such houses were frequently used in Hollywood movies of the 1920s and stimulated in millions of Americans, many of whom were buying their first cars, the desire to own miniature versions of these dream houses in the period's burgeoning suburbs. Inevitably many of these districts were littered with repetitive houses and laid out with minimal imagination and no vision of a public streetscape. But there were also many suburbs which maintained the high standards that had been achieved in suburban design before and during the First World War. These characteristically had a mix of house types that avoided repetition, well-designed streets and intersections, and coherent commercial centers.

Although an increasing number of suburban residents traveled to and from home by car, the network of streets in these areas was usually still designed as if commuting was done by train. Creating a residential area based on the automobile was a task that was undertaken by Clarence Stein (1882–1975), Henry Wright (1878–1936), Lewis Mumford (1895–1990), and other members of the Regional Planning Association of America. The ultimate purpose of this group was to develop a comprehensive approach to regional planning which would prevent piecemeal land development. The association's concept of community design came largely from Ebenezer Howard's ideas of combining the best of town and country by carefully restricting residential and industrial growth to prescribed areas contained within greenbelts of farmland.

Members of the Regional Planning Association were able to put their ideas into practice by convincing Alexander M. Bing, a successful apartment

164 Radburn, New Jersey, 1929.

house developer, to finance the City Housing Corporation, a limited
dividend housing company. The corporation's most ambitious venture was
the construction of Radburn, New Jersey, which was intended to be a self-   *164*
contained new town, but which in reality was a commuter suburb of New
York City. Radburn was based on several important planning principles. It
was located within a ring of major traffic and railroad arteries which gave
access to, but did not cut through, residential areas that were divided into
neighborhoods based on a maximum walking distance to a school.

   The neighborhoods were joined together by a continuous greenbelt with
pedestrian underpasses to avoid traffic intersections. Within a neighborhood, houses were laid out on automobile cul-de-sacs, thus leaving the   *165*
house to front on a hedge-lined path that led to the shared greenbelt. Because
a group of cul-de-sacs formed a larger block, fewer streets were necessary
than in an ordinary suburb. This principle had been developed in housing
schemes designed in the 1920s in New York by Andrew Thomas and at
Sunnyside Gardens, an earlier and more restricted venture of the City
Housing Corporation. However, its first complete adaptation to the
automobile and a suburban context occurred at Radburn.

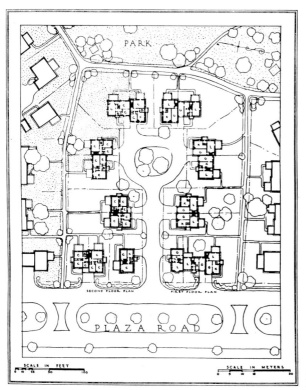

165 Plan of Burnham Place,
Radburn, New Jersey, 1929.

The first homeowners moved into Radburn in May 1929. For several years after the stock market crashed the City Housing Corporation continued to buy land and build houses, but at a reduced rate. Finally the company went bankrupt. Houses at Radburn are today eagerly sought after, but, though a success in many ways, the planning principles embodied in that development can be faulted on two major grounds. Radburn was an alternative to the suburban street, which its planners considered visually monotonous and dangerous, especially with increasing automobile traffic. Undoubtedly many such streets were monotonous, but some landscape architects and planners understood this fact and had elaborated many techniques for coping with it. Equally important, the areas that replaced the street were not problem free. Since the front door did not face the cul-de-sac, it was necessary to walk around the side of the house to get to it. Few people made the effort, and the back door and kitchen became the main entrance. In addition, though the cul-de-sac was meant primarily as a utility area, children often used those spaces more than they did the greenbelt.

182

The planning of commercial facilities at Radburn was also problematical. In earlier suburbs and small towns, shopping had been placed in the center of the community. At Radburn it was located on the periphery, at the intersections of the main traffic arteries that led to the neighborhoods. Not only, therefore, was the idea of a physical focus of the community abandoned—the school and the greenbelt were never adequate substitutes— but the planners of Radburn also grossly underestimated how large those shopping centers had to be and how much space automobiles would consume in gaining access to them. Nevertheless, by giving priority to the automobile they paved the way for the huge shopping centers and automobile dominated communities built after the Second World War.

The banning of shopping from the center of Radburn was only one of many manifestations of a continuing and broadly shared uneasiness about the culture of commerce. Architects designed office buildings, stores, and factories, but no one was sufficiently convinced about what these structures stood for to be able to articulate a comprehensive language that could be adapted to commercial as well as public, educational, religious, and domestic architecture. Even though the government regulated it, universities trained people to administer it, churches derived income from it, and houses received its products, the world of commerce and industry was a category apart as far as architecture was concerned.

The most attention-attracting commercial building continued to be the office skyscraper. When Louis Sullivan died in 1924, he was all but forgotten by the profession and so was his attempt to base the skyscraper on the expression of the structural frame. Instead, as Harvey Wiley Corbett (1873–1954), one of the chief designers of skyscrapers, explained in the same year, since "advertising, exploitation, and publicity were the animating agents behind the commercial age," the job of the architect was to give expression to these forces. The skyscraper must have a distinct physiognomy which would readily identify the company that erected it.

Although individuality was the goal, several distinct patterns for achieving it were defined in the 1920s. If expressing the structural frame was pursued at all, it received vague lip service in attempts to make the skyscraper a Gothic tower. In 1913 Cass Gilbert designed the Woolworth Building, *166* New York, in a distinctly Gothic manner, complete with gargoyles and flying buttresses. This approach received support from the 1922 Chicago Tribune Competition, which was won by John Mead Howells (1868–1959) *167* and Raymond Hood (1881–1934) with another Gothic-inspired design. However, as much notice went to the runner-up, Eliel Saarinen (1873–1950) *168* of Finland, who also submitted a distinctly vertical design, more abstract in its detail than Howells and Hood's entry. Because of its verticality and

166 Cass Gilbert: Woolworth Building, New York City, 1913.

167 John Mead Howells and Raymond M. Hood: Chicago Tribune Tower. Winning entry in the 1922 Chicago Tribune Competition.

abstractness, Louis Sullivan hailed Saarinen's design as a "lonely cry in the wilderness," a fact that has often led critics to assume that all the vertical members in Saarinen's scheme were direct echoes of structure. They were not, and in this respect Saarinen's building was as contrived as other entries.

Other skyscrapers followed the lead of McKim, Mead & White who, especially in their Municipal Building (1914) in lower Manhattan, made no pretense at revealing the frame. Instead they clad the entire building in a stone skin. Having made this decision, determining the appearance of the building was mainly a matter of architectural composition. McKim, Mead & White used the tripartite formula of classical architecture, but then further divided the building into several horizontal layers, each differentiated by an elaboration of various orders. Welles Bosworth's (1869–1966) American Telephone and Telegraph Building, New York (1923), was probably the extreme manifestation of this approach. To compose the building Bosworth

184

168 Eliel Saarinen: Chicago Tribune Tower. Runner-up in the 1922 Chicago
Tribune Competition.

169 Hugh Ferriss: Image of "The Future City," from *The City of Tomorrow*,
1929.

piled eight tiers of Ionic on top of a Doric hypostyle hall. The building was
completed with a frieze of triglyphs and metopes, carried on thirty-foot
Doric columns.

Although tall buildings based on this approach to architectural
composition were erected throughout the 1920s, the most distinctive
skyscrapers were those that were shaped explicitly in response to the New
York City zoning law of 1916. This law required that above certain neights
buildings be set back from the lot line to allow more light into the streets
below. In a sense the building envelopes that resulted from these laws
provided a rational or at least nonaesthetic basis for determining the
physiognomy of a skyscraper. But the set-back skyscraper was soon seen as a
style in itself. When an architectural renderer such as Hugh Ferriss   *169*
(1889–1962) drew hypothetical skyscrapers based on the zoning laws, he
projected more than a strict reading of what was contained in those

185

regulations. The same was true of artists like Georgia O'Keefe and John Marin, who were interpreting the skyscraper in cubist compositions, and of those architects who started to think of the set-back building in terms of Mayan prototypes and who designed buildings with stepped profiles in cities which did not have New York's regulations.

There were, in fact, two types of set-back skyscrapers. The first, and probably the more pleasing, stepped up and back in even increments. *172* Raymond Hood's American Radiator Building (1924) and Voorhees, Gmelin & Walker's Barclay-Vesey Building (1926) were the notable examples of buildings with these pyramidal profiles. However, a different configuration occurred on larger sites, because the zoning law specified that a quarter of a lot could be built upon without any height restriction. The other type of set-back skyscraper, therefore, terraced up to a given level and then had a straight tower superimposed on top. The only restraint to the height of the tower was an economic one. Since more elevators, staircases, and service risers were needed the higher the building rose, the percentage of floor space these facilities consumed was usually the controlling factor.

The architects of these set-back skyscrapers often praised their unadorned masses. It was for this reason that Arthur Loomis Harmon's (1878–1958) Shelton Hotel, New York (1924), was lauded and also why in 1925 this building was awarded the gold medals of the Architectural League of New York and the American Institute of Architects. Yet, all the Shelton Hotel's critical intersections, especially the corners, cornices, and balustrades, were celebrated with ornament, and in fact no skyscraper of the 1920s was designed without some kind of elaboration.

The source of such embellishment varied, but much of it can be classified under the vague term Art Deco, a style which was vitalized by many of the designs at the Exposition des Arts Décoratifs in Paris in 1925, but which had its origins several years earlier in both European and American manifestations of expressionism. Art Deco, or Jazz Modern, had many able practitioners and it was as much a style of office interiors and store fronts as of entire buildings. But its most thorough manifestation, and the building for *170* which it is best known, was the Chrysler Building, New York (1930), designed by William Van Alen (1883–1954). As a critic in 1930 pointed out, the Chrysler Corporation should have been pleased with its building, because it had earned more publicity for the company than any other more conventional form of advertising. This feat was accomplished primarily through the building's striking profile. The corners of the set-backs were marked by striking gargoyle-like figures and the tower itself ended in the building's most identifiable feature—a series of rounded shapes that telescoped into a culminating pinnacle.

186

171 Raymond Hood: Rex Cole Showroom, Bay Ridge, New York, 1931.
172 Raymond Hood: American Radiator Building, New York City, 1924.

Art Deco, as exemplified by the Chrysler Building, was a style that architects trained at the Ecole des Beaux-Arts could use for commercial buildings instead of the traditional languages of ornament. The problematical nature of the style's broader applicability, and of the period's architecture in general, was epitomized by the career of Raymond Hood.
167 Shortly after he won the Chicago Tribune competition with a Gothic
172 skyscraper, Hood designed the American Radiator Building with a stunning exterior of black bricks and gold pinnacles and trim. Because of its dark exterior the building glowed when illuminated at night, as was appropriate for the headquarters of a company that sold radiators. In designing a series of showrooms for a refrigerator distributor, Hood was similarly commercial
171 in topping the building with a huge refrigerator, much in the same way that a cylindrical compressor was then placed on top of this modern

173 Raymond Hood: Daily News Building, New York City, 1930.
174 Raymond Hood: McGraw-Hill Building, New York City, 1932.

appliance. Nevertheless, Hood had no compelling allegiance to this or any other style. The buildings he designed in the late 1920s and early 1930s, especially the Daily News (1930) and McGraw-Hill (1932) buildings, were 173, 174 more austere, echoing modern European architecture. One was basically vertical in composition, the other horizontal. In fact, the pragmatic Hood readily acknowledged that he had no firm opinion about whether a skyscraper should be treated "horizontally, vertically, or cubically."

The same aimless superficiality characterized the way architects thought about the appropriate setting for the skyscraper. The passage of the New York City 1916 zoning law was a recognition of the fact that rules were necessary to govern how one tall building was sited in relation to another. The effect of the law was to isolate each building from its neighbors. Raymond Hood sensed that the logical conclusion of the pattern of development implied by the law was a "City of Towers" in which the smaller buildings that spread out evenly over New York's blocks would eventually be replaced by isolated towers. Anticipating this state, Hood did not make the side walls of the American Radiator Building blank, as would have been the custom. Instead, he cut the corners and made the side elevations similar to the front and back, thus implying omnidirectionality.

Even though, as Hood recognized, the zoning laws implied a city of isolated towers, throughout the 1920s many New York architects called for the opposite pattern of development. Hugh Ferriss frequently did renderings that showed traffic-bearing bridges leaping from one tall building to another. In fact he took the idea of a connected fabric of tall buildings so far as to prophesy the construction of a network of huge skyscraper bridges, the top decks of which would be used as airplane runways. Provocative as this idea was, architects were hesitant to elaborate upon such visions in more detail. Harvey Wiley Corbett wrote about the need for a network of multilevel streets, each with a different type of traffic. But he was unable to put this idea into the context of a comprehensive vision of the urban environment, in the manner of Le Corbusier. Nor did Corbett back up his ideas with compelling statistics, as the British town planner Raymond Unwin did in his 1935 study of the impact of skyscrapers on the volume of street traffic.

Because the possibility of connecting skyscrapers was only discussed in a rudimentary manner, it is not surprising that attempts to build upper-level

175 Hugh Ferriss: An advanced stage of "The Future City," from *The City of Tomorrow*, 1929.

176 Rockefeller Center, New
York City, 1931–40.

walkways failed, as is amply illustrated by Rockefeller Center. Conceived in   *176*
the late 1920s and finished in 1940, this vast complex of buildings covered
three New York blocks and contained probably the most urbane public space
in the United States. Yet the group of slabs that surrounded the plaza was a
far cry from the architects' first conception of a network of tall buildings connected by upper-level walkways. They did not have to pursue the idea very
far to understand that, even at this vast and intensive scale of development,
such bridges did not make sense.

   With a few notable exceptions, such as the plaza at Rockefeller Center, the
great public spaces of the period were not squares, streets, or parks, but the
interiors of buildings. Skyscrapers often had impressive elevator lobbies, but
these spaces usually had no significant function. Visitors or workers wanted
to get to the elevator as quickly as possible and loitering in the lobby was
discouraged. One exception was the Cunard Building, designed in 1921 by   *177*
Benjamin Wistar Morris (1870–1944). The exterior of the Cunard Building
was an undistinguished agglomeration of classical elements, but the interior
stood out because the Cunard Company used the first floor as a huge

177 Benjamin Wistar Morris: Cunard Building, New York City, 1921. The
Great Hall.

booking office as well as an elevator lobby. At a time when steamship travel was in its prime, Cunard was able to celebrate the purchasing of a ticket in a magnificent space that the critic Royal Cortissoz described as "Medician." When you were in it, you felt "a sense of business raised to a higher power." The center of the Great Hall was capped by a seventy-foot-high dome which was embellished with scenes from the history of sea travel.

Magnificent public spaces were also to be found in the huge hotels that were built in American cities throughout the 1920s. A hotel such as the Stevens in Chicago, designed in 1927 by Holabird & Root, could accommodate almost three thousand guests. The heart of this building was a grand stair hall, 46 feet by 140 feet, designed in the Louis XVI style and modeled after a space in the Petit Trianon. The stair hall gave access to the building's many public rooms, including a grand ballroom for three thousand which was decorated with gilded plaster work, mirrors, and murals but which, nevertheless, could serve for events as diverse as a formal banquet, an automobile show, or a small circus. On the West Coast certainly the most sumptuous hotel of this kind was Schultze & Weaver's Los Angeles Biltmore (1923), which had a three-story-high lobby that culminated in a marvelously elaborate staircase with a richly wrought balustrade. The fact that there were ten floors of hotel rooms above this space did not inhibit the 178

178 Schultze & Weaver: Biltmore Hotel, Los Angeles, California, 1923. Lobby.

179 Joseph Urban: Reinhardt Theater, New York City, 1928.

architects from decorating the ceiling with elaborate wooden beams in the Spanish Renaissance style.

The design of movie theaters of the period was even more lacking in restraint. In the 1920s new opera houses and theaters for drama continued to speak to a high culture, but the movies were for a mass audience, and no other building type was more responsive to what the public, in the broadest sense, wanted. The main exterior expression of these buildings was usually a lavishly lit marquee. Joseph Urban (1872–1933), who emigrated to the United States from Austria in 1911, was one of the few architects who tried to celebrate the theater building itself. Urban had designed many opera sets and had a great sense of the theatrical. In his Reinhardt Theater (1928) in New York he used the electric light as the dominant motif not just of the marquee but of the entire facade. Strung out in long lines that illuminated emergency exterior staircases at night, these lights produced a brilliantly glowing facade that culminated in a spire-like pattern that advertised the theater. Urban's Ziegfeld Theater, New York (1927), was even more self-consciously theatrical. The front of the building took the form of a huge proscenium. The pilasters that framed this baroque fantasy and many other details all gave the theater a larger-than-life quality that heightened the expectations of arriving moviegoers.

179

194

The plan of the Ziegfeld Theater departed from the traditional fan-shaped form and was an oval. The walls and ceilings were decorated with floral patterns of bright colors that recalled those used by Urban's Viennese contemporary Gustav Klimt. But the outstanding theater of this era was the Radio City Music Hall (1932) in Rockefeller Center. Radio City largely *180* resulted from the efforts of Samuel Lionel Rothafel ("Roxy"), a theater entrepreneur who in 1927 built the Roxy Theater which seated 5920. Designed in a mélange of styles, the Roxy had a huge circular lobby that opened into an ornate auditorium.

At Radio City, Roxy used the same format—a low ticket lobby leading to a sumptuous hall and then to a lavish auditorium—but on an even more elaborate scale. The object of the ticket lobby was to marshall the customers through in orderly lines so that they would quickly proceed to the grand lobby, a space 140 feet long, 45 feet wide, and 60 feet high, culminating in a grand staircase that led up to the balconies of the auditorium and down to a basement lounge. However, the building made its impact not so much from a dramatic sequence of spaces as from a careful choice of colors and details for each area. The color scheme of the grand hall consisted basically of reds and browns, but these were vitalized by a carefully conceived pattern of mirrors, lights, black carrara glass, and polished metals, all of which, together with a golden ceiling, produced a sparkling effect. Although the grand hall was dramatic, the auditorium was the true climax. The great stage was approached under huge arches, patterned after the sun's rays, that telescoped toward the proscenium. A light orchestration was capable of producing

180 Radio City
Music Hall,
Rockefeller Center,
New York City,
1932.

numerous effects, from the light of dawn to the aurora borealis. Clearly subtlety was not what Roxy, the designers, and the audience were after.

Although the major theaters were in New York, it was incumbent on every city to have a movie-showing facility that at least aspired to the standards of the picture palaces of the Empire City. It is in the nature of such buildings that it is difficult to disentangle the memories associated with a particular theater from the architecture itself. Even so, a few theaters stand out. Meyer & Holler's Grauman's Chinese Theater, Hollywood, California (1927), for example, was famous in the late 1920s because movie stars began to leave their foot- and handprints in the sidewalk in front of it. But it was significant as a building because in making one of the more extreme statements about the association of a movie theater with the exotic, its architects were innovative in their casting of ornament in concrete. The Winema Theater in the small town of Scotia, California, was of a completely different scale, but in its consistent use of Tyrolean motifs was as delightfully obsessive as any of its big city counterparts.

Dozens of sources were drawn upon for the interiors of movie theaters, but certainly one of the most ingenious was John Eberson's Capitol Theater in Chicago. The auditorium was meant to simulate an Italian garden under a Mediterranean sky, featuring a moonlit night. On the left side was a *trompe-l'oeil* version of an Italian palace facade. The right side represented a terraced roof garden with a small temple. The ceiling of the auditorium suggested a deep blue sky with moving clouds and twinkling stars. Thus, not only was indoors completely transformed into outdoors, but simply by paying the admission price, Chicago's weary workers could also enter an Italian garden which, its architect admitted, took its motifs as much from a Persian court and a Spanish patio as from sources in Milan, Pavia, and Verona.

The movie theaters and virtually everything that was built in the 1920s can serve to remind us that architecture has a scenographic function. In fact some of the most vivid images of the period's architecture are preserved in movies made in the late 1920s and early 1930s. But architecture can be more than scenery design. Through a compelling interpretation of its elements, architecture can engage the deepest levels of thought and feeling. Because no one in the 1920s was able to respond convincingly to this challenge, the loss of momentum probably would eventually have resulted in a standstill and then a major reorientation, even if events outside the immediate concerns of architecture had not intervened. But the Great Depression did happen and could not be ignored. With its onset, mannerisms that had been popular only a few years earlier suddenly seemed dated. Once they were stripped away, little remained to serve as the foundation for an architecture of the New Deal.

CHAPTER SEVEN

The International Style and Beyond

The Architecture of the New Deal

By 1932 manufacturing output had fallen to 54 percent of what it had been in 1929. The automobile industry was operating at one-fifth its 1929 peak; steel plants were producing only 12 percent of their capacity. In the same three years American foreign trade declined from $10 billion to $3 billion. A year after the stock market crash, 6 million Americans were unemployed. Between August 1929 and March 1933 employment in the building industry had fallen 63 percent; by the end of 1932, 85 percent of the architects in New York City were out of work.

The crisis in the nation's economy confirmed doubts about the future of architecture that at least a few American practitioners had already begun to sense in the late 1920s. These doubts had many sources, but they were accentuated by the knowledge that a new architecture was emerging in Europe. This architecture was troubling because of its austerity and the fact that it seemed to make reference neither to the historic styles nor to the forms that had become so popular after the Exposition des Arts Décoratifs in Paris in 1925. More important, it was accompanied by prophetic statements about the changing nature of industrial production and a new order of society.

The first articles about modern European architecture began to appear in American magazines in 1927. By 1932 it was clear that it was not just a passing idiosyncrasy. A small but vocal group of European architects who had emigrated in the previous decade and a few American converts were announcing that the new architecture should and would be adopted in the United States. Therefore, as the Great Depression dragged on, those architects who still believed in the values that had sustained the profession through the previous decade were forced to begin to entertain the possibility that they were hopelessly behind the times. The irony, of course, of this confrontation with new ideas was that by 1930 the period of greatest innovation in modern European architecture was over.

One of the first American architects to try to come to terms with this radical shift in architectural values was George Howe (1886–1955). Educated at Harvard College and the Ecole des Beaux-Arts, Howe returned from his training in Europe to a comfortable architectural practice in Philadelphia.

181 Mellor, Meigs & Howe: Newbold Estate, Laverock, Pennsylvania, 1924–25.

Howe's approach to architecture at this time was epitomized by the
181 Newbold Estate (1924–25), which was built on the outskirts of Philadelphia as
a weekend escape house. The architecture was completely consonant with
this purpose. Howe converted a modest eighteenth-century stone house into
an extensive grouping of buildings modeled after a farm complex he had
admired in Normandy. A conical stone tower on the main house was the
Newbold Estate's most prominent feature. It could be seen from a great
distance as visitors approached by a long winding driveway that passed fields
with grazing sheep, pigeon tower, cattle barns, goose pond, potager,
bosquet, and a farm court.

In a book about the house, Howe's partner Arthur Meigs (1882–1956)
mentioned that he saw nothing inappropriate in the choice of a Norman
farm for an American house in the 1920s. Industrialization would never
influence architecture; nor would politics. To prove this point Meigs showed
two contrasting photographs. One, to demonstrate the "capitalistic order,"
illustrated all the people who had been involved in the job in descending
order—starting with Mrs. Newbold, then the architect and foreman, and
eventually down to the lowest unskilled laborer. The other photograph
showed the "communistic order." It had the same format, but the hierarchy

was reversed. The fact that Meigs had taken the effort to stage these photographs left no doubt not only about which order he thought was best, but also about his disdain for bringing such issues into the discussion of architecture in the first place.

By the late 1920s George Howe had become discontent with such complacency. In 1928 he left his firm and began a new one. With William Lescaze (1896–1964), a Swiss architect who had emigrated to the United States in 1920, Howe soon produced his most accomplished work, the Philadelphia Savings Fund Society Building (1929–32). By 1929 European *183* architects had been designing modern skyscrapers for a decade. Mies van der Rohe had published a well-known project for a glass skyscraper in 1918; Walter Gropius (1883–1969) and Adolf Meyer (1886–1950) as well as Max *182* Taut (1884–1957) and Johannes Duiker (1890–1935) had submitted modern designs to the Chicago Tribune Tower competition in 1922. Those entries were never mentioned in the American architectural press, and by 1929 a modern skyscraper had yet to be built. The PSFS building was, therefore, a significant departure not only in American, but also in international, architecture.

182 Walter Gropius and Adolf Meyer: Chicago Tribune Tower. Entry in 1922 Chicago Tribune Competition.

174   Unlike Raymond Hood's McGraw-Hill Building, the PSFS building did not achieve modernity by wrapping a contemporary-looking skin around a conventional interior. Its elevations were overtly unornamented, but Howe's primary departure was to separate out and explicitly express the different parts of the building. The elevator and service core, the office slab, and the public functions on the first floors were all distinctly recognizable. Each was clad in its own materials and had its own window system. The parts were also massed in a way which deliberately avoided symmetry and axial views. In fact, entrances were deliberately placed where functional necessity seemed to call for them rather than where the compositional devices that until that time had been the staple of the profession demanded they be. Most important, whereas vertical columns were revealed on two sides of the office slab, the Market Street facade appeared to be slung between rows of supports and thus was horizontal in orientation.

The PSFS building definitely looked "modern," but not all buildings that were described by this suggestive word had the same attributes. It was clear from those American magazines that published articles on modern architecture in the late 1920s and early 1930s that there was no consensus of opinion as to what exactly modern architecture was. European buildings were treated almost indiscriminately, with little understanding of the context in which a particular architect worked. One result of this insular ignorance was that certain buildings and movements which were of great importance to the European avant-garde were completely ignored in the United States, whereas great significance was sometimes attached to secondary works.

184   The most important attempt to clarify this matter was an exhibition on "Modern Architecture," mounted at the Museum of Modern Art in 1932 by the historian Henry-Russell Hitchcock (1903–87) and the critic Philip Johnson (1906–   ). The exhibition contained photographs, drawings, and models of recent European buildings as well as a few American examples. Hitchcock had previously written about modern architecture in numerous magazine articles and reviews, the content of which he summarized in *Modern Architecture: Romanticism and Reintegration*, which appeared in 1929. The overriding thesis of this work and of the 1932 exhibition was that modern architecture had gone through a pioneering phase that peaked shortly after the turn of the century in the work of Frank Lloyd Wright, H. P. Berlage, Otto Wagner, and a few others. From these salutary but diverse and romantic beginnings, a definite language of modern architecture had been distilled in the 1920s and was being adopted throughout the world. In effect, a new style, an International Style (the name by which the exhibition came to be known) had come into being.

183 George Howe and William Lescaze: Philadelphia Savings Fund Society
Building, Philadelphia, Pennsylvania, 1929–32.

184 "Modern Architecture—International Exhibition," staged by Henry-Russell Hitchcock and Philip Johnson at the Museum of Modern Art, New York, 1932. View showing model of Le Corbusier's Villa Savoye.

In *The International Style: Architecture Since 1922*, which was issued simultaneously with the Museum of Modern Art exhibition, Hitchcock and Johnson outlined three principal attributes of the new style. It was, first of all, concerned with volume rather than mass. The authors argued that because the cage of skeletal supports had replaced masonry bearing walls, greater spatial freedom was possible on the inside of a building. Exterior walls could thus be a light skin that served mainly for weather protection. Hitchcock and Johnson's second principle was that the chief visual motif of a modern building should be a reflection of the underlying regular rhythm of the structural system. This regularity could be modulated by an expression of the varied purposes of the building, but all attempts to compose the elevation of a building were artificial. The final principle of the International Style concerned the role of ornament and applied decoration. Hitchcock and Johnson were categorical that the elaboration of architecture, especially as it had taken place throughout the nineteenth century, served no positive function.

Only a handful of buildings can be said to have consistently and conscientiously put Hitchcock and Johnson's principles into practice. A small house and office building in Palm Springs, California (1934), by Lawrence Kocher (1886–1969) and Albert Frey (1903–98) and the

185 Tuberculosis Sanatorium in Waukegan, Illinois (1938), by William Pereira, Ganster & Henninghausen were the most accomplished demonstrations

185 William Pereira, Ganster & Henninghausen: Lake County Tuberculosis
Sanatorium, Waukegan, Illinois, 1938.

of the principles pronounced at the Museum of Modern Art in 1932.
Nevertheless, the exhibition was important because it provoked sustained
discussion about modernism in architecture and forced many architects to
come to terms with European architectural developments. Most rejected
that architecture, but in doing so they found that they could not return, at
least not directly, to the principles that had earlier guided them.

One group at odds with Hitchcock and Johnson was composed of
architects and reformers interested in housing. At the Museum of Modern
Art, in addition to the main exhibit on architecture by Hitchcock and
Johnson, Clarence Stein, Henry Wright, and Catherine Bauer (1905–64)
arranged a separate show on housing with its own catalog introduction by
Lewis Mumford. Such a division would have been unthinkable in Europe
where discussions about housing had been an integral part of the
development of modern architecture. In the debates of the 1920s, questions
of ideology, social purpose, and architecture had been all but inseparable.
However, Hitchcock and Johnson focused on aesthetic principles and thus
divorced their subject from its ideological and intellectual base. They were in
one sense simply continuing what by 1932 was an old tradition of American
architecture. Americans have often borrowed the forms of European
buildings with little understanding of their original context. Once
disassociated from their origins, these forms have often been manipulated in
ways that probably would intrigue, astound, or appall Europeans. Usually

203

the results have been naive, but some architects have used their detachment to produce highly original and challenging work.

However, the consequences of this process for the discussion and subsequent building of housing in the United States were not salutary. With no encouragement from critics like Hitchcock and Johnson to make the connection between architecture and housing, most architects continued to think that housing occupied a low level in a hierarchy of building types and, therefore, was hardly worthy of their efforts. In reaction to this attitude, housing advocates often overstated their case. For example, at a symposium on the International Style exhibition at the Museum of Modern Art, Lewis Mumford advised his audience that his main message to anyone who wanted to design housing was to undertake this task "as though you were working for a communist government."

Such confrontations led to a polarization of attitudes, and throughout the New Deal housing was never treated as an architectural issue, at least not to the degree that it had been in Europe. The profession, therefore, had little impact on Franklin Roosevelt's housing policies. The most significant of these, in terms of the number of people affected and the precedents they set for the boom years that followed the Depression, were programs to stabilize mortgages. Franklin Roosevelt never wavered in his commitment to home ownership, and certainly one of the most important measures of his administration was the establishment of an elaborate bureaucracy to regularize the practices and procedures of lending institutions.

A second aspect of federal housing policy was the construction of new towns. This approach was favored by many architects, city planners, and landscape architects, especially those who were associated with the Regional Planning Association of America. During the 1930s, about thirty communities of "subsistence homesteads" and three "greenbelt towns," one each in Maryland, Wisconsin, and New Jersey, were begun. Talented landscape architects, city planners, and architects took part in the design of the new towns, but work proceeded slowly and the results never fulfilled initial idealistic expectations. At best these were interesting experiments, but with few lasting consequences. The same can be said of the work undertaken by the Tennessee Valley Authority (TVA). This independent government agency was created in 1933 to undertake the planning and development of the Tennessee River basin, an area of 41,000 square miles with a population of 3,000,000. TVA was much discussed as a prototype for what should be done elsewhere. However, its example was not soon followed and, though many of its public works projects were provocative both in scale and in their utilitarian aesthetic, the community buildings and housing promoted by TVA were undistinguished.

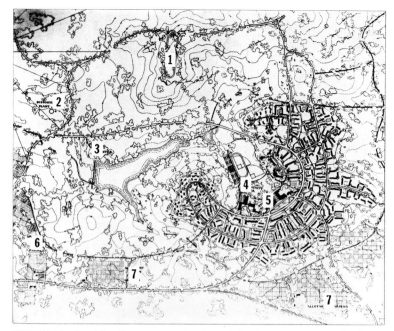

186 Greenbelt, Maryland, Plan, 1936.

A third area of housing activity was the direct promotion and construction of low-cost projects for those for whom private enterprise did not provide. The original approach, conceived in the waning days of the Hoover administration, was to make funds available for limited dividend companies, private organizations based on the semiphilanthropic model favored by nineteenth-century reformers. Hoover expected, as Charles Abrams (1901–70) later wrote, that developers would be content with a 6 percent profit simply because the public welfare was involved. Few were, and when Roosevelt took office, he authorized the Public Works Administration (PWA) to build housing directly.

Between 1932 and 1934 the PWA built forty-three projects. Many of these exemplified both the initial aspirations that reformers had for public housing and the problems the program later encountered. Of all the PWA projects the Carl Mackley Houses in Philadelphia was conceived with the most advanced architectural and programmatic ideas. Its architects were Oskar Stonorov (1905–70) and Albert Kastner (1900–75), both recently

187

188

205

arrived from Europe, and its sponsor was the progressive Full Fashioned Hosiery Workers' Union.

The Carl Mackley Houses contained more than housing. The project also had tennis courts, an underground garage, a filling station, a laundry, stores, and several other community facilities, some of which were to be run on a cooperative basis. The framework for these facilities was not the block of row houses that had been so favored by Philadelphia's working population since the early nineteenth century. Nor was it the perimeter apartment blocks developed in the 1920s in New York. Instead, Stonorov and Kastner designed a series of parallel walk-up apartment blocks, with reentrant angles on the end and setbacks in the middle. This configuration produced a series of court spaces which were joined by passages underneath the blocks. The buildings were oriented north–south to allow light into all the apartments. Facades were flat, with severely punched-in windows and porches. Flat roofs were used for laundries and roof terraces.

The project's site plan was different from anything in the immediate context. Nevertheless, the Mackley Houses development was still small enough (4.5 acres) not to seem like a project. It still fitted into the pattern of city blocks that would be used in the development of the adjacent vacant land. The same can be said of the scale and detailing of the buildings. The large-paned windows with minimal trim, the stark brickwork, and the flat roof all established these buildings as distinctly different from anything in the surrounding neighborhood and all, incidentally, caused great maintainence problems. Even so, since the project was only three and four stories high, it was not so out of character with adjacent buildings as to preclude a sense of continuity in the area.

This was less the case with the projects that were constructed by the United States Housing Authority (USHA), which superseded the PWA in 1937. Many of the projects the USHA built in small towns had only several dozen units and therefore were innocuous, but those in large cities tended to overstate the qualities that were evident, but not yet so pronounced, in the Carl Mackley Houses. They often covered dozens of acres and their characteristic housing type increasingly diverged from anything in the surrounding area.

Although some critics faulted the International Style because it divorced architecture from social purpose, many others criticized the narrow and exclusive nature of the aesthetic categories and principles that Hitchcock and Johnson elicited from the work that they included in their exhibition and subsequent book. Some architects who took exception on these grounds favored the approach to architecture, derived from Beaux-Arts precepts, that sustained the profession throughout the 1920s. Of these the most telling

187 Public Works Administration: Williamsburg Houses, Brooklyn, New York, 1938.

188 Albert Kastner and Oskar Stonorov: Carl Mackley Houses, Philadelphia, Pennsylvania, 1932–34.

was Albert Kahn (1867–1942), because by the early 1930s he was the most highly regarded designer of industrial buildings in the United States. Having started a practice in Detroit just before the turn of the century, Kahn was well placed to receive commissions from the soon burgeoning automobile industry. In 1903 Kahn was appointed architect for the Packard Motor Car Company, and he eventually also worked for Ford and General Motors. At a time when the assembly line was becoming the basis of industrial production, Kahn almost single-handedly transformed the American industrial plant from a multistory, small-span building to a single-story, large-span structure that spread out over many acres and was lit through a saw-tooth roof.

189

In 1929 in his book *Von Material zu Architektur* Laszlo Moholy-Nagy included a photograph of one of Kahn's factories and by the early 1930s, as more American architects were becoming interested in the kind of architecture then being designed in Europe, Kahn's factories were frequently cited as examples of what the future held in store. But factories represented only a part of Kahn's work. In addition, his office turned out a vast array of other buildings, from houses to libraries. Unlike the factories, which on the whole were frank expressions of the components of which they were made, Kahn's houses and institutional buildings drew directly upon historical sources for their expression. For example, the Detroit Athletic Club, Detroit, Michigan (1913–15), was a modified Italian palazzo, the William L.

189 Albert Kahn: Ford Glass Plant, Dearborn, Michigan, 1922.

Albert Kahn: William L. Clements Library, University of Michigan, Ann
Arbor, Michigan, 1920–21.

Clements Library at the University of Michigan, Ann Arbor, Michigan   *190*
(1920–21), had a Renaissance loggia, and many of Kahn's houses can best be
described as colonial.

Kahn had no doubt that it was this side of his practice that was most
significant. Although he did not attend an architecture school, he developed
an early interest in the great works of architecture and won a scholarship to
travel in Europe. His companion was Henry Bacon, the future designer of
the Lincoln Memorial. Thus, when he started his own practice, Kahn had
digested and endorsed the approach to architecture that was then being
articulated by American advocates of classicism and the methods of the
Ecole des Beaux-Arts. Fundamental to this viewpoint was a belief in the
hierarchy of building types. Those that served purely ceremonial purposes
were the most significant; those for functional ends the least. This concept of
hierarchy explained Kahn's antipathy toward the International Style. Of
Gropius's Bauhaus buildings at Dessau, he asked: "Is it architecture at all?"
Le Corbusier's work he dubbed "utterly stupid." The error Gropius, Le
Corbusier, and others made was that they designed all buildings to look like

factories. For Kahn, as for other American architects who were not swayed by modern European architecture, a language of flat roofs, horizontal windows, large glass surfaces, white walls, and freestanding columns was not sufficiently expressive to encompass all building types.

Kahn's pragmatic attitude explains his success in the Soviet Union. In 1929 he received an offer to build a $40 million tractor plant at Chelyabinsk. When more work followed, he set up an office in Moscow. By 1932, when the Russians could no longer pay in gold and the office had to be disbanded, Kahn's practice had designed 521 factories in the Soviet Union. In contrast, Mart Stam (1899–1986), André Lurçat (1894–1970), and Hannes Meyer (1889–1954) went to the Soviet Union hoping to erect a new architecture for a new society, but they soon became disillusioned. The Russians were only interested in technical knowledge and organizational expertise, both of which Kahn had and the idealistic Europeans did not.

It was not surprising that traditionalists like Albert Kahn took exception to the ideas proposed by Hitchcock and Johnson. The more troubling disagreement, however, came from those architects and designers who had different ideas about what modern architecture was. One such group was in part composed of the industrial designers who in the late 1920s had begun to turn out products characterized as "moderne." The origins of this style, at least in the case of its primary practitioner, Norman Bel Geddes (1893–1958), probably stemmed from European expressionist design of the immediate postwar period. But the explanation the industrial designers gave for the basis of "moderne" focused on the fact that speed was the essence of the modern age and that the shape which was most conducive to speed was the

191 Albert Kahn: Stalingrad Tractor Plant, USSR, 1929. General perspective.

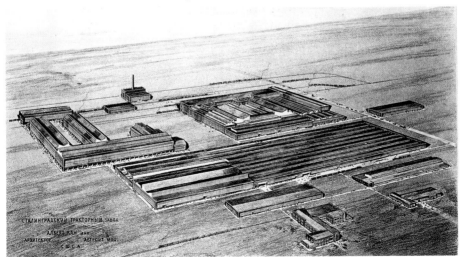

192 Kraetsch & Kraetsch: House for Earl Butler, Des Moines, Iowa, 1937.

ovoid or tear-drop. Thus, Bel Geddes, Raymond Loewy (1893–1986), Walter Dorwin Teague (1883–1960), and Henry Dreyfuss (1904–72) designed cars, trains, boats, and airplanes with distinctive streamlined forms.

Although they often talked about the expression of function, all these designers also used the same form for static objects. The interior of a theater and the casing of an alarm clock were as likely to have a streamlined shape as a train or airplane. Moderne's broad appeal—which its advocates well understood—therefore went well beyond the fulfillment of functions. It stemmed from the fact that moderne projected an image of a future in which technology would produce a flourishing economy which, in turn, would foster a cohesive society.

Given the suffering and divisiveness that occurred during the Great Depression, a style tantamount to moderne probably would have been invented then had not designers like Bel Geddes already begun to describe its outlines in the late 1920s. Because there was little construction during the Depression, few buildings were actually designed in this style. It was manifested mainly in consumer products, store fronts, and interior decoration. But the style was extremely popular, and was adopted in unlikely places throughout the nation. Probably the most elaborate moderne *192* house was built in 1937 in Des Moines, Iowa. Designed by Kraetsch & Kraetsch around a switch-back ramp which united the four stories of the house, the building was made of concrete shaped in curved and undulating forms. The fully air-conditioned interior incorporated every known

193 Norman Bel Geddes: Visitors Viewing Futurama Exhibit, New York
World's Fair, 1939.

mechanical convenience. Its kitchen was filled with gadgets including a
garbage disposal, dishwasher, refrigerator, and ice-cube freezer. The ten
bedrooms were "perfectly illuminated" to prevent eye strain. An electric eye
opened and closed the garage doors. The whole house was knit together by a
communications system that included eight internal and three door
telephones.

By the late 1930s, this consumer-oriented style was familiar to every
American, but the most thorough exposure to it occurred in 1939 at the New
York World's Fair and in particular at the General Motors "Futurama"
193   exhibit designed by Norman Bel Geddes. The scope and audacity of
Geddes' exhibit were breathtaking. The immediate purpose of Futurama
was simply to show how traffic problems would be handled by 1960, but the
broader goal was to give visitors a rosy vision of the future. The exhibit was
1583 feet long. Visitors observed it by sitting in a "sound-chair" on a
conveyor system which took fifteen minutes to travel the length of the
exhibit. The display consisted of a series of animated models which gradually
increased in scale. At first the visitor's vantage point was that of an airplane

pilot looking down on a motorway. As the conveyor passed over a mountain, into foothills, and across a valley, the visitor gradually approached a city which contrasted the sorry conditions of 1939 with the wonderful future of 1960. The center of the city was shown in great detail; it was less congested than contemporary downtown areas and had huge skyscrapers which were joined together by elevated pedestrian sidewalks that bridged across streets. Finally the spectator was brought down to a part of the city where it was possible to see only about six blocks. People were relaxing on roof gardens, shoppers were walking on the elevated streets, cars were conveniently tucked out of the way, and children were happily playing in parks. Suddenly, the conveyor swung around, and the visitor to Futurama saw a full-size version of the intersection he had just been looking at. He then got off the conveyor and became part of the crowd.

The forms and attendant vision of moderne differed sharply from the cubical shapes, undifferentiated surfaces, and austere, factory-like way of life that came to be associated with the International Style. The two aesthetics could overlap, but those who were insistent on the rigid characteristics of the International Style were quick to point out the difference. Thus, even though the exterior of Joseph Urban's New School of Social Research, New York (1929–30), was composed of horizontal panels and strip windows, the shiny metallic quality of the cladding was too exuberant for the building to be characterized as International Style. The same was generally true of William Lescaze's work.   194

194 George Howe and
William Lescaze: Lescaze
House, New York City,
1934.

Although different, both styles were often criticized because they were too concerned with an image and not enough with demonstrating the application of technology to architecture and the building process. The work of Richard Buckminster Fuller (1895–1983) was the period's most forceful statement about this issue. With inventions such as the Dymaxion car, which had two wheels in front and one in back so that it could turn in a minimum diameter, Fuller was as able to capture and manipulate media attention as a designer like Norman Bel Geddes. But Fuller's work, especially that which focused on the design of the house, was more significant because it went well beyond surface gestures about a "machine for living in." For better or worse, Fuller came as close to rethinking every part of the house, with efficiency always the ultimate criterion, as anyone before or since.

195   Fuller's most radical design, the 4D or Dymaxion House, was first made public in 1927 and continued to be a subject of discussion throughout the 1930s. Designed to hang from a central mast that contained a utility core, the house was factory made, quickly erected, and stabilized by guy wires. Its purpose was to reduce drudgery to a minimum. Virtually free of water, it contained a ten-minute atomizer bath which used only a quart of water, which was then filtered, sterilized, and recirculated. The toilets contained a packaging system that mechanically stored wastes for pickup and processing. Laundry was automatically washed, dried, ironed, and placed in storage units. Dusting and sweeping were done by compressed air and vacuum systems. Beds had air-filled mattresses; other furniture was made as light as possible. The house had no rooms in the traditional sense. Instead, space was divided by storage units with movable shelves and hangers.

Because Fuller assumed that the Dymaxion House would be mass-produced like an automobile, he designed every detail in anticipation of an industry that would be able to make thousands of houses. When asked how much the Dymaxion House would cost, Fuller answered that $100 million was an appropriate figure; what was important was the cost of the industry, not the house. No one was willing to put up a hundred million dollars, so the Dymaxion House remained unbuilt and was not exhibited at the Century of Progress exhibition in Chicago in 1933. Nevertheless, there were two other houses at that world's fair that did show how the technology then available could be applied to the home. By the early 1930s machines and gadgets had become common in the home, and the equipment of the bathroom and kitchen was often designed with streamlined styling to suggest industrial products and processes. George Fred Keck (1895–1983), the designer of the two houses, understood that the task that lay ahead was to make the structure and skin of the house commensurate with the equipment inside. Thus, his

195 R. Buckminster Fuller: Dymaxion House, 1927. Model.

House of Tomorrow and Crystal House were both supported by a steel 196, 197 frame and a battledeck steel floor system. The exteriors were composed of a store-front technology of plate glass, light steel structural members, sheet metal panels, venetian blinds, and tubular pipe railings. The House of Tomorrow borrowed from Fuller a multisided plan with a circular staircase wrapped around a utility space in the middle. The Crystal House had a more conventional, rectangular plan, but the bar joist bracing members on the

196 George Fred Keck: The House of Tomorrow, 1933.

197 George Fred Keck: The Crystal House, 1933.

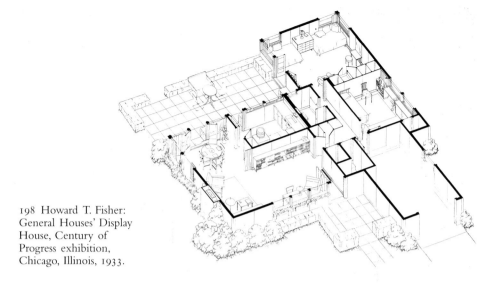

198 Howard T. Fisher:
General Houses' Display
House, Century of
Progress exhibition,
Chicago, Illinois, 1933.

exterior gave it an articulate quality that separated it from buildings that used glass as a smooth skin.

Keck, who by the mid-1930s had joined with his brother William Keck (1908–95), was able to use this level of technology in houses for a few private clients, most notably in 1937 in a semicircular house with a sun-protected south-facing all-glass facade in Lake Forest, Illinois. However, the challenge for housing was to live up to the analogy with automobile production. Although the public and the building industry proved recalcitrant, especially during the Great Depression, the fact that total mass production was neither feasible nor desirable did not mean that some level of standardization or prefabrication could not be achieved.

Throughout the 1930s architects and engineers worked on plans to rationalize the construction and therefore lower the price of houses. None approached the problem more intelligently than Howard T. Fisher (1903–79), whose firm General Houses, Inc. was based in Chicago. Fisher was trained as an architect, and his first house, in Evanston, Illinois, completed in 1929, was described by Henry-Russell Hitchcock as "very nearly the first in America to which the most rigid international standards of architectural criticism may profitably be applied." Fisher's approach to standardization was to design a system of prefabricated panels that could be assembled in a variety of configurations to meet the needs of different clients. His initial designs were for two- and three-story cubical buildings with modernist aspirations, but his later houses were less challenging, primarily because by then he had learned that to survive it was necessary to adjust to the

198

217

tastes of the market. Instead of basing the panels on a steel frame, General Houses, Inc. reverted to wood stud construction. More important, small-paned windows and entrance trellises were introduced to give these flat-roofed houses a domestic feeling.

Rudolph Schindler (1887–1953) and Richard Neutra (1892–1970) also took a rigorous approach to the construction of their buildings and in doing so were at odds with the idea of an International Style. Both were European émigrés who had settled in California in the 1920s. Schindler graduated from the Vienna Academy of Fine Arts, where he came into contact with Otto Wagner, Josef Hoffmann, Adolf Loos, and Joseph Olbrich. Attracted to Frank Lloyd Wright's buildings through the Wasmuth publication of 1910, Schindler agreed in 1914 to come to the United States to work for a firm in Chicago, with the ultimate goal of employment with Wright, which he finally began in 1917. From 1917 to 1921 Wright shifted the base of his practice from Chicago and Taliesin to Los Angeles and was frequently in Japan. Schindler was, therefore, often left to execute projects in California for which Wright had done only the initial design. However, in Wright's absence, Schindler was also starting his own practice.

The task Schindler set himself was both individual and synthetic. Highly aware of what was happening in European architecture in the 1920s, Schindler sought to combine those tendencies with his interpretation of the meaning of the work of Wagner, Loos, and Wright. He did this most *199, 200* convincingly in the Lovell Beach House, which was designed and built in Los Angeles from 1922 to 1926, but which was not published in a national magazine until 1929. The house was for Dr. Phillip Lovell, who wrote a column on health and physical fitness for the *Los Angeles Times*. Schindler's beach house provided Lovell with an environment that was consonant with his progressive views. The building was supported on five concrete frames, allowing the beach to extend underneath the house where Schindler provided a kind of outdoor living room. Schindler interwove these strong vertical members with horizontal balconies and supports, also in concrete. Floor to ceiling glass walls formed the major separation between indoors and out.

By the late 1920s the interpenetrating horizontal and vertical forms of the Lovell Beach House were becoming even more pronounced in Schindler's work. Sloping sites often gave him the opportunity to design houses on at least four levels and thus to exaggerate the stepping qualities of his architectural volumes. His buildings were equally fragmented in plan, and became all the more complex when he started to use nonorthogonal geometries. Schindler also made many specific gestures in elevation, such as interrupting parapets and stepping the sills of windows, which accentuated

218

199, 200 Rudolph Schindler:
Beach House for Dr. Phillip
Lovell, Los Angeles, California,
1922–26. Exterior and living
room.

the nervous quality of his architecture. The same motifs appeared throughout other aspects of his buildings, especially his built-in furniture. Trained as an engineer, he thoroughly understood the plastic qualities of reinforced concrete and felt no compulsion to conceive a building as a rectangular solid wrapped by a uniform skin. Because of the highly personal nature of his buildings, Schindler was not included in the exhibition at the Museum of Modern Art. In his temperament and his architecture he seemed too much in the spirit of the individualistic Wright to be considered part of the International Style.

Schindler's career made a telling contrast with that of Neutra. Like Schindler, Neutra was trained in Vienna and was influenced by Otto Wagner and Adolf Loos. With the publication of the Wasmuth portfolio, he also became fascinated by Frank Lloyd Wright's work, but unlike Schindler, Neutra remained in Europe throughout the First World War, worked in Berlin for several years, and did not arrive in the United States until late in 1923. Thus, Neutra was much more familiar than Schindler with the kind of modern architecture being designed in Europe in the early 1920s. Neutra settled first in Chicago and eventually worked for several months for Wright. Although he deeply admired Wright, Neutra's ties to him were not substantial, and he did not have to struggle like Schindler to disentangle himself from the master.

Neutra moved to Los Angeles in 1925 and soon began a productive and prosperous practice. By 1932 he had completed enough work to be included in the exhibition at the Museum of Modern Art. His buildings seemed, at least on the surface, to be acceptable to the canons established by Hitchcock and Johnson; but those appearances were deceptive. How a building was made was far more important to Neutra than it was to Hitchcock and Johnson. Because of this interest in applying up-to-date building techniques to architecture, Neutra was the designer who most directly carried on in the United States the European polemic about modern architecture.

In 1927 Neutra wrote a book entitled *Wie Baut Amerika*, which was primarily about American construction techniques and in particular the steel frame. He put his fascination with American fabricating techniques directly into practice in one of his first and probably his best-known buildings, a house for Phillip Lovell, who several years earlier had commissioned a beach house by Schindler. Unlike European buildings of the same period with a similar appearance, the Lovell House had a steel skeleton, in which steel casement windows were fully integrated. The structure was fabricated in sections in a factory, transported to the site on a truck, and erected in forty hours. What appeared to be cantilevers in fact were supported by steel cables from a roof structure.

201

201 Richard Neutra: House for Dr. Phillip Lovell, Los Angeles, California, 1927–29.

Neutra's other significant interest in architecture focused on how buildings were used and how they could provide a physically and psychologically suitable environment. This concern informed all his work, but it was most evident in his continuing interest in schools. Influenced by John Dewey's theories on education, Neutra tried to provide young children with an easy transition between home and school; at the same time he wanted an environment in which it would be possible to "learn through doing." Neutra's architectural response to these concerns was a one-story building with classrooms opening directly onto a patio. He first put these principles into practice in his 1928 Ring Plan School project in which *202* classrooms circled a large field. Each had a patio area intended for instruction. Such ideas were completely novel, and Neutra did not have the opportunity to build such a school until 1935. The Corona Avenue School, Los Angeles, was a simple but remarkable one-story building with one wing for classrooms and another for a kindergarten. The classrooms were arranged in a row. One side had a covered outdoor corridor which led to the

202 Richard Neutra: Ring Plan School, 1928.

rooms; the other an electrically operated glass door which gave access from each classroom to an outdoor space. All classrooms were lit on two sides and because there was no fixed seating, the teacher was free to arrange the space to suit any type of lesson.

The presence of the movie industry rendered the Depression less severe in the Los Angeles area than in most other parts of the United States. Neutra's practice prospered, and he continued to design houses, apartment buildings, and schools. What distinguished this work was a level of consistent experimentation. No matter what the job, Neutra tried to introduce innovations in construction, thermal control, or the organization of functions. Thus, at a time when he could have settled into a comfortable practice, he continued to be interested in designing inexpensive houses, and used his larger commissions to test out materials and techniques that could be used to further that end. Between 1933 and 1936 he designed twenty houses, each costing less than $5,000.

By the mid-1930s both Neutra and Schindler were using materials that had not previously appeared in their work. Most of their buildings had been clad with stucco, not only because the resulting continuous surface was an important part of their image of a modern building, but also because they

222

found that material to be compatible with the climate of Southern California. However, by the mid-1930s both architects began to clad their houses in wood. Architects with modernist ambitions had often used wood, but in ways that mimicked or aspired to materials that were more suggestive of an industrial civilization. Neutra's and Schindler's use of wood was different; they accepted and even celebrated its rustic qualities.

Many architects experienced a similar shift from an aesthetic that aspired to an image of machine production to one which was rooted in local building traditions. Some did so out of necessity. For example, in working for the Farm Securities Administration Vernon DeMars (1908–   ) found 203 that the only feasible way to build housing for a farm cooperative in Chandler, Arizona, was to use labor-intensive, but material-cheap techniques. He therefore designed the housing out of cement-covered adobe, a material with which the local laborers were familiar. In another Farm Security Administration rural community, one appropriately named "Woodville," de Mars used wood because it was the cheapest material available.

Nevertheless, most architects who began to use local materials in the mid-1930s did so out of choice rather than necessity. Many of the most notable ones, for example William Wurster (1895–1973), worked in the San 204 Francisco area, where they discovered a local tradition of wood-frame houses with pitched and erratic roofs, simple "carpenter style" detailing, and modest clapboard or shingle siding. Architects like Wurster were attracted to this seemingly unaffected architecture, and yet their work differed from it. A knowledge, no matter how rudimentary, of modern architecture

203 Vernon de Mars and Burton D. Cairns: Farm Cooperative Housing, Chandler, Arizona, 1936–37.

204 William Wurster: Clark House, Aptos, California, 1937.

enabled them to edit and simplify older forms and details. In some cases that impulse allowed them to revitalize a tradition; in others it produced impoverished versions of something far richer.

Although the revival of vernacular forms centered around San Francisco, it was a national phenomenon. No work was more representative of it than "Square Shadows," a house in Whitemarsh, Pennsylvania designed by George Howe in 1935. The ambiguous name perfectly summarized the design, which was a synthesis of or compromise between the historicism of Howe's early work and his International Style buildings of the early 1930s. The reason for the revival varied from architect to architect, but usually reflected a deep-seated distrust both of modernism and a machine-oriented civilization. Some who adopted these regionalisms may never have had any sympathy for modern architecture as it was introduced to the United States in the late 1920s and early 1930s. Others, however, were already looking beyond modern architecture. Lewis Mumford succinctly and presciently summarized the issue in *Technics and Civilization* (1934). First it was important to "assimilate the machine," to absorb "the essence of objectivity, impersonality, neutrality. . ." Then a reorientation was necessary in which "the diminution of the machine" would take place. Mumford favored a regionally based economy in which the small productive unit would again dominate. Of course most of the architects who adopted regionalisms in their architecture did not connect that aesthetic to the "Basic Communism" outlined by Mumford. Nevertheless, by the end of the 1930s there was virtual unanimity that it was essential to diminish the machine.

As early as 1928 Mumford had written that Frank Lloyd Wright was the true successor to Le Corbusier, not, as Hitchcock and Johnson implied in 1932, vice versa. During the 1920s Wright also experienced a loss of momentum. He dealt with it largely by removing himself from the American scene. He lived for a short time in Los Angeles, spent much of a five-year period in Japan, again tried to set up a practice in Chicago, and then finally settled in Arizona, where he built Taliesin West (1937) in the desert several miles outside of Phoenix.

One result of this peripatetic life was a loss of productivity. While living in Southern California, Wright received commissions for five houses, four of which were built with a novel system of reinforced hollow concrete blocks. Since he had moved to Japan mainly to design the Imperial Hotel in Tokyo (1916–22), the detailed design and construction of the California houses was largely supervised by Wright's assistants, his son Lloyd (1890–1978) and Rudolph Schindler. When Wright returned to the United States, he devoted more time to writing and lecturing than designing. He did receive several large commissions and made intriguing designs for them, but none of these projects was built.

The 1920s may not have been a productive period for Wright, but he used this time in which he no longer had a clear direction to make preparations for another burst of creativity. He did this in part by searching further back into the history of architecture for sources of renewal. Contact with Japanese and pre-Columbian buildings gave him clues about the very origins of architecture, but it was his reaction to the International Style which largely catalyzed these intuitions and helped him to create an architecture for the New Deal and beyond.

Throughout the 1920s Wright was in touch with architectural developments in Europe, especially in Holland. The International Style seemed to him impoverished in its formal possibilities. In his speeches and writings he often showed his concern not only about its narrowness, but also about the dangers of establishing one approach to design as correct. When the exhibition opened in 1932, he could not restrain himself, and branded the International Style the "new eclecticism," an easy formula that anyone could copy. In 1932 Wright was sixty-nine years old and it was easy to dismiss his outburst as the rantings of an old man. George Howe, for example, in an article entitled "Moses Turns to Pharaoh" (1932) claimed that though

Wright had once led architecture out of slavery, he now wanted to reinstate the shackles. Yet the most surprising and significant architectural development of the 1930s was the reemergence of Frank Lloyd Wright.

As in his early career, Wright continued to make a sharp distinction between buildings in the public and private realm. His most important work of the first category was the Johnson Wax Administration Building (1936) and Research Tower (1944) in Racine, Wisconsin. Wright conceived of this building as an enclave in an unevenly developed section of Racine. He turned the complex inward and based its organization on a memorable route from the exterior to the interior. One version of this route proceeded along the blank walls of the building, through an imposing gate, and then underneath a kind of *porte-cochère* to the main entrance. The other route started at the back of the site, traveled on axis through a courtyard, past the Research Tower, under a parking structure, and to the entrance. From the entrance, the route continued through a tall transverse space, then briefly under a low balcony, and ultimately into the building's main work space. Elevators and staircases on either side led to secondary areas.

Wright used an extraordinary set of formal and structural inventions to charge every step along this sequence with significance. He supported the roof of the parking structure and of the entry area with his famous "lily pad" columns, and then reintroduced the same elements at an entirely different scale in the main work area. The special quality of light in that space resulted from a doubly ambiguous structure. Because the exterior wall rose only to a clerestory window that wrapped around the space, the roof seemed to be held up only by the forest of columns. But the capitals of those columns appeared unconnected to one another because the space between them was filled with a membrane of pyrex tubes through which daylight was filtered. These stunning effects clearly were made to enhance what was intended as a place of work. Nevertheless, though the building was precisely constructed and contained a laboratory, it made no suggestion that the model for it had been a machine or mechanical processes. This unsentimental humanism was the most important legacy of the Johnson Wax Administration Building.

Wright's summary statement about domestic architecture was the Kaufmann House, "Falling Water," in Connellsville, Pennsylvania (1935; 1938; 1948). In this building, more decisively than in any of his other work, Wright broke from the format of a constrained box. He did so in part by separating horizontal and vertical planes. The terraces and roofs of Falling Water had smooth concrete balustrades that in their intersecting and overlapping appeared to be interwoven. These planes were held together by walls made of rough stone which nevertheless were deliberately laid in alternating courses of different thicknesses.

205, 206

206

207

205, 206 Frank Lloyd Wright: Johnson Wax Building, Racine, Wisconsin. Research Tower, 1944, and Administration Building, 1936 (interior below).

207 Frank Lloyd Wright: Kaufmann House, "Falling Water," Connellsville, Pennsylvania, 1935; 1938; 1948.

Falling Water also made an unequalled accommodation to the landscape. The house straddled a stream called Bear Run. At the back of the site, the ledge of rock to which the house was rooted was represented in plan by a dense pattern of rough stone walls. Toward the front these walls became more pier- and column-like, as the house opened up to terraces that looked out on Bear Run emerging from underneath the building and then cascading down a hill. The contrast between the densely structured and introverted back of the house and the open front served as the basic organizing principle for the sequence into and through the house.

Although the Johnson Wax Administration Building and Falling Water were his most accomplished works of the 1930s, Wright considered his solution to the problem of the small house his most important contribution. 208 The first of these so-called Usonian houses, the Herbert Jacobs House, Westmoreland, now Madison, Wisconsin, was designed in 1936 and completed in 1937. In the January 1938 issue of *Architectural Forum* Wright published his manifesto about the Usonian ideal. The Jacobs and subsequent houses demonstrate his complete rethinking of the small house. Instead of putting a miniaturized villa or manor house down in the middle of a small suburban lot, Wright tried to use the potential of the site to its maximum by turning the back of the house to the street and organizing the building in an L-shaped courtyard. On the interior, Wright's main innovation was to abolish the separate dining room. He oriented the kitchen adjacent to a small dining area so that, almost without moving, the housewife could watch her children playing outdoors, converse with guests, and put a meal on the table.

These novel ideas about the siting and organization of a house were put into physical form by three innovations in construction. Wright made the walls of the Usonian houses of a composite panel construction which was easy to install and which eliminated much of the time and expense usually associated with finishing and decorating. These panels were laid out on a two-foot by four-foot grid, which controlled the entire plan and thus allowed a degree of prefabrication. Wright's final innovation was the use of lightweight floor slabs, cast on grade and containing steam or hot water

208 Frank Lloyd Wright: Herbert Jacobs House, Madison, Wisconsin, 1936–37.

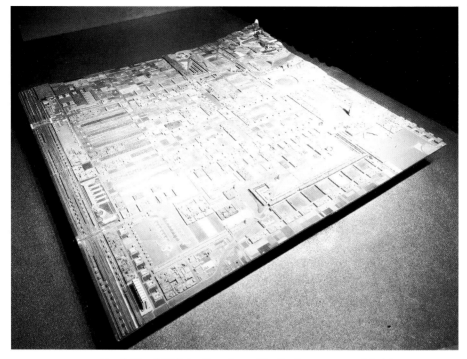

209 Frank Lloyd Wright: Broadacre City Project, 1934–58. Model.

piping for heating. At one stroke, Wright thus did away with the underused basement, provided continuous heating that was warm to the feet and cool to the head, and in eliminating awkward radiators made it possible to have floor to ceiling windows and glass doors to connect exterior and interior.

The buildings Wright designed after the late 1920s were for specific sites, but were also intended to be examples of the kinds of structures that would *209* exist in Broadacre City, a theoretical city which he started to design and write about shortly after the onset of the Depression. The important question Wright asked in these studies was how the development of vast areas of the United States could best take place, given the prosperity and broad ownership of property he anticipated once the nation emerged from the Depression. However, few people were ready to listen to what Wright had to say about this subject partly because, although he had in mind a broad strategy for land development, he illustrated it in a model that showed only a typical four-mile-square area. The model and several perspective drawings

230

allowed critics to focus too easily on eccentric details. From that angle they dismissed the whole enterprise as a simple-minded back-to-the-land scheme.

The revival of interest in the work of Frank Lloyd Wright the architect, but not the planner, was a clear repudiation of the International Style, but what it implied for the future was uncertain. In 1939 the awarding of the first prize in a competition for an addition to the Smithsonian Museum to a project by Eliel and Eero Saarinen (1910–61) seemed to indicate an official acknowledgment of a change of values. The fragmented composition of the Saarinens' scheme was more animated than the severe categories of the International Style allowed, but it was still clearly modern and therefore made a telling contrast to the classical principles and details, however attenuated, of John Russell Pope's Jefferson Memorial (1934–43) and the National Gallery of Art (1937–41). What little discussion those works received when their designs were made public was almost unanimously negative. In 1945 Joseph Hudnut (1886–1968), who by then had already initiated reforms in architectural education at Columbia and Harvard, simply dismissed Pope in a review of the buildings as "the last of the Romans." Yet whereas Pope could have easily and eloquently described what his architecture was about, it was unclear what the Saarinens stood for, especially at a time when the United States was emerging from a period of deprivation to one of unprecedented prosperity. Because no one could yet give a definitive and compelling interpretation of modern architecture and its necessity, the spirit of John Russell Pope may not have been banished as completely as Hudnut and others assumed it had.

CHAPTER EIGHT

From Less Is More to Less Is a Bore

The Architecture of Postwar America

In the quarter century after the end of the Second World War the American city was all but remade. The "Federal Bulldozer" cleared huge districts of supposedly substandard buildings in the inner city; at the same time an extensive highway program linked the downtown to sprawling areas of sparsely settled land. The essential outlines of what took place had been described much earlier, and many steps had been taken in the 1930s to establish the legal and administrative machinery that would be used to implement these changes. But the Depression and the Second World War largely postponed the construction that was then increasingly considered necessary. Thus, with the prosperity and the baby boom of the postwar decades American architects had unprecedented opportunities to build. Corporate headquarters, government centers, and buildings for learning and the arts sprang up in downtown areas while the suburbs were quickly filled with tracts of houses, shopping centers, schools, industrial parks, and even airports. During this period American architects also found many opportunities to build outside the United States, as military bases and a new generation of embassies had to be constructed to house the United States' increased presence throughout the world.

Most architects and city planners assumed that all this construction would help to create a new urban order. Sigfried Giedion (1888–1968) disclosed the essential outlines of this urban context in *Space, Time and Architecture*. This work was first given as a series of lectures at Harvard University in 1938 and 1939, was published in 1941, and as it went through many editions came to be known by architecture students and members of the profession as "Giedion's Bible." The first item on Giedion's new urban agenda was to abolish the "rue corridor" with its rigid lines of buildings and its intermingling of traffic, pedestrians, and different building types. What Giedion and others called for was not only the separation of pedestrians and traffic, but also the parcelling out of the city through zoning into separate areas, each of which would be devoted exclusively to a single purpose. These units would be larger than the outdated city block. In such generous surroundings buildings would not have to hold to a street line; they could instead "float freely" in space.

These ideas were at the root of what has often been called the "suburbanization of the city," which took place in the postwar period. But it is important to recognize that during the same years the physiognomy of the American suburb also changed. The residents of the suburbs built in the 1920s and 1930s may have owned cars, but their communities were usually still planned around a nucleus of a commuter railroad station, a business and commercial center, and nearby municipal buildings, churches, and schools. Residential areas were located on the periphery. Once the automobile became the main method of transport, the primacy of the center was undermined. Shopping and administrative centers, offices and industrial parks began to be located along highways. Similar forces changed the suburban street. If the primary means of transport was an automobile parked in a garage at the back of a house lot, the pedestrian's procession from sidewalk to front door was no longer necessary. So in the postwar suburbs much of the culture of the front yard was abandoned, as the sidewalk, lawn, porch, and sometimes even the front door itself disappeared.

Although architects and city planners agreed in principle, if not in detail, about the need to remake the American city, there was no consensus about what architectural values should be brought to bear upon its new buildings. One easy response was that everything should be modern. During and directly after the Second World War there was a remarkable change of opinion among both professionals and the public about modern architecture. The fact that the Nazis had closed the Bauhaus and branded the new architecture decadent and the knowledge that some of the founders and most ambitious practitioners of modern architecture had been stifled by the Soviet government caused modern architecture to be equated with the ideology of democracy and freedom.

Of course, a few traditionalists held out, and derogatory comments continued to be made in the popular press. But even if no one had spoken for the values that had sustained the profession through the 1920s and even the 1930s, a reactionary enemy would probably have had to have been invented. A whipping boy was necessary so that no one had to ask the basic question: what exactly is modern architecture? By harping so long upon the distinction between the traditional styles and the modern way the advocates of the new architecture were able to gloss over an issue which had been obvious to a few discerning Europeans by the turn of the century, and which was even apparent to a handful of perceptive American architects and critics by the late 1920s. They knew that it was all but fruitless to try to formulate a unified modern style or approach to architecture. Modern architecture at best was a broad term that encompassed many attitudes toward design, some of which were directly irreconcilable. By 1945 this should have been clear to all, but in the postwar rush to build few architects allowed themselves to dwell too long upon this knotty problem.

Because of the constant emphasis on the difference between modern and traditional architecture, another equally important issue was neglected. No matter how diverse it had been in its early years, modern architecture was largely spawned in Europe by avant-garde groups as a response not only to an official architecture but also to an outmoded society. The nature of the relationship of the new architecture to the new society was rarely well defined, but most European exponents of modern architecture in principle thought the connection important. Similarly, the outlines of the new society to be ushered in with the new architecture were also usually left vague, but they did at least often encompass ideas about the increased presence of the state and new economic policies.

Once modern architecture was endorsed by a society which had the same political structure as, and was certainly more prosperous than, the one that had been building Roman banks and Gothic churches ten years earlier— once it became, in effect, the official style of a democratic country that largely championed the free market and a government with a low profile— the time had come to reassess its basic premises. However, the leading architects, including many European emigrés, were reluctant to do this. If they thought about these complex matters at all, they usually dispensed with them by simply positing a consonance between modern architecture and the United States because America was a land of freedom. Louis Sullivan and Frank Lloyd Wright had made a similar point much earlier, but no one in the postwar period tried as rigorously as they had to extrapolate an architecture from this premise.

Although there was no clear discussion of these issues, it is obvious in retrospect that modern architecture had several distinctly different meanings in the postwar period. One interpretation was that the modern architect should serve society rather than represent it through the symbolic character of a building. This was not a new idea. It had a long lineage in European architectural thought; it had always been at least latent in American discussions about whether the art of architecture was more than just an indulgence; and by the late 1930s some American architects and critics were trying to describe its appropriateness for the contemporary context. Lewis Mumford, for example, in "The Death of the Monument," an essay written in 1937, argued for an ever changing architecture, one which did not have the weight and pretensions of traditional buildings, but which instead could

210 Walter Gropius
(associated with Boston
Center Architects): Boston
Back Bay Center
Development, Boston,
Massachusetts, 1953. Model.

respond because of its lightness to the varied and changing needs of its physical and social context.

Ideas similar to these were elaborated by and quickly became associated 210 with the German architect Walter Gropius. Gropius left Germany in 1934, spent the following years in England, and arrived in the United States in 1937 to become Chairman of the Department of Architecture at the Harvard Graduate School of Design. Of course, Gropius had formed impressions of the United States and American architecture long before he arrived in his adopted country. He had visited the United States in 1928 and, more important, he was familiar with American architecture through discussions that had taken place in German architectural circles ever since the turn of the century. In effect, Gropius arrived with strong preconceptions, and it is hard not to conclude that in the thirty years he lived in the United States he paid attention to whatever confirmed those ideas and dismissed whatever did not.

Reacting in part to the conditions and people responsible for the mass movements that had brought the National Socialists to power in Germany, Gropius tried to define a more wholesome context to fit and nurture his conception of the ideal citizen. Gropius's American was a practical person, more a doer than a thinker, someone who knew how to fix his car and who enjoyed building an addition onto his house on weekends. Such people did not thrive in large, chaotic cities dominated by the alluring culture of commerce; the more salutary environment was the small community in which a grassroots democracy could flourish. The architect's role was to serve such people by interpreting their social and psychological needs and by applying technological innovations to the buildings that housed their institutions.

In conjunction and sometimes in conflict with Joseph Hudnut, who left Columbia in 1936 to serve as the Dean of the Harvard Graduate School of Design, Gropius initiated studies about the use of buildings and how construction could be rationalized. Subsequently, many other American architecture schools mounted programs of research in these areas. Some even established research organizations which published their work. The history of the issues addressed in research, especially the technological roots, was described in several significant works, the most important of which were Giedion's *Space, Time and Architecture* and *Mechanization Takes Command* (1948).

Although many architecture schools have continued to undertake research into the making and use of buildings, the impact of this work on American practice has been marginal. The involvement of the federal government in the regulation and promotion of building has been weaker in the United States than in other countries, so there has never been a direct and forceful channel through which to turn research into practice. But the ineffectiveness of this work has also been due to its poor quality. Architecture schools have often produced and endorsed badly conceived projects, the work too obviously of second- and third-rate engineers, sociologists, and psychologists.

The more important difficulty with architectural research of the postwar period was that no matter how objective it claimed to be, it was often based on assumptions that were not shared by its supposed beneficiaries. Much of the work on housing suffered from this problem. Catherine Bauer, the most distinguished American student of housing, was explicit about this matter in a revealing self-criticism made in 1965. She claimed that throughout the postwar period, American architects persisted in thinking about housing as if they were still living in the 1930s, a time when there was no expectation of economic growth. "Existenzminimum," standardization, and collectivism, therefore, continued to be the three principles that guided architects in their investigations of housing. However, the vast majority of Americans wanted none of this. Their dream was individualism in the suburbs. Thus, Bauer contended, by continuing to conceive of housing in terms of existenz-minimum, standardization, and collectivism, architects merely established a

211 Demolition of part of Minoru Yamasaki's Pruitt-Igoe public housing project, St. Louis, Missouri, 1972.

separate standard of housing that served further to divide poor and low-income groups from other Americans.

The distinction was readily apparent. In the postwar period many small, low-rise projects continued to be built. These developments have usually had long waiting lists for apartments, and in many other ways they have largely been successful. The more problematical projects were the vast tracts of high-rise buildings constructed in American cities from the late 1940s through the 1950s. This configuration of apartment towers set in open space may have been encouraged by the federal agency that administered the housing program, but it certainly was never mandated. Rather it was chosen by local housing authorities and their architects through a usually vague sense that its supposed efficiency and repetitive appearance was tantamount to or symbolized progress. From their opening most of these projects experienced administrative and maintenance problems, both of which were exacerbated when the resident population shifted from the working poor to the city's disturbed, disabled, and dispossessed. The descent from idealistic beginnings was most starkly dramatized by the part-demolition in 1972 of *211* St. Louis' once-heralded Pruitt-Igoe project (1958), designed by Minoru Yamasaki (1912–86).

237

Preconceptions and misconceptions about what was good for Americans also had important consequences for the suburbs. On the whole American architects joined sociologists in condemning the suburbs for creating a lonely crowd of organization men, consumption-crazed housewives, and spoiled children. Hence, their primary response to the burgeoning culture of tract developments, shopping centers, drive-in theaters, chain restaurants, motels, and gas stations was to sit moralistically in judgment. They therefore took little or no part in determining how these vast areas of new development should be designed and built. Architects often complained that they were involved with only a small percentage of construction, but their basic stance toward the culture permitted no more.

Even if research is more able and is founded on clearer assumptions about whom it serves, there will never be a direct and obvious way to apply it to practice. No architect has ever been more doctrinaire about the primacy of the need to serve than Hannes Meyer, a former director of the Bauhaus. Yet his projects of the late 1920s were obviously influenced as much by a love of industrial imagery, which he must have absorbed from Russian constructivism, as they were by technical and programmatic requirements. American architects who endorsed the ethic of service did not allow themselves such liberties. Their buildings may have been influenced by the space-time themes of artists like Klee and Moholy-Nagy. They may also have drawn sustenance from features of the landscape in which they were set. But the overriding objective was a building that derived its form from no external source whatsoever. As it is all but inconceivable to design buildings on this basis, certain architectural motifs that had been devised to fulfil functions became instead emblems of service. Examples were the flat roof, sun screens, concrete block corridors, and the all but invisible entrance of the postwar, suburban elementary school.

The inherent difficulty, the impossibility even, of an architecture based purely on the fulfillment of function soon became apparent, even to some of its most ardent advocates. Thus in "The Need for a New Monumentality," an essay of 1943, Sigfried Giedion acknowledged that it was also necessary "to create symbols in the form of monuments." Whereas Giedion was concerned primarily about the future of public buildings, few of which had been designed or built by modern architects in the 1920s and 1930s, Joseph Hudnut discussed the same matter in terms of housing. In "The Post-Modern House" of 1945 he argued that a house was not just a machine; it also had to express "the idea of home."

Of course, the rhetoric about the need for architecture to serve continued. Throughout the postwar period to be called a "formalist" was the worst insult, designing a single-family house was equated with social irresponsibility, and using conventional construction techniques was tantamount to a betrayal of the mission of the twentieth century. Nevertheless, the need to represent values could not be stifled. Different architects came to this realization at different times and in different ways, but the February 1950 issue of *L'Architecture d'aujourd'hui* devoted to "Walter Gropius et son école" and edited by Paul Rudolph, was the most significant milestone marking this transition. The issue was meant to summarize and celebrate Gropius's achievement, but at the same time it can be read as his students' way of saying farewell to his influence.

Rediscovering how to represent values in buildings was not an easy task. Some architects traveled to Europe to draw inspiration, however furtively, from the great monuments that their history of architecture courses omitted when they were students. However, what to make of these works was unclear; given the climate of opinion that prevailed in architecture schools, it was unthinkable for a young practitioner to consider himself, at least overtly, a possible successor to John Russell Pope. Most, instead, looked for guidance to those figures who were already considered the "masters of modern architecture."

In trying to find a modern idiom that went beyond an architecture of mere service, many young architects were first attracted to the work of Ludwig Mies van der Rohe (1886–1969). When Mies arrived in the United States in 1937, he was fifty years old and might have been expected to live out his years in semiretirement as Director of Architecture at Armour Institute, now Illinois Institute of Technology, in Chicago. Mies was an effective teacher, but he made his reputation in the United States mainly through his surprisingly productive practice. Mies did not talk or write much about his work, and it has now long been customary to discuss his buildings as an architecture of fact, partly because he made painstaking studies about the components of his buildings and how they were to be assembled. Yet it is also clear that his work was guided by a conception of architecture's significance that encompassed far more than a concern for the making of buildings. From his first American design, the 1938 project for the Resor House in Jackson Hole, Wyoming, to his best-known work, the Seagram Building (1954–58) in New York, Mies tried to articulate a language of architecture that could give expression to his vision of a new, postwar and American world. This quest was guided as much by his interpretation of the special qualities of the American landscape and his knowledge of the history of architecture as it was by his proficiency at detailing corners and other critical building intersections. As such, Mies's American work was both a continuation of themes that had informed his designs of the 1920s and 1930s and a new departure.

215

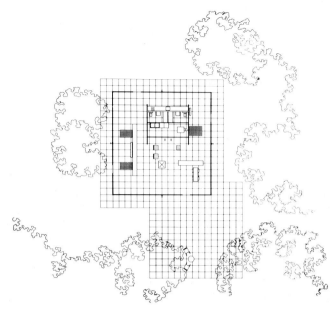

212 Ludwig Mies van
der Rohe: "Fifty by Fifty"
house project, 1950–51.
Plan.

213 Ludwig Mies van
der Rohe: Convention
Hall, Chicago, Illinois,
1953–54 Photomontage
of interior.

Mies was able to accomplish his objective in a remarkably short time. The Resor House was only the first of several significant projects that tried to reconstitute the very basis of the house in its siting, planning, and construction. The Farnsworth House of 1945–50 in Plano, Illinois, was his most widely discussed statement about domestic architecture. This exquisitely detailed glass-walled box was lifted off the ground and supported by four pairs of I-beams. As in many of Mies's other buildings, the Farnsworth House's interior had no dividing walls. It was zoned only by carefully chosen and placed furniture and the location of bathrooms and a

212   kitchen service wall. These ideas were taken to an extreme in Mies's "Fifty by Fifty" house project (1950–51). A square in plan, this house had a flat roof supported only by four columns, one each at the mid-points of a side.

The "Fifty by Fifty" house was as much a prototype for the vast public spaces Mies was building as it was a house. Mies's attempt to give public institutions a proper presence began with his 1942 project for a museum for a small city and culminated in his massive New National Gallery, Berlin (1962–68). In between he designed a series of equally provocative buildings including the Architecture and Design Building for Illinois Institute of

213   Technology (1952) and a Convention Hall for Chicago (1953–54) which had a 720-foot clear span. All these buildings were conceived as bounded figures with none of the dynamic interpenetrating planes that had characterized

240

earlier works such as the Barcelona Pavilion of 1929. It has often been said that the spaces Mies created in these buildings were not shaped to accommodate the activities they were to contain. Mies did undoubtedly aspire to universality, but as his photomontages show, he also had an image of how and what was supposed to happen within.

Mies's other significant contribution to American practice was his solution to the tall building. He had designed several projects for glass skyscrapers shortly after the end of the First World War, and a multistory apartment house of his was built in Chicago in 1949. But his first and most forceful statement about the tall building came two years later. The two apartment towers at 860 Lake Shore Drive in Chicago set an image of the tall building that was imitated and elaborated upon for the next quarter century. These towers were glass and steel cages that aspired on the exterior to complete uniformity. Mies applied window mullions to steel columns to achieve this effect.

214

214 Ludwig Mies van der Rohe: 860 Lake Shore Drive Apartments, Chicago, Illinois, 1949–51. Horizontal section showing relation of window mullions to steel column at corner of building.

The matter-of-fact quality of Lake Shore Drive's construction has often been contrasted with the self-consciously sophisticated materials and detailing of the Seagram Building. For Mies, however, the distinction was 215 simply a reflection of the difference between a speculative apartment building and a corporate headquarters. The same distinction accounted for the Seagram Building's pyramidal massing and suggestively classical composition. Similarly, whereas the Lake Shore Drive towers were placed obliquely to the roadway that separated them from Lake Michigan, the Seagram Building had its front on Park Avenue, as was appropriate to its urbane setting and its location opposite McKim, Mead & White's Racquet and Tennis Club.

Mies's work had an immediate but varied impact on American practice. For some architects his buildings suggested only a vocabulary of metal details; for others its statement of the primacy of the steel frame showed how to give an order to architecture that went beyond the mere accommodation of functions. The architect with the closest and most sustained tie to Mies was Philip Johnson. Johnson had conspicuously included Mies in the 1932 Museum of Modern Art show on modern architecture and had commissioned him to design an apartment in New York for Eddy Warburg, one of the Museum's trustees. In 1934 Johnson left the Museum of Modern Art to embark on a strange and distasteful political career in which he first worked as resident intellectual for Huey Long, the Louisiana senator then running for president, and later for Father Coughlin, a populist demagogue with fascist sympathies. After running unsuccessfully for Congress in Ohio in 1936 on Coughlin's ticket, Johnson helped to found the ominously named organization Youth and the Nation. These dubious escapades ended with his enrollment at the Harvard Graduate School of Design in 1940.

Johnson's preference for the luxurious dimensions and materials of Mies's architecture, especially in comparison to the work and precepts of Walter Gropius, was already evident in 1932. His championing, not of Mies, but of his own interpretation of Mies appeared again in his final project at Harvard, a box-like house based on one of Mies's courtyard designs of the mid-1930s, and in his Four Seasons Restaurant (1958) in the Seagram Building. It was also evident in his 1947 book on Mies which, unlike Ludwig Hilbersheimer's more informative work of 1956, did not include illustrations of working details. But it was most explicit in his own house of 1949 in New Canaan, 216 Connecticut. Ostensibly a Miesian box, Johnson's house contained one space which was interrupted only by bathroom and kitchen facilities. The structure and skin, however, did not have the freshness of invention that informed the detailing of the Farnsworth House, nor was the house sited in as aggressively challenging a way as Mies's best houses. More interesting to

243

215 Ludwig Mies van der Rohe and Philip Johnson: Seagram Building, New York City, 1954–58.

216 Philip Johnson: Johnson Residence, New Canaan, Connecticut, 1949.

Johnson were the sources on which his design drew. In an article about the house, Johnson claimed a lineage from not only Mies, but also Le Corbusier, Theo van Doesburg, Kasimir Malevich, Auguste Choisy, Karl Friedrich Schinkel, and Claude-Nicolas Ledoux.

Many of the Case Study Houses sponsored by *Arts and Architecture*, an influential California-based magazine edited by John Entenza (1905–84), suggested a more direct extension of Miesian principles in residential architecture. The Case Study Houses were largely conceived as a response to what by 1945 already appeared to be the "wacky googy" quality of recent attempts to reorient modern architecture in a regional or vernacular direction. One of the first and most influential Case Study Houses was designed by Charles Eames (1907–78), who was primarily a furniture and industrial designer. Eames was trained at the Cranbrook Academy of Art in Michigan under Eliel Saarinen. In 1940 he won a furniture competition sponsored by the Museum of Modern Art. His molded plywood chairs and many of his subsequent designs soon became all but essential fixtures in the postwar modern house. His Case Study House drew its language more from Albert Kahn's factories, which he must have seen when a student at Cranbrook, than from a knowledge of Mies's buildings. Its walls were made of glazing elements drawn from catalogues used for industrial buildings, and its roof and floor were supported by bar joists. Unlike Mies's houses, the implicit expandability and interchangeability of Eames's construction implied a less deterministic attitude both toward the pattern of use within and the building's relationship to the site. Eames's house was soon filled with clutter, and it was not unthinkable to photograph it with a tree in the foreground.

By 1950 the Case Study Houses became more decisively Miesian. Raphael Soriano (1907–88), Craig Elwood (1922–92), and others based their houses on a steel structural frame which was then infilled with glass. Unlike Mies, however, the California architects did not aspire to a constant, completely air-conditioned interior environment. The California houses often had plans which were not just rectangles, but which tried to incorporate decks, terraces, and swimming pools to mediate between interior and exterior.

Exemplary as the Case Study Houses may have been as individual works, they did not make a substantial impact on the design and construction of the ordinary developer's house, mainly because steel always seemed an inappropriate material for a house; nor was it as malleable as wood for small-scale construction. Mies's more lasting impact, therefore, was on commercial and office buildings. He was not in fact the first architect to use the glass curtain wall for a tall building. The Equitable Life Assurance Building in Portland, Oregon (1944–47), by Pietro Belluschi (1899–1995), *218* and the United National Secretariat (1948–51), designed by a team of *219*

217 Charles Eames: Eames House, Los Angeles, California, 1948.

architects coordinated by Wallace K. Harrison (1895–1981) with Le
Corbusier's participation, both used this technique before Mies did. Another
significant use of it was Eero Saarinen's General Motors Technical Center
(1948–56), but the firm which made the glass and steel curtain wall virtually
synonymous with American corporate architecture was Skidmore, Owings
220   & Merrill. Their Lever House in New York City (1951–52) was important
because it was the first New York office building planned around a public
plaza and set back from the street. But Lever House and other Skidmore,
Owings & Merrill buildings of the same period were also of note because
they were among the earliest and most successful elaborations of the metal
and glass curtain wall. Mies had set a high standard in establishing a dialogue
between the articulation of the parts of the curtain wall and the statement
of a compelling profile. In its early office buildings Skidmore, Owings &
Merrill was able at least to approach this standard, but especially as such
buildings became larger, this highly rarefied discipline was easily violated or
ignored. Toward the end of his life even Mies could not convincingly sus-

218 Pietro Belluschi: Equitable Life
Assurance Building, Portland, Oregon,
1944–47.

219 Wallace K. Harrison *et al.*: United
Nations Secretariat, New York City,
1948–51.

220 Skidmore, Owings & Merrill: Lever
House, New York City, 1951–52.

tain it. Even in the 860 Lake Shore Drive Apartments the critical relationship
between the skin and the structure had been more implied than real. Once
this dialogue was abandoned, the appearance of the skyscraper became arbitrary, determined as much by the glass manufacturer's latest gimmick as by
the architect.

One reason many architects did not continue for long to design in a
Miesian manner was that they were looking for an architecture that could be
more obviously monumental than even the Seagram Building's understated
classicism. By the time the Seagram Building was finished many American
architects, especially those designing major cultural institutions, were
already making more pronounced allusions to the classical tradition. Two
embassies, one for India, the other for Great Britain, epitomized the
problems inherent in this approach.

Before the commission for the American embassy in New Delhi, the
work of Edward Durrell Stone (1902–78) had gone through several phases.
Stone was educated at the Boston Architectural Club and in the architecture

221

221 Edward Durrell Stone: United States Embassy, New Delhi, 1954.

programs of Harvard and M.I.T. At M.I.T. he started to absorb modernist ideas and on a scholarship traveled to Europe to see some of the significant modern buildings of the 1920s, including Mies van der Rohe's Barcelona Pavilion. Stone was impressed by the exhibition at the Museum of Modern Art in 1932, and in the following years he designed several International Style houses as well as the new building for the Museum of Modern Art.

However, by the late 1930s Stone had become disillusioned with the International Style, because he felt that it would never be acceptable to the public. He began to revert to regionalist gestures in his domestic architecture and to a kind of decorative classicism for his public buildings. Stone's solution at New Delhi, and in other buildings such as the Kennedy Center for the Performing Arts, Washington, D.C. (1961–71), was to retain the axial nature of the classical plan and the columnar basis of its architecture, but to infuse the building elements with a sense of lightness, a quality that he associated with both a modern and an American sensibility. Thus, the embassy was set up on a podium and was surrounded by a colonnade of gently tapering gilded columns. Its walls were, in effect, a sun screen that was detailed both to hover above the ground and not to touch the roof. Throughout the embassy Stone tried to reduce every surface to an intricate pattern made of small units so that nothing would seem monolithic or overbearing.

The American Embassy in London was designed by another prominent member of the profession, Eero Saarinen. Born in Finland, Saarinen came to the United States with his father in 1923. After graduating from Yale University, he worked with his father until 1950, when he became principal

248

222 Eero Saarinen: TWA Terminal at John F. Kennedy International Airport, New York City, 1959–62.

partner of Eero Saarinen and Associates. By then his work increasingly showed evidence of the need to break away from the craft-oriented architecture of his father. As Saarinen often put the matter, modern architecture, especially as it was understood in the United States, lacked drama. His goal above all was to create buildings with a memorable image, one which preferably capitalized upon a daring structural technique. His most noted examples were several large-span structures, such as the 630-foot-high and 630-foot-wide Jefferson National Expansion Memorial, St. Louis (1947–48; 1959–64). In one of his most controversial works, the Trans World Airlines Terminal at Kennedy (Idlewild) Airport (1959–62), Saarinen 222 not only wanted to distinguish TWA from the other airlines but his goal was also to "express the drama and specialness and excitement of travel." Saarinen's theme was the terminal as a place of movement; to express it he used a structure based on four intersecting barrel vaults supported by four Y-shaped columns. The result was a vast concrete shell, 50 feet high and 315 feet long, which made a huge umbrella to protect all the passenger areas.

The American Embassy in London had no space that could be covered 223 with a striking structure to identify the building. In fact, the embassy largely contained offices, and although the project was exempt from local zoning laws, Saarinen felt obliged to respond to the Georgian context of Grosvenor Square. Even so, the features and motifs of the building emphatically announced it to be an American embassy. It held the roof line of adjacent buildings, but was set back from the street on a podium that made it seem aloof from its surroundings. Like the Georgian houses, it used repetitive window elements, but they were designed with a nervous rhythm that was

249

223 Eero Saarinen:
United States
Embassy, London,
1955–60.

uncharacteristic of the adjacent buildings. However, the most distinctive features of the embassy were its "costume jewelry" gold anodized aluminum trim and an eagle with a thirty-six-foot wing span that was mounted at the roof over the entrance.

Given classical architecture's longevity and the fact that the most significant modern architects—Wright, Le Corbusier, Mies, and Alvar Aalto—had all taken a close look at classical buildings in defining their own language of architecture, it was not a betrayal of principle for American practitioners again to turn to these works. The problematical aspect of what followed was not the sources, but the interpretation. The platitudinous planning and cosmetic details of the buildings at the Lincoln Center for the Performing Arts in New York City (1959–66) revealed all too clearly the superficiality with which analogies to ancient works could be made.

The only architect to undertake a more than perfunctory study of classical architecture in the postwar period was Louis I. Kahn (1901–74). Born in Estonia, Kahn came to the United States with his parents in 1905. He received a degree in architecture under Paul Cret at the Beaux-Arts oriented University of Pennsylvania in 1924, and then began an apprenticeship that extended through the Second World War. During this lengthy period Kahn worked for and with, among others, Cret, George Howe, and Oskar Stonorov.

The immediate reason Kahn was so slow to make his own statement in architecture was that very little work was available during the Depression and the Second World War, especially for a Jewish architect with no substantial connections. But Kahn was also hesitant to commit himself in practice because he was uncertain about the nature of modern architecture, at least as it was interpreted in the United States throughout the 1930s and 1940s. It was only when Kahn was able to reconcile the premises of modern architecture with his early training that he was ready to receive and execute major commissions. The significance of his education was clarified for him by a stay at the American Academy in Rome, travel in Greece and Egypt, and perhaps the publication in 1952 of Emil Kaufmann's influential article on the work of Boullée, Ledoux, and Lequeu in the *Journal of the American Philosophical Society*. One way or another the early 1950s marked the beginning of two remarkable decades in which Kahn produced, among many important works, the Richards Medical Research Building and   225 Biological Research Building, Philadelphia, Pennsylvania (1957–64), the Jonas Salk Institute for Biological Studies, La Jolla, California (1959–65), the   226 Kimbell Art Museum, Fort Worth, Texas (1966–72), the Phillips Exeter Academy Library, Exeter, New Hampshire (1967–72), and the Center for British Art and Studies, Yale University, New Haven (1967–74).

As Kahn became more prolific, he developed an often self-indulgently obscure explanation of his central premise: that there is an essential aspect of architecture, which he called "form," that exists beyond the ostensible function of a building. Architecture did not involve fitting uses into dimensioned areas. It was instead a "creating of spaces that evoke a feeling of use." At one level Kahn tried to achieve this end through an interpretation of the elements of which his buildings were made. In a revealing article of 1943 he wrote that a new monumentality in architecture could be attained by stretching contemporary materials to their limit and prophesied that light tubular steel members could form the basis of an updated Gothic architecture of ribs, vaults, domes, and buttresses. Not long after, Kahn   224 began to doubt whether such light structures (which, though Gothic in spirit, were at least in part a response to Mies van der Rohe's early work in the United States) could ever have the presence of great architecture. This interest in mass and solidity led him to reexamine the basis of trabeated architecture: the relationship between column, beam, and slab. Equally important was his discovery of the thick masonry wall as a device to filter a desired quality of daylight and to contain built-in furniture such as study carrels in libraries.

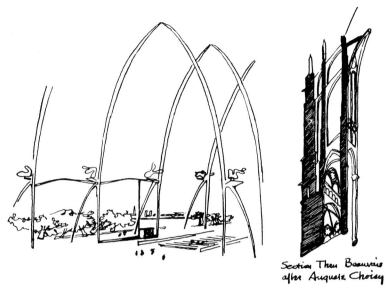

Section Thru Beauvais
after Auguste Choisy

This analysis of column, beam, and wall had immediate implications for building plans. Despite the prevalent rhetoric about the virtues of a free and dynamic plan, Kahn never relinquished a basic belief, instilled in his education under Cret, that a gridded order was essential to the organization of a building. However, especially in designing the Richards Medical Research Building, Kahn began to understand that the plan of a building for a modern institution had to be based on more than a network of walls and columns. It also had to be supple enough to channel the complex tangle of plumbing, heating, air conditioning, electrical, and other services that had become so prominent in contemporary buildings. From this fundamental distinction between "servant" and "served" spaces Kahn developed a series of memorable building plans, all based on a tartan grid.

Kahn designed the Richards Medical Research Building first by defining a unit of space to suit a laboratory. He then agglomerated a number of these units, both horizontally and vertically. All the non-laboratory functions, even the entrance, had to fit the parameters of this repetitive unit. Although the building was made out of seemingly massive concrete and brick, the emphasis on this unit of space suggested indefinite extendability and universal adaptability. Partly in response to the rigidity of this approach, Kahn's later buildings always had a more diversified plan composed around at least one focal space, the primary function of which was to celebrate the "worthiness" of the institution. So, for example, the central space in the

224 Louis I. Kahn: Beauvais Cathedral in Steel.

225 Louis I. Kahn: Richards Medical Research Building, Philadelphia, Pennsylvania, 1957–64.

226 Louis I. Kahn: The Salk Institute, La Jolla, California, 1959–65.

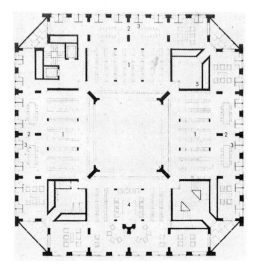

227, 228 Phillips Exeter Academy Library may serve as a passageway from one area on the main level to another and as a setting for evening concerts; it also brings light to the center of the building. But its ultimate justification is not so easily describable. In its grandeur and quiet solemnity, the space gives presence to the institution and, especially through the quality of light that filters down from above, attempts to connect those within to a sense of a higher order.

Even though the works that followed the Richards Medical Research Building had more articulate plans, Kahn's buildings have been faulted for not having a sufficiently graduated hierarchy of spaces. His entrances, for example, invariably seem abrupt. A similar question has often been posed about the quality of his detailing. Kahn had the taste and budgets to choose fine and distinctive materials, but he often detailed them in a manifestly direct or even crude manner. One reason Kahn's buildings did not have more nuance is that this would have entailed making a more complete examination of the essence of classical architecture than either he or the profession was ready to undertake. But the more compelling explanation is that Kahn may have been interpreting in his own way and for his own time an American tradition of classical architecture. American buildings in the classical tradition, even the most sophisticated works of McKim, Mead &

254

227, 228 Louis I. Kahn:
Phillips Exeter Academy
Library, Exeter, New
Hampshire, 1967–72.
Early floor plan and
central space.

229 Alvar Aalto: Finnish
Pavilion, New York
World's Fair, 1939.

White and their contemporaries, have never been as articulate as their
European counterparts. Most American architects have been apologetic
about this fact; Kahn knowingly used it as a point of strength.

Kahn's change from an interest in light tubular steel ribbed structures to a
fascination with a heavy trabeated architecture of concrete and masonry
could not have taken place without a knowledge of what Alvar Aalto, Frank
Lloyd Wright, and Le Corbusier were designing. Americans learned of the
architecture of Aalto (1898–1976) not only from published accounts of his
European work but also from his Finnish Pavilion at the New York World's   229
Fair in 1939 and, more importantly to the postwar period, his Baker House   230
(1947–48), a dormitory for the Massachusetts Institute of Technology. Baker
House was one in a long sequence of buildings in which Aalto attempted to
resolve a problematical condition of modern life: the connection between
the individual and the collective. The building thus was conceived as a
dialogue between the dormitory room and the common areas, but it was
also about the many spaces in which these two realms intersected. A similar
conversation took place with reference to the site. Baker House's undulating
front wall was a response to the river it faced; its enclosed back brought the
building into contact with the grid on which the rest of the M.I.T. campus
was based. Such juxtapositions had broad implications. Through them Aalto

255

230 Alvar Aalto: Baker House, Cambridge, Massachusetts, 1947–48. Entrance façade.

was trying to reconcile two divergent interpretations of modern architecture or even architecture in general. He gave emphasis to these issues not only through the basic themes of the building, but also through his vivid rendering of specific details and incidents such as the main door, the columns in the entry, the handrails, and the dormitory furniture.

Aalto had often been fascinated by the problem of creating sinuous shapes out of straight or rectilinear materials. Some comments about bricks he heard Frank Lloyd Wright make in a speech in 1946 provided Aalto with insights that later informed Baker House's river façade. Wright continued designing until his death in 1959. The building for which he was best known in the postwar period was the Solomon R. Guggenheim Museum in New York City. The first designs for this building to house a collection of non-objective art were made from 1943 to 1945. Work was soon halted, was then only resumed a decade later, and when the Guggenheim Museum was finished in 1959 it was evident that much of the vitality of the original design had been dissipated. The office building behind the Museum, shown in an early rendering, would have made sense of the much criticized siting and massing. Similarly, it is not implausible to think that had Wright been able to construct the building when the design was fresh, his detailing would have been more compelling and he might have devised a more convincing solution for the display of works of art.

Nevertheless, despite its many faults, the Guggenheim Museum, especially its central space which is wrapped by an ascending spiral ramp, was still a stunning accomplishment. Versions of the spiral route had appeared in several of Wright's earlier designs, ranging in scale from the gigantic parking garage of the Sugarloaf Mountain project of 1925 to the delicate ramp in the

231, 232

256

231, 232 Frank Lloyd Wright: Solomon R. Guggenheim Museum, New York
City, 1943–59.

V. C. Morris Gift Shop in San Francisco (1948–49), and of course predecessors of the Guggenheim's central space date back to Unity Temple and the Larkin Building, if not before. But in the Guggenheim Museum Wright most fully attained his ideal of an organic architecture in which plan, elevation, and section truly interact.

Le Corbusier's (1887–1965) relationship with American architecture extended back at least to his publication of photographs of grain silos in *Vers une architecture* (1923). He visited the United States in 1935 and recorded his impressions in *Quand les cathédrales étaient blanches* (1937; English edition 1947). Because he emphasized the "engineer's aesthetic" and chided American architects for being timid, Le Corbusier's architecture was usually summarized, and dismissed, by his phrase "a machine for living." In fact, by the mid- to late 1920s both his painting and his architecture were beginning to assume a different, perhaps more melancholy but certainly more profound aspect. Le Corbusier's attempt to make contact through personal but highly charged metaphors with a world of forms drawn more overtly from nature and the history of architecture than from machines reached its fruition in the postwar period in a series of masterworks that included the Unité d'Habitation in Marseilles (1947–53), Notre Dame-du-Haut at Ronchamp (1950–54), the La Tourette monastery, Eveux-sur Arbresle, near Lyons (1955), the Maisons Jaoul, Neuilly-sur-Seine (1956), and a series of remarkable buildings in India.

219

233

Except for the United Nations Headquarters, in the design of which he was only partially involved, Le Corbusier's one building in the United States was the Carpenter Center for the Visual Arts at Harvard University, Cambridge, Massachusetts (1960–63). This building primarily contained open studio, workshop, and exhibition spaces, with a few offices and classrooms. Le Corbusier dealt with this program by interweaving cubic and curved volumes within a grid of concrete columns. The armature of the design was a ramp that rose from ground level to the second floor and penetrated completely through the building. Although the concrete was finished with a smoother surface than had been used in his other postwar works, Carpenter Center had many recognizable motifs of Le Corbusier's architecture, such as thin concrete mullions, *brise-soleils*, and walls of glass block. These have often made the Carpenter Center seem discordant with its predominantly red brick and Georgian neighbors, but it can also be understood as Le Corbusier's interpretation, through his own architectural metaphors, of the pattern of buildings and space in nearby Harvard Yard.

Aalto, Wright, and Le Corbusier, like all great artists in their maturity, were reinterpreting themes developed in their youth, which in turn had been formulated in response to the work of their masters and to their

233 Le Corbusier: Carpenter Center for the Visual Arts, Cambridge, Massachusetts, 1960–63.

234 José Luis Sert: Peabody Terrace, Cambridge, Massachusetts, 1964.

understanding of the significant buildings of the history of architecture. In the postwar period, Wright, Le Corbusier, and to a lesser extent Aalto had American disciples who tried to draw out the implications of the master's work. The Taliesin Associated Architects executed, in both senses of the word, Wright's unfinished projects, and in new commissions produced a version of Wrightian architecture that bordered on kitsch. José Luis Sert (1902–83) was more successful in extending and developing some of Le Corbusier's principles, especially in the design of housing. But most American architects, including those who had worked with the masters, did not try to draw direct implications from the buildings of Aalto, Wright, and Le Corbusier. Works like Baker House, the Guggenheim Museum, and Carpenter Center simply seemed to say that modern architecture did not have to be limited by the straightjacket of the International Style, Mies's discipline, or references to the classical tradition. Instead, they suggested that it was both possible and desirable to develop a more subjective language. This conclusion was affirmed by critics as diverse as Ayn Rand and Norman Mailer who advised architects that they could best contribute to the culture by creating works of striking invention and individuality.

234

In postwar domestic architecture, many of the more eccentric houses, especially those with flamboyant roof structures, followed the cue that Wright had given in recent houses such as the Richard Davis Residence ("Woodston"), Marion, Indiana (1950), with its "teepee" roof. But the champion of individual expression was Bruce Goff (1904–83). Born in Kansas, Goff began working in an architectural office in Tulsa, Oklahoma at the age of twelve. At the firm of Rush, Endacott & Rush, Goff discovered Frank Lloyd Wright's 1908 "In the Cause of Architecture" article and was soon producing Wrightian designs. In the 1920s Goff's buildings for Rush, Endacott & Rush revealed his familiarity with German and Austrian expressionism. His Boston Avenue Methodist-Episcopal Church in Tulsa, Oklahoma (1926–29), was one of that decade's few buildings for a significant institution to depart from the safety of the established styles. Goff was largely unproductive during the Depression, spent the Second World War in the navy, but in 1945 was able to design the Seabee Chapel, Camp Parks, California out of Quonset huts and other scavenged materials.

Goff's most productive period began with the end of the war. His practice's staple—the building type which allowed him and his clients the most freedom of expression—was the private house. Some of the plans of these houses were amorphous, but most were based on geometries of circles, spirals, triangles, and squares. Goff used exotic roof structures to transform the sections of these houses. For example, the Bavinger House in Norman, Oklahoma (1951–55), spiraled up to a fifty-five-foot-high mast from which radiating cables supported a copper covered roof. To emphasize the ends of the ridges of the sloping planes of the gold anodized roof of the Price House in Bartlesville, Oklahoma (1956; 1966; 1974), Goff used sharply projecting metal spikes.

Just as important to Goff as the highly individual volumes of his houses were the materials out of which they were constructed and with which they were decorated. The walls of the owner-built Bavinger House were largely made of rough stone from nearby fields. The mast was fabricated from oil well drilling pipes. The Price House was for a wealthy client, but it was made of equally unconventional materials. Its retaining walls were composed of anthracite coal and glistening glass cullets; the studio's ceiling was covered with acoustically absorbent and light-reflective goose feathers.

An eccentric house can always be explained by the fact that an individual, whether architect or client, wanted it that way. The issue of expression and symbolic meaning in public institutions is more complex. In museums, libraries, and city halls a statement about societal values is inevitable. In the 1950s and 1960s architects who received such commissions often elaborated a language of sculptural shapes in rough masonry and concrete. The three-

235 Bruce Goff: Bavinger House,
Norman, Oklahoma, 1951–55.

dimensional nature of these forms, with consequent pronounced shadows, was seen as a humane alternative to the repetitive gridded surface of the bureaucratic curtain wall, the roughness of the surfaces was a response both to the detachment of Miesian steel and glass and the tinsel-like prettiness of 1950s classicist works, and masonry and concrete gave buildings a sense of gravity and purpose without the need to replicate or elaborate upon the language of details that had traditionally been associated with buildings for significant institutions.

Works of this type were designed by Ulrich Franzen (1921–), John Johansen (1916–), Kallmann, McKinnell & Knowles, and many others, but the most skilled and noteworthy practitioner in this manner was Paul Rudolph (1918–97). Educated first at Alabama Polytechnic Institute and then at the Harvard Graduate School of Design, Rudolph quickly rebelled against Walter Gropius's functionalism. From 1948 to 1957 he worked primarily in Florida, mainly designing houses. The influence of Mies van der Rohe was evident in the structural discipline he brought to bear upon many of these buildings. However, the statement of structure was never enough

236 Paul Rudolph: Walker Guest House, Sanibel Island, Florida, 1952–53.

236 for Rudolph. In works like the Walker Guest House, Sanibel Island, Florida
(1952–53), he constantly tried to elaborate upon the capabilities of the
structural frame. Rudolph also applied this inquiring attitude, one which
often led to an exploration of triangulated structures, to larger commissions
237 such as the Jewett Arts Center, Wellesley, Massachusetts (1955–58).
However, by the late 1950s Rudolph became dissatisfied with the discipline
of structure, no matter how broadly it was interpreted, and soon started to
work in a manner which enabled him more fully to achieve the Wrightian
238, 239 goal of breaking the architectural box. In his major works—the Art and
Architecture Building, Yale University, New Haven, Connecticut
(1958–64), the Interdenominational Chapel, Tuskegee Institute, Tuskegee,
Alabama (1960–69), the Boston Government Service Center (1962–69), and
the Southeastern Massachusetts Technical Institute, North Dartmouth,
Massachusetts (1963–68)—Rudolph used reinforced concrete, which he
sometimes finished with a corduroy-like texture, to create an architecture of
extraordinary intricacy in plan, elevation, and section.

   Rudolph's buildings were usually based on a twisting route that started
well outside the walls, extended to terraces, and culminated in a winding
staircase. Along the way this route intersected with or gave access to a major
outdoor or enclosed area. These spaces did not have the sense of repose that
was typical of the focal rooms in Louis Kahn's buildings. Instead, they were
defined by jutting balconies, stepping profiles, diagonal geometries, and
animated surfaces, all of which were further accentuated by daylight
pouring in from a variety of angles and directions.

237 Paul Rudolph: Mary Cooper Jewett
Arts Center, Wellesley, Massachusetts,
1955–58.

238, 239 Paul Rudolph: Art and
Architecture Building, New Haven,
Connecticut, 1958–64. View and section
perspective.

240 Robert Venturi: Franklin Delano Roosevelt Memorial Competition, 1960.

The sheer virtuosity of Rudolph's labyrinthine plans and multifaceted forms was undeniable. Nevertheless, there was something fundamentally troubling about the overwrought nature not only of Rudolph's work, but also of that of many of his contemporaries. This seemingly obsessive desire for formal variety was Rudolph's way either of compensating for what he perceived to be the lack of content in the contemporary building program or of masking the fact that he had lost touch with the culture of those for whom he was building. The unfortunate abuse of the Art and Architecture Building, culminating in 1969 in an extensive fire of suspicious origin, was one indication that something was askew. Another was the demolition in 1981 of Rudolph's Oriental Gardens housing project in New Haven, Connecticut. In designing this development in 1970 Rudolph used mobile home units in an attempt to align himself both with the future inhabitants and a rapidly growing segment of the housing industry. The project turned out to be so technically and socially ill-conceived that it was soon declared uninhabitable.

The aimlessness of many of the attempts to find an appropriate language for postwar American architecture was epitomized in 1960 by the entries to a competition for a memorial to Franklin Delano Roosevelt to be located near the Mall in Washington, D.C. There have never been many regrets that the winning scheme (by Pederson & Tilney), featuring eight Stonehenge-like slabs on which were to be inscribed excerpts of Roosevelt's speeches, was not built, mainly because Congress could not agree to appropriate funds for it. 240 The only memorable entry to that competition was by Robert Venturi (1925–), with John Rauch, George Patton, and Nicholas Gianopoulos. This project did not have as its focus a sculptural shape to compete with the Washington, Lincoln, and Jefferson memorials. Instead it featured a promenade along the Potomac River flanked by marble walls and a continuous grass mound.

264

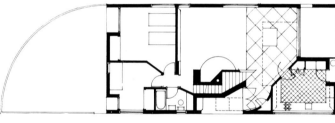

241, 242 Venturi, Rauch and Associates: House for Mrs. Venturi, Chestnut Hill, Pennsylvania, 1962–64. Facade and plan.

Venturi's scheme, his other projects of the early 1960s, and his book *Complexity and Contradiction in Architecture* (1966) all indicated a way to resolve, or at least to go beyond, the postwar dilemma of how to represent values in architecture. At one level Venturi's intention was to present an alternative to the blandness of conventional architecture. Venturi in part summarized his point by changing Mies van der Rohe's dictum "less is more" to "less is a bore." He argued for an architecture that sought neither clarity nor picturesqueness, but which instead capitalized on complexities, contradictions, ambiguities, and paradoxes—qualities which he thought consonant with the temper of the times.

Venturi's best known works were a house for his mother in Chestnut Hill, Pennsylvania (1962–64) and the Guild House, an apartment building for the elderly in Philadelphia (1962–66). Both were full of incidents and details which embodied the qualities that he enjoyed. Critics and architects have generally been put off by the second floor staircase leading to nowhere, the

241, 242
243

243 Venturi, Rauch and Associates; Guild House, Philadelphia, Pennsylvania, 1962–66.

244 Robert Venturi, Denise Scott Brown and Steven Izenour: Frontispiece of *Learning from Las Vegas*, 1972.

applied wood mouldings, and the distortions of symmetry in his mother's house. They have been equally offended by the Guild House's anodized aluminum television antenna, its round column of polished black granite at the entrance, and the perforated steel plate balcony railings. But in dismissing Venturi's architecture as coy, eclectic, and obscure, they avoided coming to terms with his more important point, one implicit in his design work, hinted at in *Complexity and Contradiction in Architecture*, and drawn out in greater detail in *Learning from Las Vegas* (1972), which he wrote with Denise Scott Brown (1931–) and Steven Izenour (1940–2001). *244*

In effect, Venturi said that architecture did not have to be "heroic and original." Instead it could draw upon a rich history. Venturi's buildings and writings contained a broad range of references, but he was especially partial to works of the Baroque period and, even more provocatively, to buildings in the American landscape, a source which he sanctioned with the phrase, "Main Street is almost all right." Hence, the house for his mother overtly drew upon the domestic architecture that Vincent Scully (1920–) had described in *The Shingle Style* (1955), the Guild House was an adaptation of an ordinary apartment house, and his F.D.R. memorial competition entry took as its point of departure an interpretation of the intentions of L'Enfant's plan.

Of course, huge questions remained about what in fact the temper of the times was, about an architect's relationship to the culture dealt with in *Learning from Las Vegas*, and about how to balance originality and learning in formulating a compelling language of architecture. Nevertheless, Venturi's work was so trenchant, especially in its critique of postwar American architecture, that no thinking member of the profession could avoid coming to terms with it.

CHAPTER NINE

Looking Backward and Forward

The practice of architecture in the United States underwent a radical transformation between 1975 and 2000. For centuries, ever since at least the Renaissance, architects made drawings to forecast what their buildings would look like and how they would be built. By the end of the twentieth century, except for initial sketches, architects no longer drew. In a period of no more than ten or fifteen years all the paraphernalia that had accompanied the hand-made drawing—the array of pencils, different types of tracing paper, erasing shields, circle and ellipse templates, etc.—was swept away by computer-aided design (CAD) software and display monitors. By 2000 it was also common to transmit drawings by email and to use digital cameras to send photographs back from building sites, thus making site visits, if not unnecessary, then certainly at least less important than they had been. By the same time the World Wide Web gave architects access to a wealth of product information that only a few years earlier took days or weeks to obtain.

Such changes were both part of and responsible for a dramatic increase in the complexity of architectural practice. As architects were making the transition from hand- to computer-generated drawings the number of consultants necessary for even the simplest project increased enormously. The usual consultants—structural engineer, mechanical engineer, landscape architect and a few others—were joined by an ever diversifying group of sub-specialists, from code consultants to curtain wall engineers, signage designers and telecommunications experts. These consultants had to be masters not only of their particular areas of expertise, but also of a myriad of regulations, as the number of building codes and related laws, often with conflicting and contradictory requirements, grew exponentially.

All of these developments were manifested in an astonishing increase in information, whether digital or on paper. The size of contracts, the thickness of specifications, and the number of drawings to produce even a small building were vastly greater in 2002 than previously. A product that an earlier generation had specified in two lines or less now needed many pages. Phrases such as "good workmanship" or "as is customary" that had served the profession so well for so long were now replaced by a numbing battery of test, submittal, and approval requirements.

Architecture, like the other professions, entered the information age awkwardly and grudgingly. However, architects were probably separated from other professionals by the sense that in this transition their very existence was at stake. It was hard enough to assimilate computers and everything they entailed. But this sea change in the culture of architectural practice was all the more difficult because it happened at the same time that other people were using computers to produce an explosion of images—the virtual world of movies, animated advertisements, and videos—which made the real environment, especially buildings, often seem nothing less than tame and boring. This fear that the built environment was losing its grip on the imagination of those who used it had a long lineage. But in the last decades of the twentieth century, as "web architects" commanded higher salaries and more glamour than traditional architects, this sense that the built environment was no longer where the action was became ever more real.

A few architects, especially in paper projects, tried to explore the interface between the virtual and the real. The New York-based firm Diller + Scofidio, for example, in 1990 designed a house (unbuilt) that ostensibly was a vacation retreat. However, it was equipped to be connected "at a moment's

245

245 Diller + Scofidio, Slow House,
Long Island, New York, 1990 (model).

notice back to the sites of anxieties" through a network of video cameras and telecommunications equipment that also gave universal access within the house to the prized "natural" view of the waterfront on which it was located.

Most American architects responded in more prosaic ways to this challenge from the world of virtual images. One reaction, especially in the face of this glut of paperwork and project coordination, was to abandon the age-old role of designer and to become a manager. Architects have always had to manage projects to see that their designs were properly constructed. But in the last decades of the twentieth century, as the balance of time and effort between design and management shifted so heavily toward the latter, it was tempting to think that design was almost an irrelevancy. The assumption of management as the primary role of the architect was all the more urgent as clients increasingly hired independent project managers to usurp some of the architect's previous role in mediating between the owner's and the contractor's interests. The donning of the garb of, if not the manager, then at least the facilitator, was also favored by architects with a populist agenda. Claiming that architecture is foremost a service, they argued that a design had to emerge from a dialogue with diverse constituents rather than be imposed by one author.

The more common response of architects to the proliferation of images and thus, as they perceived it, to the degradation of the value of architecture was to reestablish the cultural role of buildings by reassessing and reasserting the importance of their communicative power. Whereas a previous generation of architects had aspired, at least in public or written statements, toward symbolic objectivity, by the mid-1970s discussions of "meaning" in architecture were common. That topic was then expanded and expounded in a flood of publications from critics and theorists who drew upon works of anthropology, philosophy, and linguistics to make the case, in language that too often slipped from the obscure to the obscurantist, for the cultural significance of architecture.

In this quest for meaning architects all too easily concluded, especially as they were aided and abetted by critics and theorists, that—to borrow a phrase from advertising (an increasingly competitive field)—"image is everything." Thus, the complex and subtle Vitruvian discourse between *commoditas* (convenience), *firmitas* (strength), and *venustas* (beauty) that had so long sustained the profession, even in the preceding periods of modernism, was often quickly jettisoned. By the last decades of the twentieth century it was tempting to leave all of those troublesome *commoditas* and *firmitas* issues to the engineers and managers and to think of buildings as first and foremost attention-grabbing advertisements for the institutions they housed.

246 Santiago Calatrava, Quadracci Pavilion, Milwaukee Art Museum, Milwaukee, Wisconsin, 1998–2001.

This desire above all for the photogenic effect left its impact on all building types, but no institution felt the pressure to use its building as a means of self promotion more heavily than the museum. Museum directors and trustees frequently seemed to lack the confidence that the art within their buildings would attract visitors. The building itself had to be an alluring spectacle. Charismatic architects, superstars, were given commissions to design buildings in places they may never have previously visited and knew nothing about. Thus, Norman Foster (1935–), Renzo Piano (1937–), Raphael Moneo (1937–), Yoshio Taniguchi (1937–), Tadao Ando (1941–), Zaha Hadid (1950–), and Santiago Calatrava (1951–) *246* received commissions in the United States. Correspondingly, I. M. Pei (1917–), Frank Gehry (1929–), Robert Venturi, Richard Meier (1934–), *258, 259, 255* and Steven Holl (1947–) built on foreign soil. Brought in as exotic *247* imports, these architects rarely disappointed their clients. They delivered spectacular designs whose primary purpose seemed to be less the display of a collection of works of art and more the making of an iconic image, one which would promote not only the museum but also the city in which the museum was located.

247 Steven Holl, Kiasma Museum of Contemporary Art, Helsinki, Finland, 1992–98.

One source of this imagery was the history of architecture. By the late
1970s it was no longer, as it had been only a few years earlier, unacceptable
to pattern new buildings overtly after historical precedents. In part, this
response resulted from the renewed interest in the communicative power of
buildings. The historic styles and periods of architecture had associations that
modern buildings, especially those that aspired to symbolic objectivity,
lacked. This renewed interest in the historic styles over modern design,
however that was defined, was given a further boost by the technical
shortcomings of so many modern buildings, especially those that had been
based on lines of thought that were conveniently but not very knowingly
summarized by the word "functionalism." Compared to the glass prisms
and concrete bunkers of the recent past, the visual richness and common-
sense building techniques of the historic styles of architecture started to
seem attractive.

Architects came to this conclusion in response to forces outside the
profession as much as those from within. A growing interest in historic
preservation put them at the least on the defensive. The desire to save
historic buildings was slow to develop in the United States. At the beginning
of the nineteenth century it was a concern of only a handful of people,
mainly antiquarians. For the following hundred years there were isolated
efforts to save buildings such as Independence Hall in Philadelphia and the
Old South Meeting House in Boston. But these were exceptions.

The first broad federal legislation on this subject was the Antiquities Act of 1906, which allowed the federal government to save as national monuments properties that were significant to the nation. In 1935 the Historic Sites Act broadened the federal role. However, the major turning point in the legitimization of historic preservation was the passage in 1966 of the National Historic Preservation Act that established the National Register of Historic Places. By then historic preservation was no longer the interest of an exclusive blue-blooded, antiquarian-minded elite, but instead was a broad-based and self-confident force in shaping the future of the American city.

The interest in historic buildings manifested itself in practice in several ways. Unlike a quarter century earlier, by 2000 it was much more difficult to tear down older buildings of merit, and laws requestnly required the owners of historic properties to maintain and refurbish them. The contrast between the fates of Pennsylvania Station and Grand Central Station in New York City is telling. In large part due to the revulsion that ensued from the destruction of Pennsylvania Station in 1965, the attempt in 1966 to impose a forty-story tower on Grand Central was disallowed in a ground-breaking legal decision. In the late 1990s the station, which had deteriorated badly, was refurbished in an expensive but meticulous restoration by the firm of Beyer, Blinder, Belle.

In the last quarter of the twentieth century architects who specialized in historic preservation not only increased in number, but also secured a place of respectability within the profession that they had not previously occupied. These firms frequently also made the case that new buildings, and not just those in historic districts, should be designed in a recognizable historic style. First and foremost, especially after the Beaux-Arts exhibition at the Museum of Modern Art, New York, in 1976, that meant the classical tradition. If that architecture had been vital in fourth-century BC Greece, first-century AD Rome, the Italian Renaissance, eighteenth-century France, and the United States of 1900, why could it not still have value and meaning in the late twentieth century?

In response to this fundamental question, classical architecture was rendered in several ways. The architect who became known as the strictest interpreter of this tradition was Allan Greenberg (1939–). A careful student of the history of architecture, especially that of the colonial period, Greenberg argued that classical architecture's strict canons not only could be maintained but also should be. After all they were rooted in anthropomorphic realities that through the centuries had become embodied in the humanistic traditions of Europe and America. His projects, few in number but carefully detailed, were knowing adaptations of age-old details, motifs and elements to solve the design problems at hand.

248

248 Allan Greenberg, the Beechwoods residence, New England, 1988–92.

249 Robert A. M. Stern, Spangler Campus Center, Harvard Business School, Boston, Massachusetts, 1997–2001.

Robert A. M. Stern (1939–) was more prolific than Allan Greenberg. His work was also more programmatically varied. Nevertheless it was based on similar principles and assumptions. The author of a valuable book about George Howe and the lead co-author of a monumental multi-volume study of the architecture of New York City, Stern made the case that new buildings should follow past prototypes. For his vacation houses he frequently drew upon the body of work that Vincent Scully had included in his path-breaking book *The Shingle Style* (1955). For public architecture, especially buildings within classically planned campuses, Stern produced works that, when finished, could easily have been mistaken for having been constructed well before the phrase "modern architecture" came into common currency.

The Spangler Center at the Harvard Business School (1997–2001) was a case in point. The commission for the planning of the School was won in a competition in 1927 by the firm of McKim, Mead & White, which by then no longer included any of the founding partners, and the original buildings, constructed in the following five years, were in an adulterated brick Georgian style. Subsequent additions to the campus, especially a chapel by Moshe Safdie (1930–) in the shape of a copper-clad cylinder intersecting a glass pyramid, had been more adventurous. At the Spangler Center, containing student dining halls, lounges, and recreation facilities, Stern in effect turned the clock back. The language of brick walls with inset arched openings for tall ground-floor windows, projecting end and center bays, slate and copper roof, white-painted dentilled cornice, limestone quoins and stringcourse, and leaded glass side-lights, was predictable to the point of banality. A smug complacency suffused everything. In the ascendancy of American corporate culture in the late 1990s, as MBA graduates made their way from such environments into the similarly paneled and sheltered club and boardroom world, that attitude may have been defensible. But the ensuing corporate scandals, especially given that the most disgraced of the bankrupt companies was the largest employer of newly minted MBAs, should have cast doubt not simply on this approach to architecture but on the state of mind that gave rise to it.

Such questions were certainly raised earlier. Thus, another approach was to adopt the principles of classical architecture—axial planning and distinctions between base, middle, and top—but to render them in a manner that was thought to resonate more compatibly with a contemporary state of mind. That usually entailed a degree of abstraction, attained by jettisoning the tradition of moldings and shades and shadows to which previous generations had given so much thought and care. Successful buildings along these lines were designed by Michael Dennis & Associates at Carnegie

249

275

250 Michael Dennis & Associates, University Center, Carnegie Mellon University, Pittsburgh, Pennsylvania, 1991–95.

Mellon University in Pittsburgh, Pennsylvania, as part of a master plan competition that Dennis (1937–) had won in 1990. The campus had originally been designed by the firm of Palmer and Hornbostel in 1909 in a style that mixed classical composition techniques and motifs with freely rendered materials and details. From the 1930s through the mid-1980s, as the Beaux-Arts-inspired plan fell into disrepute, the integrity of the master plan was largely ignored and a discordant series of modern buildings was constructed. Dennis's plan sought to reestablish the intention of
250   Hornbostel's work by locating a student center at the core of the campus, and thus creating two new quadrangles, one oriented around a new playing field. Dennis used Hornbostel's industrial brick with white stone trim for an architecture of brick piers filled in with metal-framed windows and spanned by steel lintels.

251   Michael Graves (1934–) has produced the most sustained body of work that has at its core interpretive rather than literal themes from classical architecture. Graves began his career as a committed modernist. His work was included in the influential 1975 book *Five Architects*, which also presented projects by Peter Eisenman (1932–), Charles Gwathmey (1938–), John Hejduk (1929–2000), and Richard Meier. Shortly thereafter Graves lost confidence in modern architecture's ability to be meaningful to the broad public that uses and experiences buildings. He then began to elaborate his own classical language, drawn from a variety of sources

276

but especially from French neoclassicism. In projects that ranged from beach houses to office buildings, Graves used axial planning and symmetry to govern a distinctive architecture that included cylindrical columns, towers with attenuated pyramidal roofs, elemental pergolas, walls composed of flat piers arranged in tight geometrical grids, pronounced cornices, and exaggerated arches.

Because of its overscaled keystone motif, Graves's fourteen-story Public   *252*
Service Administration Building in Portland, Oregon, attracted much attention and criticism when it was completed in 1982. From around 1900 until the building slump of the Great Depression, American architects had of course struggled to give appropriate expression to that supposedly most contemporary building type, the skyscraper. In the period after the Second World War the glass and steel prism was favored, as mirror-glass windows and spandrel panels became indistinguishable on the exterior. In reaction, architects such as Graves and the firm Kohn Pederson Fox looked back to the beginning of the twentieth century when skyscrapers had windows that looked like windows, were clad in stone, and had a distinguishable base,

251 Michael Graves, Benacerref House Addition, Princeton, New Jersey, 1969.

252 Michael Graves,
Portland Public Service
Administration Building,
Portland, Oregon, 1981–82.

253 Kohn Pederson Fox,
225 West Wacker Drive,
Chicago, Illinois, 1985–89.

253 middle, and top. KPF projects such as 1325 Avenue of the Americas in New York City and 225 West Wacker Drive in Chicago recalled the Art Deco skyscrapers of the 1920s.

When such buildings are compared with the ones after which they were modeled, it is difficult not to conclude that, even as antidotes to the banality of the post-Miesian boxes they replaced, there was something lacking in this approach. The abstract way in which both specific details and larger architectural elements were reduced too often betrayed a lack of conviction about what this rummaging through the history books was all about.

Other architects came to terms with such feelings by designing with irony, or at least with an overtly expressed self-consciousness about the appropriation of historical elements. This was true of much of the work of Venturi and Rauch, which became Venturi, Rauch and Scott Brown in 1980 and Venturi, Scott Brown and Associates in 1987. In the last quarter of the twentieth century this firm had ample opportunity to give specific

278

254 Venturi, Scott Brown
and Associates, Seattle Art
Museum, Seattle, Washington,
1984–91.

255 Venturi, Scott Brown
and Associates, Sainsbury Wing,
National Gallery, London,
1985–91.

expression to the ideas articulated in *Complexity and Contradiction in Architecture* and *Learning from Las Vegas* (see above, p. 267). The results were full of interest and ingenuity. Some of them, notwithstanding Venturi's stated preference, were more "heroic and original" than "ugly and ordinary." Nevertheless, they invariably lacked the kind of authenticity that is the hallmark of accomplished architecture.

The equivocal nature of the built work of Venturi's firm resulted from the fact that their buildings too often were illustrations of ideas, and from their preference, in a quest for complexity and contradiction, for mannerist and therefore unsettling gestures. Such qualities were especially evident in projects that were additions to or near historic structures. These designs were ostensibly shaped by specific architectural devices supposedly chosen to show deference to the buildings in whose shadows they were located; but the working out of those devices invariably resulted in the upstaging of the building to which the addition was supposed to be subordinate.

These complex problems, illustrating both the strengths and weaknesses of Venturi's approach, were evident in university projects such as the Allen Memorial Art Museum at Oberlin College, Ohio (1973–77), and the Charles P. Stevenson, Jr., Library at Bard College, Annandale-on-Hudson,

New York (1989–93), but they can best be understood in two prominent commissions for art museums, the Seattle Art Museum in Seattle, Washington (1984–91), and the Sainsbury Wing of the National Gallery in London (1985–91). Both were set in complex contexts of older structures and surrounding streets. In both cases the architects were deferential to that context. Both buildings have curved or eroded corners that join and thus undercut the potential monumentality of two prominent facades. Yet both contain specific eye-popping, even tortured, gestures and details that belie the larger strategy. At the Seattle Art Museum the exterior is decorated with a pattern that incorporates segmental, triangular and ogee arches which recall the arcaded ground floors of nearby commercial buildings. At the Sainsbury Wing, the architects used the entablature and Corinthian pilasters of Wilkins's National Gallery, but given the irregular shape of the facade, the latter are spaced out in an irregular and unsettling manner.

254
255

Perhaps the most ambiguous aspect of the work of Venturi and Rauch and its successor firms is whether it is the product of a traditional or a modern sensibility. When Venturi reintroduced the discussion of historic buildings into the discourse on architecture, that approach was novel and provocative. Ten or twenty years later, as the possibilities of various forms of historicism were played out, modernist forms again seemed promising. Some architects had never given them up; others, especially a younger generation, discovered them afresh.

The discussion about modernism in the last quarter of the twentieth century repeated, often with a disturbing lack of awareness of what had gone on from 1925 to 1975, themes that had been touched upon earlier. In Europe in the period immediately after the First World War the new architecture had been associated with, often without precision, visions of a new society. In the United States that idea was greeted toward the end of the century with even less conviction than it had been earlier. Modern architecture was sometimes deemed to be an appropriate response to events that culminated with the collapse of the Soviet Union and the consequent triumph of consumer capitalism and globalization. Those sentiments were associated with Rem Koolhaas (1944–), who wrote about shopping as the quintessential experience of modern culture. But his understanding of capitalism was tenuous, and of the relationship between capitalism and democracy even more so. In all of this the necessity for modern design, as opposed to any other approach, remained ill-defined.

Lacking a societal agenda, except as a vague evocation of a future (whether rosy or bleak), modern architecture in the last decades of the twentieth century evolved in two directions. One was a frank, if often unacknowledged, revival and at its best reinterpretation of forms from earlier periods of modern design. The forms of the white (as it appeared in black-and-white photographs) modern architecture of the 1920s were especially popular, but they were then superseded by motifs from buildings of the 1940s and 1950s. The other approach was a quest for the strikingly original. This search was often based on or justified by highly personal and intuitive leaps. Thus, for example, Frank Gehry found inspiration in childhood memories of a fish in a bathtub, while Steven Holl spoke of insights derived from a sponge in his bathtub.

At their worst these impulses resulted in a set of frequently repeated architectural clichés such as roofs in the shape of eccentric vaults, walls tilted at an angle, and the use of materials like polished concrete and acrylic resin. At their best they produced buildings of breathtaking accomplishment. However, it has to be said that no one in this period produced a body of work as coherent and compelling as that summarized in, for example, Frank Lloyd Wright's language of walls and roofs, Le Corbusier's five points of architecture, Mies van der Rohe's ruminations upon corner details and their implications, or Louis Kahn's exploration of the relationship of beam to column—certainly high and perhaps unattainable standards.

By far the most original architect was Frank Gehry. In 1985 Gehry was hardly known even within the profession. By 2000 he was the most widely celebrated architect in the world. However, this transformation did not happen overnight. Canadian by birth, Gehry was brought up in Los Angeles

256 Frank O. Gehry, Gehry Residence, Santa Monica, California,
1977–78; 1991–94.

and educated at the University of Southern California and the Harvard
Graduate School of Design. In the late 1950s he began designing buildings
that elaborated upon many formal mannerisms of other architects working
in southern California.

The project that gave Gehry wide publicity was the renovations and
additions that he did in date? to his own house, an ordinary gambrel-roofed   *256*
bungalow originally built around 1920. One distinctive quality of the
project was his use of materials such as chain-link fencing, corrugated steel
walls, and asphalt paving that are not ordinarily associated with residential
architecture. The other was the way in which the additions in these materials
changed the nature of the house. The outside and the inside, so clearly
defined in the original bungalow, were made to interpenetrate completely,
and previously distinct interior spaces were intertwined.

In the following twenty years Gehry consistently carried out this
subversion of traditional building typologies. One strategy was to conceive
of buildings not as a single entity under one roof but instead as an
aggregation of small separate structures. The result, for example in the
Winton Guest House (1982–87), was an intentionally disorienting inversion   *257*
of scale. Because of its massing the building seemed larger than its actual
area; at the same time the parts had a similarly distorted scale, a kind of
doll's-house miniaturization.

283

257 Frank O. Gehry, Winton Guest House, Wayzata, Minnesota, 1982–87.

Another theme in Gehry's works, revealed in the renovation of his own house but also present in even earlier projects, was a tendency to free the structure, whether wood studs or steel beams and columns, from an enveloping skin. However, more commonly Gehry did just the opposite. Many of his early projects had a cladding system that blurred traditional junctions, for example at corners and between walls and roof. This search for a universal cladding system was manifested in the Steve Davis Studio and Residence in Malibu, California (1968–72), a trapezoidal box, clad in corrugated steel with a slightly tilted flat roof that was like a fifth elevation.

Many of these preoccupations were prominent in other projects by Gehry. But they were brought to full realization in his Guggenheim 258, 259 Museum in Bilbao, Spain (1991–97). The museum was set in a derelict industrial area on the city's waterfront. From the surrounding hills it looked like a vast undulating organism, with its titanium skin glistening in the sun. Traditional clues to reveal its scale were lacking as it spanned highways and railroad tracks. Equally startling were the views of the building when it was first glimpsed through the tangle of traditional streets lined with masonry constructions. In brief, the museum was truly incomparable. As such, it invited questions about the possibility, as the occasion arises, to build adjacent to it or to plan a district or an entire city according to such principles. Similar questions can also be asked about its interior, which

258, 259 Frank O. Gehry,
Guggenheim Museum,
Bilbao, Spain, 1991–97:
exterior and interior.

260 Richard Meier, The Atheneum, New Harmony, Indiana, 1975–79.

was as breathtaking as the exterior. The character of the spaces was not describable in conventional terms: words like "ceiling," "wall," and "window" did not apply. Given that the building was designed from the outside in, its suitability for the display and appreciation of works of art was open to question. Such issues were apparent in other projects by Gehry. His Experience Music Project Museum in Seattle (1999–2000) also had a stunning exterior, but within this thoroughly unconventional enclosure there was an undeveloped interior with indifferent displays.

Other, perhaps more conventional, approaches to modern design have better accommodated the requirements of diverse and demanding programs. The work of Richard Meier is a case in point. Over a thirty-year period he designed a wide array of buildings that included houses, apartment complexes, office buildings, hotels, museums, and churches. They were located on dense urban sites as well as in countryside with no other structures in view. Beginning with vacation houses in the environs of New York City, Meier has now built throughout the United States, in Europe and the Far East.

These buildings drew inspiration as well as specific forms from modern architecture of the 1920s, especially from Le Corbusier's works of that decade and from specific buildings like Brinkman and Van der Vlugt's Van Nelle factory in Rotterdam. From these Meier elaborated a language of forms that had as its hallmarks flat roofs, white walls, strip windows, floating

260–262

261, 262 Richard Meier, The Getty
Center, Los Angeles, California, 1984–97:
axonometric and main court.

planes, and industrial railings, all governed by strict geometries. In effect, by deriving his work so clearly from a canonical strain of modernism, Meier disavowed the role of original form-maker that so many American modern architects have tried to assume.

The result has been a thoroughly consistent body of work that has shown remarkable resilience and inventiveness, its obvious debts to earlier buildings notwithstanding. The culmination and summary of this work was Meier's design for the Getty Center in Los Angeles, California (1984–97). Located on a hilly site, adjacent to the San Diego Freeway and near a residential neighborhood, the Getty Center was a vast complex of buildings that included a museum, a center for the history of art and the humanities, a conservation institute, an auditorium, and a restaurant. Taking advantage of the varied terrain and the distant views offered by the site, Meier used axial organizing devices to create a contemporary temple-like complex of buildings that were planned with equally pronounced geometries.

With projects now spanning the globe, there is certainly much to admire in practices as comprehensive, consistent, and resourceful as those of Frank Gehry and Richard Meier. But in an ever-shrinking world, the future of architecture may belong to practitioners who, either because they have not had the opportunity to build far-flung projects or because they simply prefer to work within a restricted context, have given intense scrutiny to local circumstances and have gradually built up a body of work enriched by the

261, 262

263 Antoine Predock, Fuller House, Scottsdale, Arizona, 1984–87.

264 James Cutler, Virginia Merrill Bloedel Education Center,
Bainbridge Island, Washington, 1992.

resulting insights. Throughout the United States many architects are now
practicing, often without much publicity, who, taken together, are defining
an architecture that is neither historicist nor modernist. It owes a debt to
specific locales or regions, but it does not employ the cloying regionalist
clichés of previous periods. Thus, the work of Antoine Predock (1936–)   263
draws great sustenance from the landscape of the Southwest, especially the
enigmatic characteristics of the desert. The buildings of James Cutler (1949–)   264
reflect both his study with Louis Kahn at the University of Pennsylvania and
a love of the materials and traditions of the Pacific Northwest where
he works. Similarly, the best work of Peter Bohlin (1937–) is rooted in the
Pennsylvania countryside.

An equivalent impulse spurred the work of Samuel Mockbee
(1944–2001) and the Rural Studio. Mockbee founded the Studio in 1992   265
when teaching at Auburn University in Alabama. He did so out of the
conviction that architectural education should not be simply about
hypothetical projects, that the profession has a responsibility to improve the

265 Samuel Mockbee and the Rural Studio, Bryant (Hay Bale) House, Mason's
Bend, Alabama, 1994.

living conditions of the poor, and that the fundamentals of construction
should be at the root of architectural form. Mockbee located the Studio in
Hale County, one of the poorest regions of the United States. There for a
period of almost ten years, until his untimely death, he directed a series of
student-designed and built projects. These were constructed on limited
budgets and often with discarded materials such as automobile windshields
and tires, combining structural inventiveness with an affinity for the humble
buildings of the region. The result was an architecture that was both highly
inventive and appropriate for its context, small buildings but eloquent
statements about important issues.

   In the aftermath of the devastating events of 11 September 2001 there was
an unprecedented amount of discussion by both architects and the public
about what should replace Minoru Yamasaki's twin towers of the World
Trade Center in New York City (1966–77), a complex of buildings that had
never been popular with either practitioners or the public. This turning
point, "the day that the world changed," could also have been the occasion
for the American architectural profession to conduct a broad reassessment of
its role in society. But that kind of inquiry was surprisingly mute. Certainly
there is a great distance, both physically and spiritually, between the Hay
Bale House in Alabama and the canyons of skyscrapers in Lower Manhattan.
However, American architecture could now benefit from an understanding
of what that gap is about and of how to bridge it.

290

Bibliography

The literature on American architecture is vast and varied. The bibliography on Frank Lloyd Wright alone occupies over 250 pages and encompasses short articles in ephemeral but significant magazines and major monographs. The following references were useful in writing this book and are cited for further reading on specific subjects.

JSAH: Journal of the Society of Architectural Historians

Chapter One

GENERAL
George Kubler, *The Religious Architecture of New Mexico in the Colonial Period and Since the American Occupation* (Colorado Springs, Colo., 1940); Neil Harris, *The Artist in American Society* (New York, N.Y., 1966), pp. 2–25; Anthony N. B. Garvan, *Architecture and Town Planning in Colonial Connecticut* (New Haven, Conn., 1951); Fiske Kimball, *Domestic Architecture of the American Colonies and of the Early Republic* (New York, N.Y., 1922; republished 1966); Henry Chandlee Forman, *The Architecture of the Old South: the Medieval Style, 1585–1850* (Cambridge, Mass., 1948); Dell Upton, "Seventeenth-Century Virginia: A New Architecture for a New Society," paper delivered at the "American Home" session, Society of Architectural Historians convention, New Haven, Conn., April 1982; Rosalie Fellows Bailey, *Pre-Revolutionary Dutch Houses and Families in Northern New Jersey and Southern New York* (New York, N.Y., 1934; republished 1966); Abbott Lowell Cummings, *The Framed Houses of Massachusetts Bay, 1625–1725* (Cambridge, Mass., 1974); Charles Albert Wright, *Some Oldtime Meeting Houses of the Connecticut Valley* (Chicopee Falls, Mass., 1911); Marcus Whiffen, *The Public Buildings of Williamsburg, Colonial Capitol of Virginia* (Williamsburg, Va., 1958); T. T. Waterman and J. A. Barrows, *Domestic Colonial Architecture of Tidewater Virginia* (New York, N.Y., 1932); Thomas T. Waterman, *The Mansions of Virginia, 1706–1776* (Chapel Hill, N.C., 1946); Aymar Embury, *Early American Churches* (New York, N.Y., 1914); Charles A. Place, "From Meeting House to Church in New England," *Old Time New England* 13 (October 1922, January 1923, April 1923): 69–77,

111–23, 149–64; On Newport: Antoinette Downing and Vincent Scully, Jr., *The Architectural Heritage of Newport, Rhode Island, 1640–1915* (Cambridge, Mass., 1952), pp. 11–42; William B. Rhoads, *The Colonial Revival* (New York, N.Y., 1977), 2 vols.; Durand Echeverria, *Mirage in the West: A History of the French Image of American Society to 1815* (Princeton, N.J., 1957), pp. 3–38.

INDIVIDUAL ARCHITECTS AND BUILDINGS
James Grote Van Derpool, "The Restoration of St. Luke's, Smithfield, Virginia," *JSAH* 17 (March 1958): 12–18; John Coolidge, "Hingham Builds a Meetinghouse," *New England Quarterly* 34 (December 1961): 435–61; Glenn Patton, "The College of William and Mary, Williamsburg, and the Enlightenment," *JSAH* 29 (March 1970): 24–32; On Independence Hall: Hugh Morrison, *Early American Architecture* (New York, N.Y., 1952), pp. 532–36; On Munday: Downing and Scully, *The Architectural Heritage of Newport*, pp. 43–71; Carl Bridenbaugh, *Peter Harrison, First American Architect* (Chapel Hill, N.C., 1949).

Chapter Two

CONTEMPORARY TEXTS
Thomas Jefferson Architect: Original Designs in the Collection of Thomas Jefferson Coolidge, Junior, with an Essay and Notes by Fiske Kimball (Boston, Mass. 1916; republished 1968); Asher Benjamin, *The American Builder's Companion, or, a New System of Architecture: Particularly Adapted to the Present Style of Building in the United States of America* (Boston, Mass., 1806; 6th edition [1827] republished 1967).

GENERAL

Harold Kirker and James Kirker, *Bulfinch's Boston, 1787–1817* (New York, N.Y., 1964); Talbot Hamlin, *Greek Revival Architecture in America* (New York, N.Y., 1944; republished 1966); Richard Carrott, *The Egyptian Revival* (Berkeley, Calif., 1978); On the adaptation and varieties of classical architecture: *The White Pine Series of Architectural Monographs* (1915–1928, 1932–1941); John W. Reps, *Monumental Washington; the Planning and Development of the Capital Center* (Princeton, N.J., 1967).

INDIVIDUAL ARCHITECTS AND BUILDINGS

Harold Kirker, *The Architecture of Charles Bulfinch* (Cambridge, Mass., 1969); On the Virginia State Capitol: Sidney Fiske Kimball, "Thomas Jefferson and the First Monument of the Classical Revival in America," *American Institute of Architects Journal* 3 (September–November 1915): 370–33, 473–91; Ihna Thayer Frary, *Thomas Jefferson, Architect and Builder* (Richmond, Va., 1931); Karl Lehmann, *Thomas Jefferson, American Humanist* (Chicago, Ill., 1947), pp. 156–76; William B. O'Neal, *Jefferson's Buildings at the University of Virginia: The Rotunda* (Charlottesville, Va., 1960); Buford Pickens, "Mr. Jefferson as Revolutionary Architect," *JSAH* 34 (December 1975): 257–79; Robert L. Alexander, *The Architecture of Maximilian Godefroy* (Baltimore, Md., 1974); Agnes Addison Gilchrist, "John McComb, Sr. and Jr., in New York, 1784–1799," *JSAH* 31 (March 1972): 10–21; Hanna Hryniewiecka Lerski, *William Jay, Itinerant English Architect, 1792–1837* (New York, N.Y., 1983); Talbot Hamlin, *Benjamin Henry Latrobe* (New York, N.Y., 1955); Fiske Kimball, "Latrobe's Designs for the Baltimore Cathedral," *Architectural Record* 42 (December 1917): 540–56, 43 (January 1918): 35–51; H. M. Pierce Gallagher, *Robert Mills, Architect of the Washington Monument, 1781–1855* (New York, N.Y., 1935); Agnes Addison Gilchrist, *William Strickland, Architect and Engineer, 1788–1854* (Philadelphia, Pa., 1950); Agnes Addison Gilchrist, "Additions to William Strickland, Architect and Engineer, 1788–1854," *JSAH* 13 (October 1954): documentary supplement; Jack Quinan, "Asher Benjamin and American Architecture," *JSAH* 38 (October 1979): 244–61; Fiske Kimball, *Mr. Samuel McIntire, Carver, the Architect of Salem* (Salem, Mass., 1940); H. Paul Caemmerer, *The Life of Pierre Charles L'Enfant* (Washington, D.C., 1950; republished 1970); Glenn Brown, *History of the United States Capitol* (Washington, D.C., 1900).

Chapter Three

CONTEMPORARY TEXTS

Arthur D. Gilman, "Architecture in the United States," *North American Review* 58 (April 1844): 436–80; Howard A. Small, ed., *Form and Function: Remarks on Art by Horatio Greenough* (Berkeley, Calif., 1947); James Bogardus, *Cast Iron Buildings: Their Construction and Advantages* (New York, N.Y., 1856; republished 1970); Alexander Jackson Davis, *Rural Residences* (New York, N.Y., 1837; republished 1980); Alexander Jackson Downing, *Cottage Residences* (New York, N.Y., 1842; republished 1968).

GENERAL

Robert W. Winter, "Fergusson and Garbett in American Architectural Theory," *JSAH* 17 (Winter 1958): 25–29; Roger B. Stein, *John Ruskin and Aesthetic Thought in America, 1840–1900* (Cambridge, Mass., 1967); Carl Condit, *American Building Art: The Nineteenth Century* (New York, N.Y., 1960), pp. 75–181, 197–222; Alan Trachtenberg, *Brooklyn Bridge, Fact and Symbol* (New York, N.Y., 1965); Carroll L. V. Meeks, *The Railroad Station* (New Haven, Conn., 1956); Henry-Russell Hitchcock, *Rhode Island Architecture* (Providence, R.I., 1939), pp. 36–43; Turpin Bannister, "Bogardus Revisited: Part I: 'The Iron Front,'" *JSAH* 15 (March 1956): 12–22; David M. Kahn, "Bogardus, Fire, and the Iron Tower," *JSAH* 35 (October 1976): 186–203; Williamson Jefferson, *The American Hotel* (New York, N.Y., 1930); Phoebe B. Stanton, *The Gothic Revival & American Church Architecture, An Episode in Taste, 1840–1856* (Baltimore, Md., 1968); Rachel Wischnitzer, *Synagogue Architecture in the United States* (Philadelphia, Pa., 1955), pp. 25–63; David Rothman, *The Discovery of the Asylum* (Boston, Mass., 1971); Dolores Hayden, *Seven American Utopias: The Architecture of Communitarian Socialism, 1790–1975* (Cambridge, Mass., 1976); John Phillips Coolidge, *Mill and Mansion, a Study of Architecture and Society in Lowell, Massachusetts, 1820–1865* (New York, N.Y., 1942); John Borden Armstrong, *Factory Under the Elms: a History of Harrisville, N.H., 1774–1969* (Cambridge, Mass., 1969); Paul E. Sprague, "The Origin of Balloon Framing," *JSAH* 40 (December 1981): 311–19; Vincent Scully, "Romantic Rationalism and the Expression of Structure in Wood: Downing, Wheeler, Gardner and the 'Stick Style,' 1840–1876," *Art Bulletin* 35 (June 1953): 121–42; David P. Handlin, *The American Home, Architecture and Society, 1815–1915* (Boston, Mass., 1979), pp. 3–88.

INDIVIDUAL ARCHITECTS AND BUILDINGS
Everard M. Upjohn, *Richard Upjohn, Architect and Churchman* (New York, N.Y., 1939); On Renwick: William H. Pierson, Jr., *American Buildings and Their Architects, Technology and the Picturesque, the Corporate and the Early Gothic Styles* (New York, N.Y., 1978), pp. 206–69; Roger Hale Newton, *Town & Davis, Architects; Pioneers in American Revivalist Architecture, 1812–1870* (New York, N.Y., 1942).

Chapter Four

CONTEMPORARY TEXTS
William A. Coles, ed., *Architecture and Society, Selected Writings of Henry Van Brunt* (Cambridge, Mass. 1969); Donald Hoffman, ed., *John Wellborn Root, The Meanings of Architecture* (New York, N.Y., 1967); Louis H. Sullivan, *Kindergarten Chats* (appeared serially in 1901–1902 in *Interstate Architect & Builder*, revised in 1918, published as Claude Bragdon, ed., *Kindergarten Chats on Architecture, Education and Democracy* (Lawrence, Kan., 1934), reprinted in Isabel Athey, ed., *Kindergarten Chats and Other Writings* (New York, N.Y., 1947)); Louis H. Sullivan, *The Autobiography of an Idea* (appeared serially in 1922–23 in *Journal of the American Institute of Architects*; published in New York in 1926; republished in 1956).

GENERAL
David T. Van Zanten, "Jacob Wrey Mould: Echoes of Owen Jones and the High Victorian Styles in New York, 1853–1865," *JSAH* 23 (March 1969): 41–57; Arnold Lewis, "A European Profile of American Architecture," *JSAH* 37 (December 1978): 265–82; Winston Weisman, "New York and the Problem of the First Skyscraper," *JSAH* 12 (March 1953): 13–21; Bainbridge Bunting, *Houses of Boston's Back Bay* (Cambridge, Mass., 1967); Vincent Scully, *The Shingle Style and the Stick Style* (New Haven, Conn., 1971); David P. Handlin, *The American Home, Architecture and Society, 1815–1915* (Boston, Mass., 1979) pp. 89–490; Winston Weisman, "Philadelphia Functionalism and Sullivan," *JSAH* 20 (March 1961): 3–19; Donald D. Egbert, "The Idea of Organic Expression and American Architecture," in Stow Persons, ed., *Evolutionary Thought in America* (New Haven, Conn., 1950); Sigfried Giedion, *Space, Time and Architecture* (Cambridge, Mass., 5th ed., 1967), pp. 368–96; Colin Rowe, "Chicago Frame," *Architectural Review* 120 (November 1956): 285–89; Winston Weisman, "A New View of Skyscraper History," in Edgar Kaufmann, Jr., ed., *The Rise of an American Architecture* (New York, N.Y., 1970), pp. 113–60.

INDIVIDUAL ARCHITECTS AND BUILDINGS
Helen Kramer, "Detlef Lienau," *JSAH* 14 (March 1955): 18–25; Montgomery Schuyler, "A Great American Architect: Leopold Eidlitz; Ecclesiastical and Domestic Work," *Architectural Record* 24 (September, October, November, 1908): 164–79, 277–92, 365–78; Paul R. Baker, *Richard Morris Hunt* (Cambridge, Mass., 1980); Winston Weisman, "The Commercial Architecture of George B. Post," *JSAH* 31 (October 1972): 176–203; James F. O'Gorman, *The Architecture of Frank Furness* (Philadelphia, Pa., 1973); Mariana Van Rensselaer, *Henry Hobson Richardson and His Works* (Boston, Mass, 1888; reprinted 1969); Henry-Russell Hitchcock, *The Architecture of Henry Hobson Richardson* (New York, N.Y., 1936; revised edition 1961); Richard Chafee, "Richardson's Record at the Ecole des Beaux Arts," *JSAH* 36 (October 1977): 175–84; Harriet Monroe, *John Wellborn Root, a Study of His Life and Work* (Boston, Mass., 1896; reprinted 1968); Donald Hoffman, *The Architecture of John Wellborn Root* (Baltimore, Md., 1973); Hugh Morrison, *Louis Sullivan, Prophet of Modern Architecture* (New York, N.Y., 1935); Philip Johnson, "Is Sullivan the Father of Functionalism?" *Art News* 55 (December 1956): 44–46; Vincent Scully, "Louis Sullivan's Architectural Ornament," *Perspecta* 5 (1959): 73–80; Willard Connely, *Louis Sullivan As He Lived: The Shaping of American Architecture* (New York, N.Y., 1960); Albert Bush-Brown, *Louis Sullivan* (New York, N.Y., 1960).

Chapter Five

CONTEMPORARY TEXTS
Montgomery Schuyler, *American Architecture and Other Writings*, ed. William Jordy and Ralph Coe (Cambridge, Mass., 1961); William Robert Ware, *The American Vignola* (Scranton, Pa., 1906; republished 1977); *A Monograph on the Works of McKim, Mead & White, 1879–1915* (New York, N.Y. 1915; republished 1977), 4 vols.; Daniel H. Burnham and Edward H. Bennett, Charles Moore, ed., *Plan of Chicago* (Chicago, Ill., 1909; republished 1970); Frank Lloyd Wright, *Ausgeführte Bauten und Entwürfe* (Berlin, 1910; republished 1975 and 1982); Edgar Kaufmann, Jr., and Ben Raeburn, ed., *Frank Lloyd Wright, Writings and Buildings* (New York, N.Y., 1960).

GENERAL

Ernest Flagg, "The Ecole des Beaux-Arts," *Architectural Record* 3 (January–March, April–June, 1894): 302–13, 419–28; 4 (July–September, 1894): 38–43; Lewis Mumford, *Sticks and Stones* (New York, N.Y., 1924), pp. 123–54; James P. Noffsinger, *Influence of the Ecole des Beaux-Arts on the Architecture of the United States* (Washington, D.C., 1955); Richard Chafee, "The Teaching of Architecture at the Ecole des Beaux-Arts," in Arthur Drexler, ed., *The Architecture of the Ecole des Beaux-Arts* (Cambridge, Mass., 1977), pp. 61–109; Roy Lubove, *The Progressives and the Slums, Tenement House Reform in New York City, 1890–1917* (Pittsburgh, Pa., 1962); Roy Lubove, "I.N. Phelphs Stokes: Tenement Architect, Economist, Planner," *JSAH* 23 (May 1964): 75–87; Leland Roth, "McKim, Mead & White Reappraised," in *A Monograph of the Works of McKim, Mead & White* (New York, N.Y., 1977); John W. Reps, *The Making of Urban America* (Princeton, N.J., 1965), pp. 240–62; David P. Handlin, "The Context of the Modern City," *Harvard Architectural Review* 2 (Spring 1981): 76–89; Leonard K. Eaton, *Two Chicago Architects and Their Clients: Frank Lloyd Wright and Harold Van Doren Shaw* (Cambridge, Mass., 1969); David Gebhard, "Louis Sullivan and George Grant Elmslie," *JSAH* 19 (May 1960): 62–68; David Gebhard, *The Work of Purcell and Elmslie, Architects* (Park Forest, Ill., 1965); Mark L. Peisch, *The Chicago School of Architecture: Early Followers of Sullivan and Wright* (New York, N.Y., 1964); H. Allen Brooks, *The Prairie School, Frank Lloyd Wright and His Midwest Contemporaries* (New York, N.Y., 1976); Robert J. Clark, *The Arts and Crafts Movement in America, 1876–1916* (Princeton, N.J., 1972); Robert Winter, *The California Bungalow* (Los Angeles, Calif., 1980); Clay Lancaster, *The Japanese Influence in America* (New York, N.Y., 1963); Esther McCoy, *Five California Architects* (New York, N.Y., 1960); Richard Longstreth, *On the Edge of the World: Four Architects in San Francisco at the Turn of the Century* (Cambridge, Mass., 1983).

INDIVIDUAL ARCHITECTS

Charles Moore, *The Life and Times of Charles Follen McKim* (Boston, Mass., 1929); Charles C. Baldwin, *Stanford White* (New York, N.Y., 1931; republished 1976); Charles Moore, *Daniel H. Burnham, Architect, Planner of Cities* (Boston, Mass., 1921); Thomas Hines, *Burnham of Chicago, Architect and Planner* (Chicago, Ill., 1979); Keith Noble Morgan, *The Architecture and Landscapes of Charles A. Platt,*

1861–1933 (Ph.D. Thesis, Brown University, 1978); Henry-Russell Hitchcock, "Frank Lloyd Wright and the 'Academic Tradition' of the Early Eighteen Nineties," *Journal of the Warburg and Courtauld Institutes* 1 (January–June 1944): 46–63; Grant H. Manson, *Frank Lloyd Wright: The First Golden Age* (New York, N.Y., 1958); Vincent Scully, *Frank Lloyd Wright* (New York, N.Y., 1960); Robert C. Twombly, *Frank Lloyd Wright: An Interpretive Biography* (New York, N.Y., 1973); Edgar Kaufmann, Jr., "'Form Became Feeling,' a New View of Froebel and Wright," *JSAH* 40 (May 1981): 130–33; John Crosby Freeman, *The Forgotten Rebel, Gustav Stickley and His Craftsman Mission Furniture* (Watkins Glen, N.Y., 1965); Los Angeles County Museum, *Irving Gill, 1870–1936* (Los Angeles, Calif., 1958); Kenneth H. Caldwell, *Bernard Maybeck, Artisan, Architect, Artist* (Santa Barbara, Calif., 1977); Randell Makinson, *Greene & Greene: Architecture as a Fine Art* (Salt Lake City, Utah, 1977); Randell Makinson, *Greene & Greene, Furniture and Related Designs* (Santa Barbara, Calif., 1979).

Chapter Six

CONTEMPORARY TEXTS

The Chicago Tribune, *The International Competition for a New Administration Building for the Chicago Tribune, 1922* (Chicago, Ill., 1923); Hugh Ferriss, *The Metropolis of Tomorrow* (New York, N.Y., 1929); Francisco Mujica, *History of the Skyscraper* (Paris, 1929; republished 1977).

GENERAL

Cass Gilbert, "United States Army Supply Base, Brooklyn, New York," *Architectural Review* 10 (July 1920): 1–4; Roy Lubove, "Homes and 'a Few Well Placed Fruit Trees': An Object Lesson in Federal Housing," *Social Research* 24 (Winter 1960): 469–86; Lois Craig and the Staff of the Federal Architecture Project, *The Federal Presence, Architecture, Politics, and Symbols in United States Government Building* (Cambridge, Mass. 1978), pp. 280–337; On Radburn: Clarence S. Stein, *Toward New Towns for America* (Cambridge, Mass., 1957), pp. 37–74; Walter Littlefield Creese, *American Architecture from 1918 to 1933 with Special Emphasis on European Influence* (Ph.D. Thesis, Harvard University, 1950), 2 vols.; Cervin Robinson and Rosemarie Haag Bletter, *Skyscraper Style, Art Deco New York* (New York, N.Y., 1975); David Naylor, *American Picture Palaces:*

The Architecture of Fantasy (New York, N.Y., 1981); Joseph Urban, *Theaters* (New York, N.Y., 1929).

INDIVIDUAL ARCHITECTS AND BUILDINGS
Theodore B. White, ed., *Paul Philippe Cret* (Philadelphia, Pa., 1973); Elizabeth Greenwell Grossman, *Paul Philippe Cret* (Ph.D. Thesis, Brown University, 1980); Albert Christ-Janer, *Eliel Saarinen* (Chicago, Ill., 1948); Walter H. Kilham, Jr., *Raymond Hood, Architect* (New York, N.Y., 1974); Richard Oliver, *Bertram Grosvenor Goodhue* (Cambridge, Mass., 1983); Ann Miner Daniel, *The Early Architecture of Ralph Adams Cram, 1889–1902* (Ph.D. Thesis, University of North Carolina at Chapel Hill, 1978); Douglas Shand Tucci, *Ralph Adams Cram, American Medievalist* (Boston, Mass, 1975); Carol Herselle Krinsky, *Rockefeller Center* (New York, N.Y., 1978); Richard W. Longstreth, *Julia Morgan, Architect* (Berkeley, Calif., 1977); On Vizcaya: James T. Maher, *The Twilight of Splendor* (Boston, Mass., 1975).

Chapter Seven

CONTEMPORARY TEXTS
Museum of Modern Art, *Modern Architecture: International Exhibition* (New York, N.Y., 1932); Philip Johnson and Henry-Russell Hitchcock, *The International Style* (New York, N.Y., 1932); Norman Bel Geddes, *Magic Motorways* (New York, N.Y., 1940); Frank Lloyd Wright, *The Disappearing City* (New York, N.Y., 1932); Frank Lloyd Wright, *An Autobiography* (New York, N.Y., 1932; revised 1943).

GENERAL
Charles Abrams, *The Future of Housing* (New York, N.Y., 1946), pp. 223–311; Joseph L. Arnold, *The New Deal in the Suburbs: A History of the Greenbelt Town Program, 1935–1954* (Columbus, Ohio, 1971); Julian S. Huxley, *TVA, Adventure in Planning* (Cheam, Surrey, 1943); Marian Moffett, *Built for the People of the United States: Fifty Years of TVA* (Knoxville, Tenn., 1983); Richard Pommer, "The Architecture of Urban Housing in the United States during the Early 1930s," *JSAH* 37 (December 1978): 235–64; Jeffrey C. Meikle, *Twentieth Century Limited: Industrial Design in America, 1925–1939* (Philadelphia, Pa., 1979).

INDIVIDUAL ARCHITECTS AND BUILDINGS
Arthur J. Meigs, *An American Country House, the Property of Arthur E. Newbold, Jr.* (New York, N.Y.,

1925); William Jordy, "PSFS: Its Development and Its Significance in Modern Architecture," *JSAH* 21 (May 1962): 47–83; Robert A. M. Stern, *George Howe, Toward a Modern American Architecture* (New Haven, Conn., 1975); George Nelson, *Industrial Architecture of Albert Kahn, Inc.* (New York, N.Y., 1939); Grant Hildebrand, *Designing for Industry: The Architecture of Albert Kahn* (Cambridge, Mass., 1974); Robert Coombs, "Norman Bel Geddes: Highways and Horizons," *Perspecta* 13/14 (1971): 11–27; Robert W. Marks, *The Dymaxion World of Buckminster Fuller* (New York, N.Y., 1960); On Keck: Dorothy Raley, ed., *A Century of Progress, Homes and Furnishings* (Chicago, Ill., 1934); Narcisco G. Menocal, *Keck & Keck, Architects* (Madison, Wis., 1980); David Gebhard and Harriet Von Breton, *Kem Weber: The Moderne in Southern California, 1920–1941* (Santa Barbara, Calif., 1969); Esther McCoy, *Vienna to Los Angeles: Two Journeys* (Santa Monica, Calif., 1979); David Gebhard, *Schindler* (Santa Barbara, Calif., and New York, N.Y., 1971); Thomas S. Hines, *Richard Neutra and the Search for Modern Architecture* (New York, N.Y., 1982); Richard C. Peters, "William Wilson Wurster: An Architect of Houses," in Sally Woodbridge, ed., *Bay Area Houses* (New York, N.Y., 1976); John Sergeant, *Frank Lloyd Wright's Usonian Houses: The Case for Organic Architecture* (New York, N.Y., 1976); Donald Hoffmann, *Frank Lloyd Wright's Fallingwater: The House and Its History* (New York, N.Y., 1978); Joseph Hudnut, "The Last of the Romans: Comments on the Building of the National Gallery of Art," *Magazine of Art* 34 (April 1945): 169–73.

Chapter Eight

CONTEMPORARY TEXTS
Sigfried Giedion, *Space, Time and Architecture: The Growth of a New Tradition* (Cambridge, Mass., 1941); Sigfried Giedion, "The Need for Monumentality," in Paul Zucker, *New Architecture and City Planning* (New York, N.Y., 1944), pp. 549–68; Joseph Hudnut, "The Post-Modern House," *Architectural Record* 97 (May 1945): 70–75; Robert Venturi, *Complexity and Contradiction in Architecture* (New York, N.Y., 1966); Robert Venturi, Denise Scott Brown, and Steven Izenour, *Learning from Las Vegas* (Cambridge, Mass., 1972).

GENERAL
Paul Rudolph, ed., "Walter Gropius et son Ecole," *L'Architecture d'aujourd'hui* 20 (February 1950);

"America," *Zodiac* 8 (1961): whole issue; Vincent Scully: "Doldrums in the Suburbs," *JSAH* 24 (March 1965): 36–47; William H. Jordy, "The Aftermath of the Bauhaus in America: Gropius, Mies, and Breuer," in Donald Fleming and Bernard Bailyn, eds., *The Intellectual Migration: Europe and America, 1930–1960* (Cambridge, Mass., 1969), pp. 485–543.

INDIVIDUAL ARCHITECTS AND BUILDINGS
Philip Johnson, *Mies van der Rohe* (New York, N.Y., 1947); L. Hilberseimer, *Mies van der Rohe* (Chicago, Ill., 1956); Werner Blaser, *After Mies: Mies van der Rohe, Teaching and Principles* (New York, N.Y., 1977); Henry-Russell Hitchcock, intro., *Philip Johnson; Architecture, 1949–1965* (New York, N.Y., 1966); Esther McCoy, *Craig Ellwood* (New York, N.Y., 1968); Alison Smithson, "Eames Celebration," *Architectural Design* 36 (September 1966): whole issue; *Skidmore, Owings & Merrill, Architects and Engineers* (New York, N.Y., 1964); Arthur Drexler, intro., *Architecture of Skidmore, Owings and Merrill, 1963–73* (New York, N.Y., 1974); Edward Durrell Stone, *Edward Durrell Stone: The Evolution of an Architect* (New York, N.Y., 1962); Eero Saarinen, Aline R. Saarinen, ed., *Eero Saarinen on His Work: A Selection of Buildings Dating from 1947 to 1964 with Statements by the Architect* (New Haven, Conn., 1968); Vincent Scully, *Louis I. Kahn* (New York, N.Y., 1962); Romaldo Giurgola and Jaimini Mehta, *Louis I. Kahn* (Boulder, Colo., 1975); Karl Fleig, ed., *Alvar Aalto* (Zurich, 1963), Vol. 1, pp. 124–32, 134–35; Solomon R. Guggenheim Foundation, *The Solomon R. Guggenheim Museum, Architect: Frank Lloyd Wright* (New York, N.Y., 1960); Eduard F. Sekler and William J. R. Curtis, *Le Corbusier at Work* (Cambridge, Mass., 1978); Knud Bastlund, *José Luis Sert, Architecture, City Planning, Urban Design* (Zurich, 1967); David G. De Long, *The Architecture of Bruce Goff: Buildings and Projects, 1916–1974* (New York, N.Y., 1977); *Paul Rudolph, 1946–1974* (Tokyo, 1977).

Chapter Nine

INDIVIDUAL ARCHITECTS AND BUILDINGS
David B. Brownlee, David G. DeLong and Kathryn B. Hiesinger, *Out of the Ordinary: Robert Venturi, Denise Scott Brown and Associates* (Philadelphia, Pa., 2001); Theresa Morrow, *James Cutler* (Gloucester, Mass., 1997); Andrea Oppenheimer Dean, *Rural Studio, Samuel Mockbee and an Architecture of Decency* (New York, N.Y., 2002); Coosje Van Bruggen, *Guggenheim Museum Bilbao* (New York, N.Y., 1998); Peter Eisenman, ed., *Five Architects: Eisenman, Graves, Gwathmey, Hejduk, Meier* (New York, N.Y., 1972); Karen Vogel Wheeler, ed., *Michael Graves, Buildings and Projects, 1966–1981* (New York, N.Y., 1982); Michael Graves et al., *Michael Graves: Buildings and Projects 1982–1989* (New York, N.Y., 1990) Karen Nichols, Lisa Burke and Patrick Burke, eds., *Michael Graves, Buildings and Projects, 1990–1994* (New York, N.Y., 1995); Richard Meier, intro. Kenneth Frampton, *Richard Meier, Architect: 1964–1984* (New York, N.Y., 1986); Richard Meier et al., *Richard Meier, Architect: 1985–91* (New York, N.Y., 1991); Richard Meier et al., *Richard Meier, Architect: 1992–1999* (New York, N.Y., 1999); Peter Arnell and Ted Bickford, eds., *Robert A. M. Stern, 1965–1980: Toward a Modern Architecture after Modernism* (New York, N.Y., 1981); Luis F. Rueda, ed., *Robert A. M. Stern, 1981–1986* (New York, N.Y., 1986); Robert A. M. Stern et al., *Robert A. M. Stern: Buildings and Projects, 1987–1992* (New York, N.Y., 1993); Terence Riley, *The Un-Private House* (New York, N.Y., 1999); Brad Collins and Juliette Robbins, *Antoine Predock, Architect* (New York, N.Y., 1994); Andreas Papadakis and Harriet Watson, *New Classicism* (London, England, 1990); Francesco Dal Co and Kurt W. Forster, *Frank O. Gehry, The Complete Works* (New York, N.Y., 1998); Oscar Riera Ojeda, ed., *Ledge House, Bohlin, Cywinski, Jackson* (Gloucester, Mass., 1999).

Acknowledgments for Illustrations

Photo Acme Photo 252; Wayne Andrews 51, 96, 99, 102, 114, 140; Associated Press 211; The Norman Bel Geddes Collection, Hoblitzelle Theater Arts Library, Humanities Research Center, The University of Texas at Austin, by permission of the executrix of the Norman Bel Geddes Estate, Mrs. Edith Lutyens Bel Geddes 193; © Guggenheim Museum, Bilbao 258, 259; Boston Athenaeum 71; Boston Center Architects 210; Jack E. Boucher 73; © Tim Buchman 248; Courtesy Santiago Calatrava SA, Zurich 246; Chicago Architectural Photographing Company 109; The Art Institute of Chicago 120; Chicago Historical Society 138; Taylor Museum Collection, Colorado Springs Fine Arts Center 4, 5; Jerry Cooke 127; Courtesy of Michael Dennis & Associates 250; Courtesy Diller + Scofidio, New York 245; Courtesy of the Library, Phillips Exeter Academy, Exeter, New Hampshire 227, 228; Farm Security Administration 203; R. Buckminster Fuller 195; Ewing Galloway 134; Estate of Bruce Goff 235; © Arthur Grice 264; Courtesy Harvard University News Office 89, 233; Hearst San Simeon State Historical Monument 162, 163; Courtesy of the Museum of Finnish Architecture, Helsinki 229, 230; Historical Society of Pennsylvania 45, 46, 52, 74, 100; Horizon Press, New York 143; © Timothy Hursley 263, 265; © Edward Jacoby 249; Thomas Jefferson Memorial Foundation, Monticello, Virginia 40; Philip Johnson 215; Photographs courtesy of Johnson Wax 205, 206; Albert Kahn Associates 187, 188 (Hedrich), 191 (Jeffrey White Studio); Louis I. Kahn 224; Keystone 178; © T. Kitajima 256; Paul Kivett, Landmarks Commission 156; Courtesy of Kohn Pedersen Fox Associates, New York 253; Reproduced by courtesy of the Trustees of the British Museum, London (plan by John White, 1585) 1; Conway Library, London 118, 166; R.I.B.A., London 37; United States Embassy, London 223; Lowell Historical Society on loan to Old Sturbridge Village, Massachusetts (Photo Henry Peach) 67; © Laurin McCracken 251;

Maryland Historical Society 44; Courtesy Richard Meier & Partners 261; © Grant Mudford, Los Angeles 257; Columbia University in the City of New York 76, 77 (Butler Library); The Solomon R. Guggenheim Museum, New York 231, 232; Photograph courtesy Museum of Modern Art, New York, 183, 184, 194, 201, 202, 208, 209, 213 (Collection, Mies van der Rohe Archive, Gift of Ludwig Mies van der Rohe); Museum of the City of New York 73, 93 (The J. Clarence Davies Collection), 87 (Gift of the Hon. Irwin Untermyer), 97, 98; New York Historical Society 70, 88, 95; New York Public Library 16, 86 (Astor, Lenox and Tilden Foundations), 92; The Free Library of Philadelphia 101; © Charles S. Rhyne and Reed College 262; Valentine Museum, Richmond, Virginia 43; Cervin Robinson 170; Courtesy The Rockefeller Center Inc. 180; Rieley and Associates 39; Paul Rudolph, Architect 236, 237 (Paul Rudolph, Architect and Anderson, Beckwith and Haible), 239; Courtesy of the Essex Institute, Salem, Massachusetts 12; Courtesy The Salk Institute, San Diego, California 226; Sandak Inc., Stamford, Connecticut 3, 7, 13–15, 18–24, 26–9, 31, 32, 35, 47–9, 54, 55, 61, 62, 66, 82, 110, 111, 116, 128, 139, 145, 149–51, 154, 157, 161, 173, 174, 176, 185, 207, 216–18, 220; Architectural Drawings Collection, The University of California at Santa Barbara 199, 200; Ezra Stoller 222, 260; Sturtevant 204; John Szarkowski 117; Ralph Thompson, Virginia 41; United Nations 219; Archives of the University of Pennsylvania 225; Courtesy Venturi, Rauch and Scott Brown 240, 241, 242, 243; Courtesy Venturi, Scott Brown and Associates 254; Virginia State Library 38; Matt Wargo for VSBA 255; © Paul Warchol 247; Fine Arts Commission, Washington, D.C. 11, 30, 50, 57–60; Copyright Frank Lloyd Wright Foundation, all rights reserved 141, 142, 144, 146; Yale University Library 65; Yale University News Bureau 238.

Illustrations have also been reproduced from the following publications:

The American Architect vol. 155 (1934) 158; *The American Architect and Building News* vol. 17 (March 1885) 113; *Appleton's Journal* vol. 6 (November 1871) 94; *The Architectural Forum* vol. 51 (November 1929) 155, vol. 67 (1938) 192; *Architectural Record* vol. 30 (October 1911) 159, vol. 35 (July 1921) 177, vol. 64 (December 1928) 179, vol. 78 (November 1935) 190, vol. 80 (September 1936) 186; *The Architectural Review* (Boston) vol. 10 (1920) 152; Daniel D. Badger, *Illustrations of Iron Architecture made by the Architectural Iron Works of the City of New York* (New York 1865) 68, 69; *Building Budget* (Chicago 1885–90) 115; D. H. Burnham and E. H. Bennett, *Plan of Chicago* (Chicago 1909) 136; Carl W. Condit, *American Building Art 19C*, from the *Transactions of the American Society of Civil Engineers* (New York 1960) 64; Andrew Jackson Downing, *The Architecture of Country Houses* (New York 1861) 80, 81; Andrew Jackson Downing, *A Treatise on the Theory and Practice of Landscape Gardening* (New York and London 1840) 79, 85; Hugh Ferriss, *The Metropolis of Tomorrow* (New York 1929) 169, 175; Henry Chandler Forman, *The Architecture of the Old South* (Cambridge, Mass. 1948) 9, 10; General Houses Inc., *Our Homes* (Chicago 1934) 198; *The Great Metropolis or New York Almanac* (New York 1850) 78; Henry-Russell Hitchcock, *Architecture: Nineteenth and Twentieth Centuries* (Harmondsworth 1958) 72; Raymond Hood, intro. by Arthur Tappan North (New York and London 1931) 171, 172; Richard Morris Hunt, *Designs for the Gateways of the Southern Entrance to Central Park, New York* (New York 1866) 91; Fiske Kimball, *American Domestic Architecture* (New York 1922) 25; *Landscape Architecture* vol. 27 (1938) 17; *Massachusetts Magazine* (January 1790) 33 (engraving by Samuel Hill), (February 1794) 36; A. J. Meigs, *An American Country House* (New York 1925) 181; *A Monograph on the Work of McKim, Mead and White* (New York 1915) 119, 123, 124, 126, 131–3; Lewis H. Morgan, *Houses and House Life of the American Aborigines* (Washington 1881) 2; Rexford Newcomb, *Spanish Colonial Architecture in the United States* (New York 1937) 6, 8; Arthur Tappan North (ed.), *Ralph Adams Cram* (New York 1931) 160; *Photographs of the Worlds Fair* (Chicago 1894) 137; *A Monograph on the Work of Charles Platt* (New York 1913) 129, 130; *Port Folio* (November 1913), 34 (engraving after a painting by Thomas Sully); Public Works Administration, *Public Buildings* vol. 1 (Washington 1939) 189; Dorothy Railey (ed.), *A Century of Progress Homes and Furnishings* (Chicago 1934) 196, 197; Mariana Van Rensselaer, *Henry Hobson Richardson and His Works* (Boston and New York 1888) 103–8; *Scribner's Magazine* vol. 16 (1894) 121, 122; Samuel Sloan, *Homestead Architecture* (Philadelphia 1861) 83, 84; C. S. Stein, *Towards New Towns for America* (Chicago 1951) 164, 165; *Trinity College Catalogue* (Hartford, 1877) 90; *Town Planning Review* vol. 2 (1911) 125; United States Shipping Board, *Types of Housing for Shipbuilding* (Washington, D.C., n.d.) 153; Frank Lloyd Wright, *Ausgeführte Bauten und Entwürfe* (Berlin 1910) 147; Frank Lloyd Wright, *Ausgeführte Bauten* (Berlin 1911) 148.

Index

Page numbers in *italic* refer to illustrations

7219 034